PRAISE FOR

GEMS OF WISDOM,
GEMS OF POWER

"Teresa Kennedy has single-handedly introduced the newest healing paradigm in the advancement of crystal healing! … This is groundbreaking material and a must-have for anyone interested in the beauty and brilliance of gemstones. She honors the realm of stone by introducing a clear and concise method for achieving what you need from earth's treasures!"
—Andrew Pacholyk, MS. Lac., Author of *Crystal Medicine: A Clinical Approach to Healing Mind, Body, Spirit.* peacefulmind.com

◆

"Helpful mineral identification information, interesting mineralogical history, and a useful, up-to-date guide to minerals and gems."
—Michael Walter, author of *Field Collecting Minerals in the Empire State: Stories of Modern Day North Country Miners*

TERESA KENNEDY is the author of more than thirty published works of fiction and nonfiction on a wide variety of subjects, including health, cooking, and well-being. A former newspaper editor, she is a frequent contributor to a variety of national and international publications. She lives in Tucson, Arizona.

TERESA KENNEDY

GEMS OF WISDOM, GEMS OF POWER

A PRACTICAL GUIDE TO HOW
GEMSTONES, MINERALS AND CRYSTALS
CAN ENHANCE YOUR LIFE

MARLOWE & COMPANY
NEW YORK

GEMS OF WISDOM, GEMS OF POWER:
A Practical Guide to How Gemstones, Minerals and Crystals Can Enhance Your Life

Copyright © 2007 Teresa Kennedy

Cover photographs courtesy of:
Kennedy and Company (peridot, amazonite, red jasper, pyrite, tanzanite)
Rob Lavinsky, irocks.com (sugulite)
Jim Butterbrodt (iolite)
Mike Walters (calcite heart)

Published by
Marlowe & Company
An Imprint of Avalon Publishing Group, Incorporated
245 West 17th Street • 11th Floor
New York, NY 10011-5300

Library of Congress Cataloging-in-Publication Data

Kennedy, Teresa.
  Gems of wisdom, gems of power : a practical guide to how gemstones, minerals, and crystals can enhance your life / Teresa Kennedy.
    p. cm.
  Includes index.
  ISBN 978-1-60094-015-6
  1. Precious stones—Psychic aspects. 2. Precious stones—Therapeutic use. 3. Gems—Psychic aspects. 4. Gems—Therapeutic use. 5. Crystals—Psychic aspects. 6. Crystals—Therapeutic use. I. Title.
  BF1442.P74K46 2007
  133'.25538—dc21

                                                             2007009868

9 8 7 6 5 4 3 2 1

Designed by Pauline Neuwirth, Neuwirth & Associates, Inc.

Printed in China

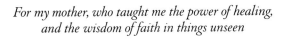

For my mother, who taught me the power of healing,
and the wisdom of faith in things unseen

◆

Contents

Introduction

A LOT OF BOOKS of this kind will almost invariably begin with words like "for centuries" and go on to offer readers a long, vague history lesson about the use of crystals dating all the way back to legendary lost continents and antique alchemical practices, or even hint at the long-lost secrets of space aliens. Unfortunately, as with many so-called alternative therapies, the traditional uses of gemstones and crystals have been overlaid with a lot of misinformation, outlandish claims, and confusing and contradictory babble. Yet at the same time, given the restrictions and superstitious attitudes on the part of scientists and conventional medicine toward such therapies, there simply isn't a lot of hard evidence, clinical trials, or press releases by huge pharmaceutical corporations touting their discoveries about what crystals, minerals, and gemstones can do.

yellow flourite

So in departure from the usual format, I am going to make a few assumptions about you, the reader of this book. Whether you are an amateur rock hound or an experienced alternative healer, I'm going to assume, first, that you are intelligent and not especially interested in having that intelligence insulted by far-fetched fantasies or unfounded theories. Second, I'm going to assume that you are genuinely interested in gemstones and crystals and in exploring their possibilities for your personal use—or you wouldn't be reading this book.

With those things in mind, I'm going to stick with the facts, keeping always in mind that "fact" is not necessarily limited to what we are able to prove in the context of modern science. After all, science did not invent reality; rather, it is merely a means of looking at physical reality in an attempt to discover and offer proof of the secrets that lie beyond our limited sensory perceptions. For example, atoms can't be seen by the naked eye, but that doesn't mean they don't exist.

In a very real sense, crystals can be seen as a symbol for seeking a "crystallization" of certain aspects of our experience. Coming to work with the power of crystals means you are ready to embark on one of the great adventures of what we call "consciousness," as their energies will assist you in manifesting your dreams and desires into beautiful reality. Because crystals, minerals, and gemstones offer us a bridge between the inner and outer world, and a means to better integrate who we are with who we would most like to become, in the introductions to each of the following chapters I will urge you to get better acquainted with your feelings and motivations. The greater understanding you have of yourself, the more effective these energies will be.

Crystal energy can be subtle or dramatic, healing or enlightening. It can help draw needed resources into your life; it can serve to attract the lover of your dreams; or it can work to effect a complete transformation of your outlook. No matter what your personal reasons are for coming to crystal work—whether your needs are physical, emotional, or material—exploring these energies will surely help to crystallize your experience and enhance every aspect of your life.

GEMS OF WISDOM, GEMS OF POWER

1

THE BASICS

ALL ROCKS ARE made up of minerals. Crystals and gemstones are therefore also made up of minerals. What distinguishes a precious or semiprecious stone or crystal from an ordinary rock is how they are formed.

All rocks fall into roughly three distinct categories: *Igneous* rocks are formed when magma from deep below the earth's crust wells up through cracks and fissures and is trapped in molten pockets. There, water, dissolved gases, and rare elements combine and crystals begin to grow as the molten mass slowly cools. The rock that is thus formed is a mixture of minerals called pegmatite, which is characterized by its large chunks, or **crystals**. With just the right chemicals present and just the right ambient conditions, pegmatite will hold precious gems. Igneous formations include diamonds, rubies, sapphires, topaz, and garnet.

Sedimentary formations may contain gems with two separate histories. Some sedimentary rocks hold crystals that were formed in one location and then moved by erosion to sediment basins where they became part of the **deposit**. Other gems of this type are formed when groundwater seeps down through the volcanic ash or other sediments, dissolving minerals and moving them into pockets. Opal and turquoise are examples of this type of gemstone.

Metamorphic rocks have been altered by tectonic processes, such as great heat, pressure, or both. The partial melting of the parent rock allows specific minerals to escape and move to areas where they concentrate into gems. Garnet, for example, is commonly found as crystals in mica schist.

To be even more specific, a *mineral* is any naturally formed homogeneous inorganic material. A *crystal,* at its most basic definition, is a solid formed by the solidification of chemicals that has a regularly repeating internal arrangement of atoms and molecules and is bounded by external plane faces. Crystal particles form a variety of geometric shapes based on their internal compressions. Finally, a *natural gemstone* is a mineral, stone, or organic matter that can be cut and polished or otherwise treated for use as jewelry or other ornament.

Every crystal has an orderly, internal pattern of atoms, with a distinctive way of locking new atoms into that pattern, which repeats again and again. In each rock formation, structure and the mineral's chemical composition combine in specific crystal properties. Crystal properties such as shape, **hardness, cleavage, luster,** and **more,** help us to identify each individual crystal's structure, gemstone species, and group.

How Minerals Are Identified

Minerals can be identified absolutely only by x-ray analysis and chemical tests. The x-ray analysis determines the structure of the mineral, and the chemical tests determine the composition of the mineral. Structure and composition are the defining marks of a mineral. For most of us, that kind of testing is beyond reach. So we use a variety of other criteria for identification.

Color: Strangely enough, the first quality that attracts us to minerals and gemstones is their color, but color is not the most reliable means of identifying a stone. Color in minerals is determined by the way they absorb and give off wavelengths of light through a process of atomic bonding. Generally speaking, the color of a stone is related to how light waves move through certain trace elements, but that isn't always the case. Traces of copper, for example, usually produce blue and green colorations in a mineral—but not always. Iron can produce not only red, but also an entire range of colors in the red-yellow end of the spectrum.

Luster: The term *luster* refers simply to the particular way light **refracts** off the surface of a stone, and is usually appended with a more descriptive adjective, such as "waxy," "greasy," "pitchy," "pearly," or "gemmy."

Structure: Crystals and minerals are classified according to seven basic structures that inform us about how they grow as well as the patterns in which they store and emit energy. Refer to the section on crystal structure (pg. 14) for additional discussion.

Cleavage: Because minerals and crystals have an internal structure, they also reveal that structure in certain ways. *Cleavage* refers to the way a stone breaks in order to produce a smooth face. Cleavage is generally defined as "perfect," "imperfect," "good," "distinct," "indistinct," or "poor," according to how easy it is to produce that smooth face from a particular specimen.

Hardness: *Hardness* is a term that refers to the strength of a mineral's structure and how tightly the atoms are packed within the structure. Since a mineral can be scratched (or its atoms displaced) only by a substance harder that itself, hardness is considered one of the best methods for mineral identification. Hardness is measured by the **Mohs scale,** conceived by French mineralogist Friedrich Mohs almost two hundred years ago. He established a scale that placed the mineral talc at 1 (softest) and diamond at 10 (hardness). The intervals between the numbers are not equal, however, and the difference between corundum at 9 and diamond at 10 is greater than the entire range of 1 to 9. Today the Mohs scale is the universal measure of hardness for minerals. At its simplest, the higher a stone's measure on the Mohs scale, the harder (and usually more valuable) the stone.

Streak: *Streak* is the color of the powder of a mineral. The proper way to test for streak is to rub a mineral across a tile of white, unglazed porcelain and to examine the color of the streak left behind. It's a great means of identification because it is consistent from specimen to specimen for a given mineral. So when it comes to determining whether you have a piece of genuine turquoise or a piece of dyed howlite, test for streak. Two minerals that look alike have different colors when powdered.

Locale: If you know where your stone comes from, you will be better able to discern its authenticity, because though the earth is always uncovering new finds and new stores of mineral specimens, a knowledge of some basic geology can tell you where a particular mineral is typically mined or located. If you happen on a huckster selling sapphire rough from a new "find" in New Jersey, you can be fairly sure it isn't the real thing.

HOW DO CRYSTALS WORK?

IF ONE ACCEPTS that earth herself is a living, integrated organism and not just a big chunk of rock floating in space, the theory behind the various forms of crystal therapy is not at all difficult to accept. Physicists tell us that all matter is made up of energy, that energy cannot be destroyed, and that it changes form. Because crystals and gemstones were and continue to be formed by ongoing changes in the earth, they are believed to be charged with highly concentrated forms of energy and to conduct energy. Therefore, that energy can be released, exchanged, and used to "energize" other forms of organic life.

Blue Fluorite specimen

The fact is, the scientific and technological communities' uses of crystal energy have been growing by quantum leaps since the days when Grandma and Grandpa referred to their radio as a "crystal set." That single development, which can be seen as the birth of modern electronics, has seen us move from semiconductors to transistors to integrated circuits to microchips. Crystals are already a mainstay of the space and military industries in making such things as space travel, satellite technology, and weapons' accuracy possible. The liquid crystals in our watches, calculators, and computer screens are just one more bit of technology waiting to be explained, explored, and expanded.

So while it might very well take a rocket scientist to explain just how crystals work, we already know that as conductors of energy, they *do* work. That's more than a fact—it's the truth.

CRYSTAL STRUCTURE— SOMETHING OLD, SOMETHING NEW

GEOLOGISTS GROUP CRYSTALS according to how they are formed. Some contemporary practitioners, myself included, believe that these essential structures affect the energy characteristics of a crystal and how it operates. The seven crystalline classes are part of a repeating pattern of symmetry and organization that can be found throughout nature, including the systems of the human body.

Galena

The Eastern traditions of crystal healing and therapy associate specific crystals with the seven energy centers in the body called "chakras." Just as the spectrum of light contains seven colors, traditional healing practice under the Eastern system tends to associate the color of a crystal with an energy center in the body as a means of balancing, strengthening, or "moving" energy through the system. Many people have used this method with fine results.

As our scientific methods of measuring mineral structure and energy patterns have become more sophisticated, however, we now know more about the energy of crystals than ever before. Simply stated, we're finding out more about *why* we know *what* we have always known intuitively about crystal energy. As a result, many contemporary practitioners utilize stones and crystals in increasingly specific ways, simply because our modern ability to identify their structure and energy patterns enables us to utilize stones for increasingly specific purposes. The stones selected for this book reflects that emerging taxonomy, while at the same time respecting the traditions that have come down to us. You will discover in the course of working with these stones that at times the structure and energy pattern of a particular stone is in complete correspondence with its history of uses under more traditional systems. At other times there will be a departure from literature and lore you may have encountered elsewhere. Certainly, there are no hard and fast rules for crystal work, but there is new promise and an increasing body of scientific evidence that beckons toward a new frontier in which to explore the powers of crystals to enhance our lives.

Without giving the average reader a crash course in chemistry and physics, it's important to keep in mind that minerals, crystals, and gemstones are scientifically classified in two important ways—by their *primary categories* and by their *structure*. Primary category tells us the essentials of how a crystal is put together atomically, or how the atoms are "packed," which tells us something about its energy pattern. Structures inform us about shapes and therefore how energy is able to move through that shape.

Primary Categories

Covalent Crystals

A covalent crystal has shared electrons, or covalent bonds between all of the atoms in the crystal. Think of this type as one big molecule. A diamond is one example of the covalent type.

Metallic Crystals

Individual metal atoms of metallic crystals sit on *lattice sites*, or the three-dimensional network of atoms that are arranged in a symmetrical pattern when a crystal is formed. This leaves the outer electrons of such atoms free to float around the lattice. Metallic crystals tend to be very dense with very high melting points.

Ionic Crystals

The atoms of ionic crystals are held together by electrostatic forces, or ionic bonds. Ionic crystals are hard and also have relatively high melting points. Ordinary table salt is an example of this type of crystal.

Molecular Crystals

These crystals contain recognizable molecules within their structures. A molecular crystal is held together by noncovalent interactions, like hydrogen bonding. Molecular crystals tend to be soft with relatively low melting points.

The Seven Structures of Crystals

While knowing the primary type of a crystal can be helpful in gaining an overall sense of its composition, the seven classifications of crystal structure will sometimes, though not always, assist you in being visually able to recognize different types of crystals and groupings, which in turn will offer clues as to why specific stones can be used for specific healing and therapeutic purposes. Keep in mind that at its simplest, crystal structure is a description of its inherent symmetry—in other words, about how the atoms are packed. So while structure can be an aid to identifying crystals visually, it's more a question of determining what patterns of energy a crystal stores and how it emits those energies as you use it.

The **cubic** or **isometric** group includes iron and a number of elemental metals. It's also one of the most common **crystal systems** in naturally occurring crystals and minerals. Crystals of this class generally form six mirror planes, just as a cube has six sides. But it's something of a paradox that such low-density structures nevertheless emit the highest levels of energy. As a result, crystals belonging to this system have an energy pattern that affects us at a very deep level and has even been said to assist in the repair of damaged cellular structures. Examples of isometric crystals include garnet, hematite, and magnetite, as well as galena and pyrite. Isometric energy is highly concentrated yet very versatile, and as the stone selections in

the following chapters will illustrate, crystals with this type of energy can be used in the widest variety of ways.

FOR PEOPLE WHO are trying to get a better grasp of crystal structure, it is sometimes helpful not to think of planes and imaginary axes, but in terms of edges. Below is a brief description of the seven crystal structures described in such terms.

1. **Isometric or cubic:** Have three edges of equal length at right angles to one another.

2. **Tetragonal:** Also have three edges at right angles, but only two of those edges are of equal length.

3. **Orthorhombic:** Have three edges at right angles, but all the edges are of different lengths.

4. **Monoclinic:** Have two edges at right angles, the other angle not, and all the edges are of different lengths.

5. **Triclinic:** All three edges are of different lengths, and none of the angles are right angles.

6. **Hexagonal:** Have two edges that are equal and form angles of 60 to 120 degrees with each other. The third edge is at right angles to them and of different length.

The **hexagonal** crystal system is divided into the **hexagonal** and **trigonal** divisions. Hexagonal crystals have seven planes, each running perpendicular to the "axis," or center. Mineral species in the hexagonal division are apatite, beryl, and high quartz. The hexagonal class emits a fluctuating, reciprocal type of energy that both gives and receives. As such, crystals of this type are particularly useful in matters of relationship and for opening the heart. Examples of minerals that crystallize in the **trigonal** division are calcite, dolomite, low quartz, and tourmaline. These crystals give off energy in a continuous fashion—always in a spinning motion that is of neither a positive nor negative nature. Crystals belonging to the trigonal class are generally used for balancing energy in the body, especially when there is a particular lack of energy or gross imbalance in one of its systems.

Tetragonal crystals tend to form short crystals of a prismatic habit. Examples include zircon and casserite. Crystals of this type have qualities allowing them to absorb negative qualities or vibrations and to transmute them

◾ A MODERN CRYSTAL PIONEER ◾

ONE OF THE early pioneers of silicon chip technology was scientist Marcel Joseph Vogel (1917–1991). Vogel was a research scientist for IBM for almost thirty years and during that time was awarded many patents for his inventions. His particular areas of expertise were phosphor technology, liquid crystal systems, luminescence, and magnetics.

Yet throughout his career Vogel became notorious among the established scientists of his day for his strong interest in metaphysics. Vogel discovered that not only can crystals be programmed as silicon chips in a computer, but his research indicates they also can be programmed with thought. After all, a person sitting at a computer inputs thought through a keyboard, which is then stored in the computer's silicon chips. Vogel reasoned that, like electricity, thought is a form of energy, which is given direction by our conscious intention. He concluded that crystals might be programmed without the need for electricity by using just thoughts or clear intention, and he undertook a multitude of experiments to validate his theories. As with all groundbreaking alternative scientists, the mainstream scientific community ostracized him.

What drew Vogel to crystal work? According to his good friend and associate Rumi Das, Vogel explained his fascination this way: "When I was between five and eight years old," he said, "I was watching TV and this strange character named Elmer Fudd—you remember Elmer Fudd?—came on dressed up like a swami, wearing a turban, and staring into a crystal ball. And I remember looking at him and saying to myself, 'That's what I want to be when I grow up.'"

into positive energy. Their particular qualities show us "transformation in action" and can be used very effectively when one is faced with circumstances that require change of some kind. Think of this group as having the same kind of energy that transforms a caterpillar into a butterfly.

The **orthorhombic** group includes peridot, olivine, and barite. Stones belonging to this system have a unique, encompassing energy pattern. They magnify consciousness in a way that allows one to switch from the perspective of the microcosm to the macrocosm and back again. If you're trying to gain a better sense of your place in the universe, carry an orthorhombic stone.

Monoclinic crystals form long prismatic shapes. This group includes gypsum, azurite, and malachite, among many others. Crystals of the monoclinic system emit a constant pulse of energy. Their nature is that of continual expansion and contraction, which helps serve as an impetus to action and growth.

The **triclinic** group includes the mineral species plagioclase feldspars and axinite. Crystals of the triclinic system form *triads* or *trinities,* a repeating form in nature and throughout the hierarchical structure of the universe. As such, their energies offer an aspect of completion and wholeness.

If you're still having difficulty understanding how human beings are continually affected and responsive to unseen energies, consider that Marcel Vogel, the world-renowned crystal expert, has said the human energy field exists as an array of oscillating energy points that have a layered structure and a definite symmetry. He points out that these properties fulfill the definition of a normal crystal in material form.

CHOOSING A STONE FOR A PARTICULAR PURPOSE

THE CONVENTIONAL WISDOM would have us believe that choosing stones for special uses and cases is largely a matter of intuition. Indeed, many writings on the subject insist that the stone should "choose you," rendering your part of the process a result of having an appropriately passive or receptive response to a stone's energy. While there's nothing at all wrong with intuition, I believe we have advanced enough in our knowledge of the measurable patterns of crystal energy to make their use a more precise art—that is, crystals and gemstones in each of the seven classifications mentioned above emit a characteristic energy that varies from stone to stone, but not from category to category.

The energy of stones belonging to the trigonal group, for example, emit energy in a constant spinning pattern. The energy of monoclinic stones emits a pulse that expands and contracts. Now, if you consciously examine the specific nature of *what you want a stone to do*—whether it be to improve your love life, heighten your sense of personal power, or increase your bank account—you will have a better and more precise understanding of what stones to look for, based upon the energies they possess.

Part of the reason this book has been organized the way it has is not simple convenience for you, the reader, but because the better acquainted we can become with the science of crystals, the more effective we will become in the art of working with them for specific purposes and in very precise ways. We are blessed with a great deal of tradition in crystal work, and a wealth of truly useful information can be found as a matter of historical record. Yet because of the sheer popularity of the subject, much of the more readily available information today is a hodge-podge of superstition, half-theory, or instruction from anonymous "intuitive sources" about how to use crystals effectively. To give credit where credit is due, however, some sources and healers have proven quite intuitively correct in using the crystals they have chosen for specific purposes. Other sources, though, can offer conflicting information and still others just offer their own best guesses.

So letting a stone choose you isn't always the best method for finding what you need. Instead, I would encourage you to participate as fully and consciously in that process as you can.

◆ Research as much as you can about the history, science, and locations where the stone you have in mind is found. Vendors selling stone from "newly discovered" deposits aren't always telling the truth. If you are aware that tanzanite, for example, just doesn't come from Arizona, you'll be way ahead.

◆ Get your information from reliable sources, and deal with reputable dealers. Many such resources and dealers are listed in the resources section (appendix 6) in the back of this book.

◆ Make sure you've got the genuine article before you put your money down. Stones can be expensive, and fakes and phonies abound. Mineral specimens are harder to fake, but it has been done. Many vendors of tumbled rocks, for example, fill selections with dyed stones or even glass. The "Buyer Beware!" sidebars throughout this book should be of some help in spotting fakes and enhanced or simulated stones, but location, color, and other basic criteria are still your own best field guide to quality.

Armed with good information, by all means allow your intuition free rein in choosing stones and minerals—go with your heart, go with your gut, or even go with your pocketbook. But don't forget to use your head.

■ BUYER BEWARE! ■

WHAT'S IN A name? When it comes to buying gemstones—plenty. The worldwide traffic in gemstones constitutes an enormous industry, worth billions of dollars every year. Stones that begin as rough from the mines themselves may make their way through dealers, wholesalers, stone cutters, enhancement processes, and an assortment of more wholesalers before they get to your local shop or retailer. And a lot of things can, and do, happen on the journey.

Trade names abound in the gemstone industry, and many of them are downright misleading to consumers. Some are inventions of clever dealers to sell inferior products; others can be an attempt by otherwise reputable dealers or merchants to recover losses when they discover they didn't get what they paid for. Such intrigues are nothing new in the history of gemology, but with the plethora of technology, enhancements, and other practices, it does help to educate yourself before you go out shopping. If you're not a professional, there are a few important things to keep in mind when buying stones in whatever form—whether as lapidary "rough" tumbled stones; loose, faceted stones; or as jewelry.

1. Real stones have real names, and reputable trade organizations hold their members to that standard. The genuine names for all gemstones are regulated through the International Association of Jewelry, International Colored Stone Association (ICA), and the Federal Trade Commission. With very few exceptions, precious and semi-precious stones have a single name—such as diamond, ruby, or emerald. Lapis lazuli is one notable exception, and while different types of agate or jasper are frequently described by qualifying adjectives, such as "poppy" jasper or "eye" agate, they are usually visually recognizable. The names for gemstones are mostly derived from root languages such as Greek or Latin, or in more recent cases, the discoverer of the stone itself.

2. So-called trade names, however, are not so obvious. A big clue to whether a stone is genuine or not is when you find stones sold by place names. This kind of "branding," although useful to merchants from a marketing standpoint, is usually a tip-off that a particular stone, while it may resemble the genuine article, is not what it's claiming to be. Such stones may be adulterated or reconstructed, despite a resemblance to their namesakes.

3. Genuine stones do not have the name of a country or even a state attached to them. There is no such thing, for example, as an "Indian topaz," a "Vietnamese

ruby," or a "Japanese amethyst." Nor is there any such thing as "Mogok diamond," which is actually a colorless topaz. "Nevada black diamond" is not a diamond at all—it is obsidian.

4. Check your spelling. "Turquoisite" is not the same thing as genuine turquoise. "Emeraldite" or "emeraldine" is not emerald; it is tourmaline. Keep a close eye on those funny little suffixes so frequently attached to a traditional designation. They almost certainly spell trouble for potential buyers. Keep an eye out for "-ite" or "-ine" in particular.

5. Things get even more complicated when you realize that genuine stones of lesser value are very frequently sold as impostors under the guise of being more expensive stones. Garnets are frequently sold as rubies under names such as "Bohemian ruby," "Australian Ruby," and even "Montana" or "Mountain ruby." Tourmalines are sold as "San Diego ruby" and "Siberian ruby." And spinels have been used as stand-ins for rubies for centuries. One fine example even graces the British Crown jewels. Remember, there's nothing at all wrong with buying these stones—unless, of course, you're paying the price of actual rubies.

6. And it doesn't get easier when you add the abundance of semiprecious stones to the mix, which, as they gain in popularity and slowly go up in price, can be just as subject to branding with all manner of confusing and misleading names. "Tanzanite," for example, is actually a brand name created by Tiffany and Company for a variety of the mineral zoisite, which has been heat-treated to acquire its beautiful, deep blue color.

7. By no means are all gem dealers crooks—and let's face it, some of these practices have been going on for a long time. Your best bet is to deal only with merchants who are registered with a reputable trade organization, and refuse to deal with anyone who won't answer your questions and concerns to your satisfaction.

For more information on some common "trade names" for stones, please refer to appendix 1.

Gemstone Treatments and Enhancements

Peridot

WHAT IS A treated stone? What is an enhanced stone? Is there a difference? And above all, how do these sometimes bewildering treatments affect a stone's energy and its ability to work for you?

In today's market, real answers are not always easy to find. But before we go into any discussion of the treatments themselves and how they might affect a particular stone's energy patterns, it's important to remember why stones are treated or enhanced in the first place: because they are not top-quality gemstones. My own feeling about purchasing stones for personal or therapeutic use is exactly the same as my feeling about purchasing coffee or chocolate—always buy the best quality you can possibly afford, no skimping.

Still, knowing that every budget has its ups and downs, it's also important to remem-

ber that generic aspirin will take away a headache just as well as the more expensive name brands, so just because your stone isn't from Tiffany, or even King Solomon's mines, doesn't mean it won't work effectively. Besides, many enhancements are accepted practice these days and are difficult or impractical to prove, as enhanced gemstones are still considered "natural." So when buying gemstones either as loose stones or set in jewelry, it's best to assume that some traditional enhancements have been made. When purchasing crystals, mineral specimens, or gemstone rough, it's much less likely that you'll encounter such processes, but again, it's not unheard of. Tumbled agates, for example, are very frequently dyed.

Before venturing out to the rock shop, gem show, or shopping mall, however, it will help to clarify some of the terms you'll encounter when purchasing gemstones, minerals, and crystals.

Simulated—*Simulated* means fake, period. It may look like a sapphire, but it won't act like one, so forget it.

Irradiated—This means a stone has been exposed to gamma and/or electron bombardment to alter a gemstone's color. The irradiation may or may not be followed by a heating process. And although you certainly can find any number of merchants out there who will insist such treatments don't affect the value of a particular stone, I disagree. As for whether or not such stones will have the same energy properties as before they were exposed to radiation? Well—would you?

Heat-Treated—The use of heat to affect desired alteration of color and/or remove **inclusions**. Since heat treating doesn't involve alteration of the stones at the atomic level, it doesn't generally affect crystalline structure or effectiveness as much as some other methods of stone enhancement.

Oiling—Some stones, such as opals and emeralds, actually require regular oiling to keep them in optimum condition and to prevent **crazing** and shattering.

Waxing—Similarly, waxing usually involves the use of innocuous substances such as household paraffin or natural resins to smooth porous stones as both a filler and polish. Neither method affects a stone's energy quality as much as it does its durability and how you care for it—in other words, no ultrasonic cleaners, acids, abrasives, and so forth.

Filling—Strangely enough, filling is different from waxing, because it implies the use of colorless plastics to smooth, coat, and fill any of nature's loopholes. Particularly prevalent in softer stones, such as corals and turquoise, it's best to go with natural specimens even if they

aren't as attractive—assuming you can find them, that is.

Diffusion—This involves the use of chemicals or acids in conjunction with heat treatments to produce fake **asterisms,** or "stars." Pretty, but for therapeutic purposes, skip 'em.

Bleaching—The use of chemicals or other agents to lighten or remove a gemstone's color. It's unknown if bleaching affects energy properties, but it's unlikely.

Dyeing—The introduction of coloring matter into a gemstone to give it new color, intensify present color, or improve color uniformity. Effects upon energy patterns are unknown.

Lasering—The use of a laser and chemicals to reach and alter inclusions in diamonds. Not recommended to use these stones for therapeutic purposes.

Lab-Grown versus Natural

Today's technology makes it possible to "grow" gemstones, such as emeralds, in the laboratory. Lab-grown gems, however, are not to be confused with **synthetic** stones. Synthetic stones may have materials that are similar in color or chemical composition to a natural stone, but they do not have the same crystal structure, and thereby lack the healing and energy qualities of the original.

Synthetic gems are often misrepresented as having been grown as crystals in a laboratory.

By contrast, lab-grown crystals are grown from smaller, *natural* crystals, rather like seeds grown in a greenhouse as opposed to being planted outdoors. Lab-grown crystals are produced by duplicating the same natural processes that grew the originals, but in a much shorter space of time. Do lab crystals have the same energy and vibrations as natural crystals or gemstones? It's hard to say—some say yes, some say no, and some insist they're even better than the originals because of the purity of the process. For any crystal to have the correct "signature energy," it is essential that the billions of atoms that constitute its atomic lattice line up exactly like its natural counterpart. When this occurs, the major difference between the two is that the laboratory crystal, because it was formed in a controlled, non-disturbance-prone environment, has fewer inclusions, color zones, **fractures,** or other flaws. Only by working with the energy of a particular stone will you be able to tell if a lab-grown stone works for you.

To Cleanse or Not to Cleanse?

THERE ARE ENORMOUS differences of opinion among alternative and New Age crystal workers. Some say cleanse, some say don't. Some insist that all crystals should be cleansed in a dark place in a bowl of sea salt or seawater for several days, but since crystals can get scratched and even react badly with salt crystals or seawater, that may not be such a great idea. Others say to run your crystals under fresh water or place them securely in a running stream. I've read that crystals should be buried in the ground under the light of a full moon, unearthed on the new moon, and set out in the sun at high noon. Still others say they should be smudged with incense or sage and even blessed with holy water.

My best advice on the subject consists of simple common sense. Having acquired your crystal, bring it home and simply let it rest for a few hours or overnight before you begin to use it. Since we do know that stones and crystals emit very specific energy patterns, it's a pretty good bet that a few hours undisturbed will allow them to slough off any undesirable vibes.

Charging Your Crystal

CRYSTALS COME CHARGED with energy—that's why we use them. However, there is a good bit of opinion that insists crystals must first be imbued with some direction or conscious intention in order to be more effective for a specific purpose. Charging a crystal through practices such as meditation or visualization is often recommended, as is contact with one of the so-called master crystals, which include amethyst, citrine, and pure **rock crystal.** Defined as simply as possible, a master crystal is one that works very effectively to enhance and augment the energy of other stones.

Personally, I've found that spending some time with your stone or crystal is as much an opportunity to attune and sensitize yourself to its energy as it is a chance to "charge" the crystal with your intentions. Meditations, visualization, or simply shutting out distractions to the point where you can feel a particular stone's energy is not a bad idea in any event, simply because such practices have a way of increasing your conscious awareness of just what you want a crystal to do.

A SENSE OF THE SACRED

Coral Kwan Yin

THE HISTORY OF crystals, gems, and minerals is impossible to ignore and as full of "facts" as geological science. Ever wonder why the Stone Age is called the Stone Age? Because it was the first period in human history, from approximately 300,000 BC to 100,000 BC, that our ancestors began to use crystals, rocks, and minerals—carefully shaping them into objects such as tools and weapons. It was also the first time in our development as a species that we began to revere stones as sacred objects—tangible evidence of our connection with the divine.

Peridot Rosary

In fact, the use of crystals, rocks, and minerals is part of what psychologist Carl Jung called the "collective unconscious." As human beings, our use of stone is a practice so intimately woven through our history, religion, and myth that it's difficult to pinpoint just when it all began. And yet it is something awe-inspiring to imagine—that moment in prehistory when a caveman scratched a symbol on a particular rock or formation and, in so doing, recognized an inherent quality and imbued it with it a magical purpose.

Every kid who ever had a rock collection or painted a face on a "pet rock," anybody whoever plucked a colorful pebble from the gravel in the driveway or the bottom of a creek bed, is responding to that same sense of the sacred. Holding a string of "worry beads" or praying a rosary speaks to that same impulse. To hold a little bit of the earth in your hand connects us with a sense of something larger—a sense of the divine.

If you consider the stone monoliths of a place like Stonehenge, the pyramids of ancient Egypt, the crystal skulls of the Maya and the Aztecs, the stone tablets of the Ten Commandments, and the rune stones used for divination by the Vikings, or the endless number of similar examples from thousands of civilizations all over the world, you begin to get a sense of just how deep our sense of connection to stone really is. It is as though we know, and have always known, that these materials hold an energy that connects us to our gods.

Pre-Christians had a stone called "bethel" for example, for which the town of Bethlehem was named centuries afterward. Jesus is referred to as the "cornerstone" in the Bible, along with hundreds of other references to rubies, emeralds, jasper, and other stones in both the Old and the New Testaments. Stones of every description are prominent in every religion in the world—as symbols of protection, strength, and enrichment. We exchange precious stones as symbols of our love for one another; they stand for wealth and worldly accomplishment; we crown our kings and queens with jewels; and they carry us to the afterlife, too. We mark our graves with stones, just as our

ancestors did. Unlike humankind, stones are invulnerable and unchanging—a symbol of eternity itself. A diamond, after all, is forever.

Ramses II as a child bas relief

Stones are sacred things; they speak of our connection to the earth as well as our connection to the divine. Natural stone formations have been used as objects of worship and sites for ritual. We know from the traditions of indigenous peoples around the world that such formations are believed to be evidence of the divine in the world. And anyone who has seen the Grand Canyon would be hard-pressed to disagree.

By 4000 BC stones became gemstones and were used for personal ornaments, sacred objects, and in all manner of armor. Numerous examples indicate that as stonework became more refined, so did our collective associations, yet the connection between heaven and earth was never quite broken, and twinkling gems came to be associated with the stars themselves.

The Babylonians first devised the system we know today as the twelve signs of the zodiac, and gemstones came to be associated with each of the twelve star signs. In the Old Testament, twelve stones are associated with the twelve tribes of Israel, and twelve jewels are also associated with the twelve gods of Olympus. An ancient Egyptian creation myth offers a slight variation on the theme, where a goddess sowed the heavens with green stones, and from these the stars were born. Among indigenous American peoples, a common myth has a powerful medicine man, or shaman, after seeing the sky in darkness, taking his magic crystal, breaking it into pieces, and throwing the crystal into the sky to form the stars. The famous crystal skulls discovered in Mexico and various locations in Central America were believed by the Maya, Aztecs, and others to be a gift from a time when human beings inhabited all the visible planets in the sky, and it was believed that the skulls had been sent to the people of earth to inform them of heavenly ways. Though shrouded in controversy as to their origins, research has indicated that each of these skulls was carved against the axis of the crystal, a seemingly impossible task for people without modern equipment. Regardless, the skulls seem imbued with special qualities. In fact, one example from the British Museum has been removed from display, because curators and other museum personnel claim that when left in a case, enclosed in glass, the skull moves on its own.

The Egyptian *Book of the Dead* offers us perhaps the first documentation of specific stones for specific uses. The sacred texts and myths were quite literally carved in stone, with each type of crystal associated with the story of a particular god. In addition, we have evidence that the living used these stones for special purposes. Scarabs, for example, offered protection when fashioned out of malachite or jasper; heart shapes were carved from carnelian and lapis lazuli; while objects of jade might be used as protection against drowning or to ensure a good night's rest.

■ DO CRYSTAL SKULLS CARRY A CURSE? ■

THE THIRTEEN CRYSTAL skulls discovered in parts of Mexico, Central America, and South America constitute one of the most compelling subjects of twentieth-century archaeology. They are a mystery every bit as profound as Stonehenge or the pyramids of Egypt. Believed to be anywhere between five thousand and thirty-six thousand years old, various examples of the skulls have made their way into modern history, sometimes with a curse attached. Given that throughout the world the skull is a powerful icon associated with death, many stories of such curses are not difficult to understand. Yet in other instances, such as the skull donated to the Smithsonian Institution in Washington, D.C., the history of misfortune is difficult to ignore.

The Smithsonian skull was donated anonymously with the following note:

> Dear Sir,
>
> This Aztec crystal skull was purported to be part of the [Mexican President] Porfirio Diaz collection, was purchased in Mexico City in 1960 . . . I am offering it to the Smithsonian without consideration. Naturally, I wish to remain anonymous.

Reported to be the largest and ugliest example of the known crystal skulls, it weighs thirty-two pounds and is not as clear a crystal as some other well-known examples, such as the Mitchell-Hedges skull. The Smithsonian skull has a smooth finish, but its features are crude and have an oddly threatening aspect.

When the Smithsonian National Museum of American History tried to track down the donor, they learned he was dead. In fact, his lawyer said that after his client sent the skull to the museum, he committed suicide. Relaying the details, he said that soon after his client bought the skull, his wife died. Shortly after that, his son had a terrible accident that left him brain-dead. The man then went bankrupt—all before he had donated the skull.

The use of gemstones as personal talismans, jewelry, and magical objects reached a high point in the ancient world with the Romans. In their continual efforts to expand the empire, Rome absorbed many cultural influences and traditions of the Persians, the Egyptians, Arabs, and others, and the love of gems was no exception. Romans incorporated precious gems into their architecture, and many temples dedicated to the gods have stones adorning them in honor.

It's worth noting, however, that although they revered these gems, the Romans believed they must first be consecrated by priests, inscribed, or otherwise imbued with magic before they could "perform." This practice may well be the antecedent for the popular modern belief that stones and crystals must first be cleansed or charged by a user or healer in order to be effective.

advent of Christianity diminished, though by no means extinguished, humanity's love of the mineral world. For example, there are a number of references to precious gems in the New Testament, and they appear numerous times in the Book of Revelations in descriptions of God and his heavenly throne.

Roman Angel

The Middle Ages saw renewed interest in crystals and gemstones, and their various powers were ascribed to by mystics, thinkers, and physicians of every persuasion. References in medieval literature abound: the stone at the base of the horn of the mythical unicorn is one example, while the Holy Grail, a vessel endowed with all sorts of magical qualities, is said to have been fashioned from a single gem. In both instances, the gemstone as an allegory for divine energy, or the life force, is clear. And the ultimate goal of the alchemists was, of course, the philosopher's stone. In fact, literature on alchemy includes numerous mineralogical references and

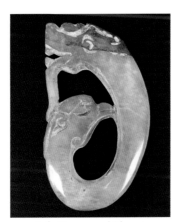

Jade Dragon and Phoenix

Though the Old Testament abounds with references to gems, as does the Talmud, the involves taking "base matter" (stone or lead, lapis, etc.) and transforming it. Much of their work was secret and allegorical, yet it is known that they spent considerable time experimenting with processes that removed impurities from gemstones and other metals. It is of particular interest that the "pure vessel" referred to in many such texts was in fact pure rock crystal. Descriptions of the famous alchemist's furnace are fascinating when compared to the process of extreme and prolonged heat that we use to enhance gemstone quality today.

Paracelsus, the famous philosopher who was in many ways a father of modern holistic healing sciences, used gems and minerals extensively in his work and research. Among other things, he saw the earth, in all its life forms, as an integrated whole, with minerals and gemstones available to us for specific purposes. He was a proponent of powdered stone and gems for medicinal purposes, and in his day the medicinal use of stones and minerals was so widespread that they were part of the regular inventory of the apothecary.

But a new view of the universe was about to emerge. Nicolaus Copernicus and Johannes Kepler, in advancing the idea of a sun-centered solar system, did not so much disparage the metaphysical universe as add to it. Later centuries saw more of a division between the emerging sciences and the more integrated worldview. Religion played a part in changing believers' perceptions as well, preaching, as it did, against worldly preoccupations and vanity.

In the centuries since then, because of the increasing division between the advancing sciences and the worldview advocated by organized religion, the use of crystals, gemstones, and minerals was relegated to the realms of mystery and fringe theory. The current advancement of crystal use and therapy in the modern era is less than twenty years old and yet, at the same time, it speaks to a tradition and beliefs that are many hundreds of thousands of years old.

Ironically, in recent years we have witnessed science find uses for crystal energy that an alchemist might never have dreamed; you have only to touch the LCD display on your computer to connect with a sense of their mystery. Yet their increasing use by alternative therapists, ordinary people, and modern-day mystics speaks to a sense of knowing that is beyond mere imagination. The connection between human beings and rocks, minerals, and crystals runs so deep within us that we respond without fully comprehending why.

The paradox is that the more science is able to accomplish, the closer we return to mystery. Mystery, in turn, renews our sense of the divine. Ultimately, science may be able to measure the energies of crystals, find new technologies for them, and harness their power. But no matter what science may be able to accomplish, it will never eradicate that sense of the sacred.

Energy is energy; science can measure it, and we use it. Crystals, gems, and minerals conduct measurable energy in specific ways. It doesn't have a religion and belongs to no area of expertise. We can harness its power, but we cannot own it. There are right ways and wrong ways in the use of energy, just as there are right and wrong ways to utilize crystals, but their nature remains ultimately mysterious—yet somehow it serves to reestablish our connections with everything around us and provide an all-important sense of the sacred forces at work in our lives.

Wulfenite Crystals

HOW TO USE THIS BOOK

MUCH OF THE information you will find in these pages is based upon time-honored traditions. The knowledge that crystals, minerals, and gemstones contain and conduct energy has not escaped the attention of any major cultural or religious tradition in recorded history. I've included as much background on the minerals as possible, wherever possible, and tried to respect tradition while at the same time incorporating as much new information as is available.

Each entry includes some basic information to help you identify your stones: their basic composition or mineral grouping; which crystal structure they have; their hardness according to the Mohs scale, as a means to help you choose your stones wisely for jewelry or other uses; and finally, where they come from, as an aid to your being better able to determine their authenticity.

The uses (and potential misuses) of gems and crystals is well documented here and carefully researched. As your guide, I have made every effort to cross-reference where possible and to exclude any recommendations that seemed questionable or contradictory. Some stones are able to assist you in more ways than one, so feel free to utilize and experiment with them in as many ways as you desire. Just because a stone has a certain type of energy doesn't mean you can't put that energy to use in a variety of ways.

This book is unique in that it is organized not as an A to Z reference, but by personal needs, be they physical, spiritual, or practical. After all, if one has heartache, one doesn't necessarily want to go thumbing through a hundred different kinds of crystals to find the one that will be most effective, and not everyone needs to be an expert to use crystals effectively in their everyday life. I've also included a selection of references and resources, as well as a glossary for quick reference in the appendixes following the text.

It's important to keep in mind that we're dealing with *energy*. Energy isn't *magic* and energy isn't *medicine*. I do not advocate the use of powdered stones or gem elixirs for the simple reason that while those alternatives have a respected historical tradition, the fact is, the ancients did *not* have the same kind of pharmacy available to them as do you and I. Further, some stones can be downright toxic when taken internally. So use your good sense, and remember that crystal work, although it can be tremendously helpful in a variety of ways, is not a substitute for more conventional forms of medical treatment.

Despite the fact that we dwell in the midst of highly advanced technology, many of us continue to seek a deeper sense of connection to ourselves, to one another, and to the energies of the planet as a whole. For that reason, a more conscious approach to life demands we become more conscious of ourselves and our motivations, and to be as specific as possible when it comes to defining what we want crystals to do for us. Thus, each chapter introduction includes a short discussion on getting in touch with your own ideas of how to best work with the selections included in that chapter. In addition, the epigraphs, or "gems of wisdom," provided for each entry are meant to assist you in better attuning to the energy of the process you are addressing, be it love, money, or transformation. They are there both to inspire and to serve as a reminder of your own inner wisdom.

The use of gemstones, crystals, and miner-als can never hurt you and can be of enormous help, whatever your situation. Working with these stones over time and experimenting on your own will educate you further in the mysteries of crystal energy, and will help to restore that sometimes missing sense of connection to the life all around us. Not only do stones offer us the most natural remedies possible, but they also provide energy that is straight from the earth, and it works.

Yet the process remains essentially mysterious, the result of an exchange of the subtle and unseen energies that make up all life on this planet and, indeed, form the essence of the life force itself. To enter into crystal work shows a willingness to enter that mystery and to experience, consciously and without prejudice, an expansion in consciousness of ourselves, our deep connections to others, and to the life force that exists in all things. To harness and direct that energy constitutes true mastery, a genuine gift of the gods.

Andalusite

2

THE LOVE STONES

There are four questions of value in life . . .
What is sacred? Of what is the spirit made?
What is worth living for, and what is worth dying for?
The answer to each is the same. Only love.
—DON JUAN, IN *DON JUAN DEMARCO*

THE PROBLEM WITH love is that it's an awfully broad category that can't really be covered in a short introduction. At the risk of sounding cliche, love simply means too many different things to too many different people. For some, it's all about that first flush of romance; for others, it's about sexual passion; for still others, love means establishing a stable, long-term situation, complete with a mortgage, kids, and white picket fence. Some people think of love in terms of finding the ultimate soul mate, while for others, it's all about a best friend and steady companionship.

Despite the fact that looking for love, falling in love, and being in love can sometimes seem like our collective preoccupation, we don't necessarily know as much about love as we think. What we do know is that love changes our energies through a host of complex psychological, spiritual, and physical responses that aren't always easy to identify or pin down. Yet as mysterious as the phenomenon of love is, we can say with some certainty that each and every love relationship is bound to teach you something important about yourself.

But while each of us might quite rightly be called a "bundle of individual needs" when it comes to affairs of the heart, we've become oddly conditioned to the idea that there's just one solution—some ultimate partner out there waiting for us. If we just manage to hang on and play the game to the best of our abilities, that person will eventually show up. *Someday, my prince will come; some day I'll meet the man or woman of my dreams. Someday my troubles will be over and I just won't have to worry about the whole relationship thing anymore.*

Wrong.

The fact is, each and every person alive will encounter any number of opportunities to experience true love during the course of a lifetime, but it's what we do with those opportunities that counts. Just like people, love relationships come in all shapes, sizes, and sexual persuasions. Some last forever and some don't, and no crystal, mineral, or gemstone in the world is going to conjure up your one and only. What stones can be used for in the arena of personal relationships is simply what they do best—they help. If you're sincerely interested in improving your love life (and who isn't?), working with these energies is sure to teach you that when it comes to love, it's all about *intention.*

Since there are so many different kinds of love, as you might expect, there is no set type of energy or crystalline structure for the type of love you may be looking for. Nevertheless, this chapter includes information about stones with a wide variety of energies to offer you the broadest array of choices for spicing up, augmenting, or overhauling your love life. You will find a number of stones here associated with the more traditional heart chakra and some associated with the sexual energy centers of the body. These stones have been chosen for both their strong erotic history and their modern associations with that ineffable thing we call romance. So whatever you may be looking for, you're sure to find something that speaks to your personal needs.

Before choosing any stone or following any of the recommendations included here, it's important that you first clarify what you're really looking for. That's going to require time, reflection, and a few long conversations with yourself. Love gems and crystals each have very specific "emotional intelligence" and energies. Those energies act in such a way that our deepest motivations and needs can surface from the unconscious with sometimes unsettling results. Like God himself, crystal energy can work in downright mysterious ways, so it helps to be as self-aware as possible before selecting any specific stones.

In a very real sense, then, working with love crystals asks us not so much to be careful of what we wish for, but to be especially mindful of what we wish for. Each of the love stones carries specific energies. Some are subtle, some are strong, some will draw passionate encounters, some will contribute to the stability of an existing relationship, so it's important to be clear about what you want before you employ a stone to help you get it.

(Also see chapter 4, The Stones of Protection)

A talisman made of carnelian brings luck and well-being to believers.
—JOHANN WOLFGANG VON GOETHE

■

CLEAR RED to brownish-red member of the chalcedony family, carnelian, or sard, is actually a variety of **cryptocrystalline** quartz, which means its crystals are too small to discern, even under a microscope. Having a hardness of 7.0 on the Mohs scale, these stones may contain small amounts of iron and can be streaked or banded with white. Sometimes called the "Mecca stone," most carnelians today are heat treated to enhance their color. Carnelian is found in many locations throughout the world, including India, Australia, Brazil, Madagascar, Russia, South Africa, and the United States.

Some of the oldest jewelry artifacts feature carnelian. The Egyptians so revered the power of this stone that it was one of three used most often in jewelry and ornament, along with turquoise and lapis lazuli. In the Bible it is one of the twelve stones used to represent the tribes of Israel. Ancient Greeks and Romans called it *sardius* and used the stone for signets, seals, and cameos. In more modern times, Goethe attributed carnelian with the powers of protection against evil, of continuation of hope and comfort, and of good luck. Rich in providing motivation, some have called it the "stone of self-esteem."

Long believed to have powers associated with the physical cycles of the body, including menstruation, the name *carnelian* means "flesh-colored," and for that reason this stone has come to be associated specifically with sexual relationships and sexual healing. Some healers associate carnelian with the second chakra, which is the body's center for creative, sexual, and emotional energies, but other practitioners associate it with the five physical senses. When you use this energy, you may simply feel more alive, more sensual, and have a deeper appreciation for both your own and a lover's body—it helps you to be more comfortable in your own skin. In addition, carnelian energy offers a greater sense of connection with friends and lovers and a reduction of guilty feelings, resulting in a more spontaneous, energetic, and generous attitude. With an energy that inspires one to focus on the here and now, carnelian will bolster your confidence, allay your fears, and enhance passion in every respect.

On the emotional level, the energy from carnelian helps to stimulate emotional balance and expression, inspire passion, and move those who wear or carry it to action. It is *the* stone to have when it's time to make your move. So turn on the soft music, lower the lights, and keep a carnelian close at hand.

EMERALD

The young emerald, evening star,
Good light for drunkards, poets, widows,
And ladies soon to be married.
—WALLACE STEVENS

■

THE HIGHLY PRIZED emerald is the grass-green variety of beryl, with essentially the same physical properties of other stones of the beryl family, including aquamarine, goshenite, and morganite. Emeralds belong to the hexagonal group of crystals and measure 7.5 to 8.0 on the Mohs scale. Today emerald is mined in Columbia, Brazil, and Zambia, but there is an increasing amount of lab-grown emerald on the market as well.

Another member of the beryl family and a relative to emerald, morganite is said to be helpful for getting rid of someone. So if you're the object of some undesired attention, wear or carry morganite until your unwanted admirer gets the message.

The name *emerald* may have come indirectly from the Greek *smaragdos*, a name that seems to have been given to a number of stones having little in common except a green color. Ancient peoples obtained emeralds from the area in and around Upper Egypt, where it was used as early as 2000 BC. The Greeks were mining emeralds in the time of Alexander the Great, while in Egypt, Cleopatra was becoming an avid collec-

tor. In the New World, sixteenth-century Spanish explorers found large emeralds in the possession of the Aztecs and Incas. And in India and areas of Persia, they were considered appropriate for the moguls and shahs, who wore them as talismans.

Traditionally, the emerald was a stone of love, domestic bliss, and loyalty, and was particularly associated with the qualities of faithfulness and devotion. It was believed to eliminate negativity from relationships, and sometimes even negative partners. As emer-

■ LET THEM EAT—EMERALDS? ■

THE ACTRESS Marlene Dietrich was a huge fan of jewelry of all kinds, but especially emeralds, a trait that undoubtedly landed her the role of a jewel thief in the film *Desire* (1938). Another famous Hollywood story claims that once, when baking a cake at Katherine Cornell's house, Dietrich thought she had lost her 37.41 carat cabochon emerald ring, which she had removed in the kitchen. The house was turned upside down, but the ring could not be found. It was only during dessert that the ring was discovered by one of the dinner guests inside a piece of the cake!

alds are very sensitive to heat and can change color, many believe that if an emerald fades, it is a sure indication of unfaithfulness.

Legend has it that the Roman emperor Nero would watch his gladiators through an emerald crystal.

THOUGH EMERALDS CAN now be grown in the laboratory, true emerald is typically heavily flawed with cracks and inclusions of fluid and minerals. These inclusions are called *jardin* (or "garden") and usually resemble leaves and branches. These characteristics are considered part of the character of the stone and are used to assure buyers that the stone is genuine.

In matters of the heart, emerald is the stone to work with when seeking (or showing to another) the qualities of constancy, deep affection, and abiding love. Use the energy of this stone when you're ready to go steady, get married, or make a similar long-term commitment, for emeralds impart faith and success in love. It is said that emerald energy also helps you to identify false friends and false promises. It promotes constancy of mind, true friendship, and the kind of sustaining energy that shows us all the healing power of true love.

Contemporary practitioners and healers employ emerald in a variety of ways, and find it particularly useful in subduing an overactive heart chakra, where emotions tend to take over and vulnerability, impulsiveness, or oversensitivity is a problem. In identifying the kinds of souls for whom emerald was a "good light" in the quote that introduces this stone, it appears that poet Wallace Stevens was entirely correct in his assessment of emerald energy.

The ruling passion, be it what it will. The ruling passion conquers reason still.
—ALEXANDER POPE

■

GARNETS GET THEIR name from the Latin *granatum*, meaning "seed of the pomegranate," an obvious reference to the deep red variety of the stone. All garnets belong to the isometric crystal group. With a hardness of 6.0 to 7.5 on the Mohs scale, garnets in various forms are found all over the world in locations such as India and parts of Europe, as well as the state of Arizona and the continents of Africa and Australia.

To geologists, garnet is really a family of stones made up of two distinct groups: (1) the *aluminum group*, which makes up the vast majority of what we usually think of as garnet gemstones, including pyrope (the red to dark red variety), almandine (orangey-red to brown), and spessartine (yellow to orange); and (2) the *calcite group*, which includes the olive-green uvarovites; grossular, which can be anything from almost clear to orange, pink, yellow, green, and brown; and finally *andradites*, which are usually brown or black, though there are yellowish stones in the group with tones ranging from green to orange.

Garnets are plentiful in crystals and small stones, though larger stones are rare. Most garnets today are dyed to enhance their color, which modern crystal practitioners and healers believe does not much affect their qualities of energy. Belonging to the igneous group, garnets are formed when high temperatures or pressure is a factor, and geologists often use garnets as a gauge of the amount of temperature and pressure that was present during their formation. Similarly, garnet energy works in much the way it was formed, exerting subtle but powerful pressure on matters of the heart.

Garnet jewelry has been found that dates back to the Bronze Age. Other ancient jewelry containing garnet has been discovered in Sweden that dates from between 1100 and 2000 BC, in Samaria (dating from 2300 BC), and in Egypt (dating from 3100 BC), where it enjoyed popularity in a variety of amulets and talismans. Garnet has also been documented as a largely admired treasure in Greece during the third and fourth centuries. Mythology tells us that garnet symbolism is used as a gift of love's attraction, a gift of quick return, or a gift of estranged love. Biblical references imply that King Solomon wore garnet and that it is one of the stones chosen to represent the twelve tribes of Israel.

During the Middle Ages, garnets were believed to protect people from poisons and other illnesses and thought to increase the knightly qualities of chivalry, loyalty, and honesty. Thus, in today's world of love and romance, garnets are the stone to wear or carry if you are, indeed, looking for that knight in shining armor.

Contemporary proponents of working with garnet energy associate the stone, in its many varieties, with romantic love, passion, and the ability to restore a sense of purity and innocence to the quest for romance. They are said to be great healers of broken hearts as well. Since garnets tend to be small, their energy is best used in combination with other stones to draw love to you. If you're simply clueless in matters of the heart, garnet is the stone to use for guidance. For that reason, it is thought to be especially appropriate

■ COLORFUL GARNETS ■

THE MANY DIFFERENT colors and chemistries of garnet varieties allow you to experiment and refine your work with this stone's energy for very specific purposes. The green garnets are thought to bring peace and to smooth over romantic troubles. Orange garnets are associated with the energy of commitment. Purple garnets increase physical and emotional tenacity and heal chronic indecisiveness. Finally, the red garnet group is particularly useful for those who desire a spark in an existing relationship or who are beginning a new one. Red stones are also for helping to heal and energize those who feel they have been sexually weakened (by self-consciousness or other means). Physically, some people have used garnets to aid in relieving the negative energy that blocks fertility. As a stone of sexual power, garnet acts to renew, awaken, and heal the sexual center.

for adolescents, or for people who are long out of the dating scene and wishing to reenter the world of romance. Offering a healing and protective energy, some believe garnet is a protection against infidelity.

On the physical level, garnet works to allay anxiety and bothersome physical symptoms such as sweaty hands and nervous giggles. The red variety, along with being one of the stones that ignites and refuels the fires of passion and romance, sets ablaze those all-important inner fires of self-confidence and creativity. Got your eye on a temperamental type? Wear or carry garnet to soothe that savage beast. The opposing positive fire of garnet energy can be used against tantrums and episodes of angst.

Gold has a value; jade is invaluable.
—CHINESE PROVERB

WHAT WE USUALLY think of as *jade* is actually a generic term for two different gems, nephrite and jadeite. Both varieties belong to the monoclinic system of crystals. Jadeite is generally considered more valuable than the nephrite variety and measures anywhere from 5.0 to 7.0 on the Mohs scale. Deep green jadeite is known as *imperial jade,* though it also comes in a variety of other colors, including pink, lilac, lavender, brown, lime green, black, and white. Both nephrite jade and jadeite artifacts have been unearthed in such places as Holland, France, Germany, Poland, Belgium, Switzerland, Finland, and Great Britain. Jade is also found in Mexico, in Central and South America, and in the western United States, including Alaska.

Always considered a sacred stone in China, where it is called *yu,* the Western name, *jade,* is derived from the Spanish *piedra de ijada,* or "stone of loins." Jadeite and nephrite are used more or less interchangeably by contemporary practitioners, and both have similar vibration and crystalline structure.

Blessed with unique energy, jade is equally unique in its mythological tradition and has held a special attraction for centuries. Among the Chinese, jade butterflies symbolize love to a bride on her wedding day, while a carved jade phoenix is offered to young girls who are coming of age. Ancient Mexicans and Amerindians placed a piece of jade in the mouths of the dead, while in ancient Europe jade was primarily used for tools and weapons. As the Bronze Age and the Iron Age approached, more suitable materials became available, and the Europeans slowly abandoned the use of jade.

Contrary to popular belief, jade cannot be carved in the traditional sense, nor can it be shaped by chiseling or chipping. Instead, the intricate working of jade, both in ancient and modern traditions, reveals a process by which jade is abraded, or worn away. Since working jade is a process that is time-consuming and requires immense patience, ancient examples of intricate jade are a testament to the skill of those ancient artisans who worked the stone several thousand years before modern tools were invented.

The Chinese believe jade is symbolic of the five highest virtues: benignity, lucidity, resonance, immutability, and purity, while Native Americans of the Pacific Northwest considered jade a stone of wisdom and luck. The Maori of New Zealand carved pictures of their ancestors in jade, handing them down through generations with the belief that some portion of the spirit remained within the stones.

Holding a strong feminine, yin energy, jade is related to the heart chakra and exerts a beneficial effect on all heart-related matters. Carried or worn, it can attract and enhance love of all kinds. Also said by some traditions to be a stone that ensures both sexual fidelity and generosity, it is also believed to enhance and improve sexual performance in both males and females.

Jade is not the stone to use if you're in search of a wild night of passion, however. Rather, its peaceful energy promotes long-term domestic bliss. Especially useful for patching up a lovers' quarrel or getting a foundering marriage back on track, the energy of jade works deeply and with long-term effect, encouraging serenity and acceptance of each other's faults.

■ COLORS OF JADE ■

VARIATIONS IN JADE color can further the stone's energy and can be useful in very specific circumstances. White jade, for example, promotes discernment in matters of the heart and is said to help control the urges of those with a wandering eye. Honey or yellow jade will increase optimism and energy. Brown jade is good for people who are entering a new phase of relationship, while the highly prized pink and lilac varieties are said to draw to one who wears or carries the stone a love match truly made in heaven.

Love is just love, it can never be explained.
—ANONYMOUS

■

A PHYSICAL COMPOSITION of the minerals lazurite, calcite, and pyrite, along with lesser amounts of other minerals, lapis lazuli is generally found as veins in limestone. Scientifically speaking, lapis lazuli is neither a gemstone nor a mineral, but a rock, because it is a conglomeration of other minerals. As such, it belongs to no specific crystal group. Measuring 5.5 on the Mohs scale, true lapis lazuli is characterized by the presence of flecks of pyrite. Today, the major supplier of lapis lazuli is Afghanistan, where the stone has been mined for more than six thousand years. Lapis is also found in some parts of Russia and Chile and in the states of California and Colorado.

The first part of its name comes from the Latin word *lapus,* which means "stone"; the second part derives from the ancient Persian word *lāzhward,* which originally was a place name but in subsequent centuries was associated both with the sky and the color azure blue. Prized for centuries for its beauty, lapis was used by the ancient Egyptians and Persians for everything from medicine to makeup, to paint pigment. An important ritual stone in many ancient cultures, lapis lazuli has always had strong mystical and occult associations. Its beautiful deep blue has been traditionally associated with the sort of royalty thought to be descended from the gods themselves. Egyptians, Sumerians, and Babylonians all associated this stone with the divine feminine and fertility, while even today Hindus believe it has strong protective powers over children.

The Romans were perhaps the first to associate lapis with love and believed it to be a powerful aphrodisiac. In the Middle Ages it was thought to keep the limbs healthy and to free the soul from error, envy, and fear. Russian empress Catherine the Great certainly responded to its vibrations, for she had an entire ballroom paneled with the stone.

Today we understand that the true energy of lapis lazuli lies in its ability to connect the mind and the heart. It is especially useful for those who experience a chronic conflict between workings of the mind (or conscience) and the more spontaneous impulse to follow their heart. The stone is perfect for those romantic situations of *Will I, or won't I? Should I or shouldn't I?* because the real gift of this

■ BUYER BEWARE! ■

TRUE LAPIS LAZULI is expensive and relatively rare, so it has become one of the most faked stones in the world. First, lower grades of lapis are frequently dyed to enhance the color. Unfortunately, lapis does not take dye well and will easily rub off with water and time. Fake lapis may also be created by dying howlite, a white stone that takes dye easily, while other imitations are made of glass or sugilite. Real lapis is best identified by its hardness (5.5 on the Mohs scale), a lack of white or calcite veins, and the all-important presence of flecks of golden pyrite.

energy is clarity. Lapis carries the unique ability to help those who work with it to come to terms with their own truth and to be more authentic in the context of their relationships.

Beyond its ability to illuminate and clarify our truest feelings, many people all over the world consider lapis lazuli to be a stone of truth and friendship. We know for certain the stone will bring about increased harmony in relationships, and will help those who wear or carry it to be more completely themselves and to openly state their opinions. Thus, it's particularly helpful for people who are perennial pleasers or who often find themselves in a position of giving more to a relationship than they get back.

Worn as jewelry, lapis is particularly effective in a pendant or brooch worn over the heart, though in a ring worn on the ring finger of the left hand, it will also serve to connect the mind and heart more effectively. Frequently cut into **cabochons** or amulets, lapis talismans are easy to keep near you, and keeping one on your bedside table is said to offer protection from false love of all kinds. Don't be surprised if your tried-and-true marriage or relationship begins to undergo long-needed changes under the influence of lapis energy; just keep in mind that perhaps a change was long overdue. Finally, if you're really uncertain about where a love relationship is going, add some lapis to the energy mix for two to three weeks. It's a sure way to establish if a relationship has "got legs."

Ultimately, lapis is of tremendous help in resolving any inner conflicts between intellect and emotions, resulting in a wonderful expansion of viewpoint and a greater openness to the infinite possibilities for love to grow without resistance from one's inner critic.

MOONSTONE

Wait for me by moonlight,
watch for me by moonlight,
I'll come to thee by moonlight
though hell should bar the way.
—ALFRED NOYES

■

MOONSTONE IS A variety of feldspar known for its spiritual powers and specifically associated with feminine energy. Moonstones come in a variety of colors, ranging from colorless to white, gray, brown, yellow, orange, green, or pink, and their clarity ranges from transparent to translucent. Measuring 6.0 on the Mohs scale, moonstones belong to the hexagonal group of crystals. Today, moonstone is found in Brazil, the European Alps, India, Madagascar, Mexico, Myanmar, Sri Lanka, Tanzania, and the United States.

Named by the Romans for its luminous resemblance to moonlight, the milky sheen of moonstone is known as **chatoyancy** or the **schiller effect**. It has been prized as a gemstone for thousands of years. In parts of Asia it is revered as a stone that can bring harmony and good fortune to marriages and love relationships. It is said that moonstone helps one to relax fully and enjoy the moment; thus, it is often used to alleviate sexual anxiety, in addition to helping one fully love and appreciate others. In India moonstone is given to engaged couples to help them understand what their lives together will be like.

Older women have found moonstone to have regenerative qualities that can reawaken passion and sexual desire. Younger females have reported it useful in matters of fertility and pregnancy.

Moonstone pendant

In general, moonstone energy is calming, gentle, and receptive. Though traditionally held forth as having female qualities, it is good for anyone seeking to strengthen their intuition, especially with regard to potential love interests. It is also reputed to have the power to grant wishes. For example, if some obstacle stands in the way of you and a lover, moonstone energy will aid you, though, of course, it will not bend another person to your will. It can also be extremely useful in smoothing out the aftermath of a lovers' quarrel and increasing understanding and harmony between the parties. Very much offering a "feeling" and intuitive energy, it can help you find your heart's desire, even if you're not sure just what that might be.

Some healers and practitioners point to the colorations of moonstone as being especially useful in particular situations. White moonstone is considered the most generally beneficial; orange is particularly recommended for sexual anxiety; silver is good for eliminating confusion and helping to make far-reaching decisions such as whether to marry or divorce; and rainbow moonstone is recommended for reviving a sense of passion and creativity in an established relationship.

Moonstone energy can be of great use in ridding oneself of so-called toxic relationships and people. In love matters especially it will help you to find the strength to change and can encourage growth and the ability to "go with the flow."

Wearing or carrying a moonstone is believed to help bring a new love into your life. Another traditional ritual instructs that lovers who have quarreled should each hold a piece of the stone over their hearts, then exchange the stones with each other to bring them back together. Place a piece of moonstone on your bedside table, and it is said your true love will appear in your dreams.

Finally, moonstone energy combines and works well with other stones, providing a steady complementary energy for more passionate, sexual, or romantic adventures.

PEARL

Does the pearl know, that in its shade and sheen
The dreamy rose and tender, wavering green
Are hid the hearts of all the ranging seas
That beauty weeps for gifts as fair as these?
—HELEN HAY

PEARLS VARY IN color from white to those with a hint of pink, to brown, or even black. Contrary to popular belief, pearls hardly ever result from the intrusion of a grain of sand. Rather, a pearl forms when an irritant such as a food particle becomes trapped in a mollusk. The object is then coated with the mineral aragonite and the protein conchiolin to form nacre, more typically known as *mother-of-pearl*. Quite soft in comparison to other stones, pearls range between 2.5 and 4.5 on the Mohs scale. Today, "natural" pearls are cultivated in various locations around the world.

A complete history of the pearl and the

mystical lore surrounding it could make for an entire book all by itself. As perhaps the world's oldest gemstone, it's likely that their ineffable beauty was first discovered sometime in prehistory. For thousands and thousands of years, pearls have been harvested from the Persian Gulf, the Indian Ocean, and the Red Sea, while Polynesia and Australia produce mainly cultured pearls. Both freshwater and saltwater pearls are now cultivated in Japan and China, and the freshwater varieties can also be found in rivers in Scotland, Ireland, France, Austria, Germany, and the United States. Before the creation of cultured pearls in the early 1900s, natural pearls were so rare and expensive that they were reserved almost exclusively for royalty and the very wealthy.

Pliny the Elder, perhaps the world's first gemologist, writes in his famous *Natural History* that two pearls were worth an estimated 60 million sesterces, or 1,875,000 ounces of silver—figuring silver at a modern price of $5 per ounce, far less than its worth in ancient times, that's $9,375,000!

The pearl's mystique reaches deep. In Chinese culture it is said that pearls fall to earth when dragons fight in the clouds. Dragons are therefore often depicted with a pearl in their mouth or claws—a symbol of immortality, magic, and luck. In feudal Japan pearls were prescribed for healing, longevity, and in love potions, while Western lore holds the pearl as the stone of Diana, the Roman goddess of the moon and wild magic. During the Middle Ages knights often wore pearls onto the battlefield for protection. Many Polynesian cultures assert that the pearl is a moon goddess in physical form. All over the world, pearls have been said to have the kind of legendary mystical, restorative, and healing powers that have fired imaginations for centuries.

Pearls have obvious associations with the

moon, the feminine, along with the fact that they grow underwater, in itself a symbol for the emotions. But pearl energy also represents purity, innocence, and integrity. Pearls have long been considered ideal wedding gifts. In the Hindu religion, for example, the presentation of an undrilled pearl and its piercing has formed part of the marriage ceremony for obvious symbolic reasons.

You can best tell that a pearl is real, whether natural or cultured, by rubbing it against your teeth. Real pearls are rough and produce vibrations that you can hear.

Because of their natural beauty, pearls are associated with the very matrix of life. Wear pearls if you are intent on wanting love to grow between you and a partner, particularly if you are seeking energetic aid in matters of fertility and reproduction. Is your biological clock ticking? Are you yearning to start a family with no prospects in sight? Male or female, pearls will draw to you a suitable prospect, for these stones are believed by contemporary practitioners to be blessed with extraordinary magnetic energy—just the right kind of power to attract true love and soul mates to one another. Offer loved ones gifts of pearls only when you are sure that the person with whom you are involved is "the one." Such gifts will ensure that the object of your affections will remain steadfast and devoted, even in cases where his or her love isn't reciprocated.

Perhaps most important, however, pearl energy better enables its owner to *accept* love. It allows the person who wears or carries it to see the good qualities in themselves and develop a higher degree of self-love, so that they can, in turn, share and love others more completely.

■ LA PEREGRINA ■

ELIZABETH TAYLOR MAY be known for her diamonds, but her jewelry collection also boasts one of the most famous pearls in the world. The pear-shaped "La Peregrina" weighs in at a whopping 203.84 grains. The pearl was discovered in the early sixteenth century by a slave on the shores of Panama, who supposedly won his freedom with his find. It was later found in England, where it was given to Mary Tudor by her husband, the Spanish king Philip II. It became part of the Spanish treasury, was painted by Velasquez, and inspired the composer Ravel. The pearl eventually made its way to France, where it was sold to save its new owner, the son of Napoleon III, from financial ruin. It finally ended up at Sotheby's in 1969, and Ms. Taylor engaged the renowned French jeweler Cartier to make it into a necklace. It's been reported that the pearl was lost at one point in the actress's Las Vegas hotel room, resulting in a frantic search until it was discovered in the mouth of her dog.

PERIDOT

Men always want to be a woman's first love—women like to be a man's last romance.
—OSCAR WILDE

■

PERIDOT BELONGS TO the chrysolite family of minerals. The stones range in color from yellowish green to bright lime green, and their clarity ranges from transparent to translucent. They belong to the orthorhombic crystal group and measure 6.5 to 7.0 on the Mohs scale. Chemically, peridot's color depends on the amount of iron contained in the stone. Today, peridot is found in many locations, including Australia, Brazil, China, Egypt, Myanmar (Burma), Pakistan, Norway, and the western United States. Much of today's supply comes from Arizona.

Peridot is a French word derived from the Arabic word *faridat,* meaning "gem." In ancient times these stones were mined in the area around the great city of Constantinople, and it is said that many of Cleopatra's famed collection of emeralds were actually peridot. The stones are distinguished by the fact that they may well be the only precious stones that have literally dropped from heaven, for peridots have been found in meteorites.

The Romans called this stone the "evening emerald" and believed it had magical powers to cure depression. Crusaders carried the stones back from the Far East as symbols of wisdom, and very large examples of the stone adorn the shrine of the three magi at Cologne Cathedral in France. During the reign of the Ottoman Empire, Turkish sultans amassed some of the world's largest collections of the stone. In Hawaii active volcanoes throw out the gem in molten form, cooling into teardrop shapes as they fall to earth. Thus, ancient Hawaiians believed the stones were the tears of the volcano goddess Pele. Believed to be a stone of springtime, some see peridot as a gift from Mother Nature.

In matters of the heart, peridot is used to help dreams become a reality, specifically with the purpose of drawing a new lover to you. It's been said that Napoleon once gave Josephine a peridot as a symbol of his undying love and admiration. This very popular stone radiates with enthusiasm and is strongly associated with yang energy and the sun itself. A stone of lightness and beauty, its vibrational aspect brings to mind new beginnings. Its energy is both subtle and light—some might call it a rather sophisticated energy. But if you visualize both the great courage and the utter fragility of a new seedling as it pushes up out of the soil, you'll have a better understanding of how to best employ this stone. For that reason, more no-nonsense types, the single-minded, those who are love obsessed, or one embroiled in overwhelming personal problems might miss the true nature of the peridot's blessings.

More specifically, peridot adds a certain intelligence to your romantic life and will draw to you the kind of lover with whom you will have a true meeting of the minds. It's also said to mitigate jealousy and protect its wearer from unnecessary heartache. This is definitely not "drag 'em off by the forelock" energy, but if you're looking for the kind of love that somebody once called "the great relief of having somebody to talk to," peridot is your stone. It strengthens fragile egos and facilitates communication on all levels.

Although it doesn't traditionally have specific sexual associations, peridot will definitely do a lot to calm the butterflies in your stomach and is considered extremely effective against nervousness. Overall, it increases strength and physical vitality, calms the heart, and truly raises the spirit.

RHODOCHROSITE

There are two sorts of romantics:
those who love, and those who love the adventure of loving.
—LESLIE BLANCH

■

RHODOCHROSITE IS DERIVED from the Greek word for "rose red." It is also known by the names *Inca Rose* and less frequently *Madagascar Star*. Rhodochrosite is its own mineral species, belonging to the trigonal crystal system. It measures 3.5 to 4.5 on the Mohs scale and ranges in color and opacity from pale pinks, often banded with orange and gold, to brilliant red crystalline forms. Inexpensive and easy to obtain, the stone's major suppliers today are found in Argentina, Germany, Romania, South Africa, and the United States.

A relatively recent discovery in the mineral kingdom, significant finds occurred in Argentina just before World War II, though archaeological remnants of this stone have been found that date from the time of the Incas; hence, the nickname *Inca Rose.* In parts of the Andes in South America, indigenous peoples believed that rhodochrosite was the blood of their former rulers turned to stone.

Its softness makes it impractical for use in jewelry and ornament, and what relics survive are deteriorated. Nevertheless, the stone has attained great popularity among New Age practitioners and in alternative therapies.

This is a stone closely associated with the fourth, or heart, chakra, and it is of considerable benefit in opening the heart center. Used wisely, rhodochrosite can make for great changes in your love life in a very short period of time—the key word being *change.* This is *the* gem for change, so if you're seeking a change of romantic partners, lifestyle, spouses, or attitudes, this is the energy to work with. But before you begin, it's important to keep in mind just how resistant we can be to making significant changes in our lives. As much as we are willing to acknowledge that change is inevitable, it takes a great deal of self-awareness and flexibility to incorporate change gracefully. So don't attempt to work with rhodochrosite unless you're really sure you need a change—really, *really,* sure. This is a crystal that doesn't fool around.

More than anything, the energy of rhodochrosite urges us to pay attention to our hearts and those things we hunger for. It reacquaints us with desire, makes us ready for adventure, and offers new chances, especially for love. It works very effectively with our resistance, avoidance, or capacity for denial, and in some cases may call forth a reinterpretation of old prejudices or outworn values.

Understanding how rhodochrosite works requires some knowledge of behavioral patterns, keeping in mind that not all behavioral patterns are negative in nature. Think of these patterns as dominoes, positioned one after the other. One represents a cause, the next is the response to that cause; the next domino is a similar cause, and the next is its response. Now pretend these dominoes are magnetically charged. As soon as you finish reacting to a certain cause in a certain way, the energy will serve to attract like energy in the form of a similar experience. The longer a pattern goes on, the stronger its magnetic charge and the more strongly it directs you to react in a certain way.

Rhodochrosite affects the magnetic charge only at the end of undesirable patterns, ideally drawing different, and healthier, responses. It increases awareness of your own patterns and can evoke the sense that you have outgrown certain circumstances and people. As you work with this energy, it may seem highly unsettling at first, so proceed with caution.

When rhodochrosite is worn or carried, its energy sweeps across your life, shaking up these unhealthy patterns. Eventually, however, it will reveal a stronger, more authentic self—open to new possibilities, new adventure, and above all, to new and significant experiences of love.

ROSE QUARTZ

Life has taught us that love does not consist in gazing at each other
but in looking outward together in the same direction.
—Antoine de Saint-Exupery

■

ONE OF THE most desirable of the quartzes, the distinct pink to rosy tones of rose quartz are generally believed to be caused by small amounts of iron or titanium. Measuring approximately 7.0 on the Mohs scale, rose quartz is used as an ornamental stone, as a gemstone, and in crystal form. A member of the trigonal group of crystals, rose quartz is found in Madagascar, India, Germany, and several locations in the United States. Today, most of the world's supply of rose quartz comes from Brazil, a country that is also the only source of true, well-formed rose quartz crystals.

The relative rarity of rose quartz in crystal form is something of a curiosity, since most other quartz varieties tend to crystallize well and are even grown in the laboratory. Occasionally the stone will show a form of asterism, or a starlike quality, but only when viewed by looking through the stone, rather than as an effect of light shining on the stones, as is the case with star sapphire.

Although not much is known historically about rose quartz, we do have evidence that it has been used as a gemstone and in other ornamental and religious objects for thousands of years. The name *quartz* derives from the Saxon word *querklufterz*, which meant "cross-vein ore." Beads made of rose quartz dating back to 7000 BC have been found in what is now Iraq, and rose quartz jewelry is known to have been crafted by the Assyrians. The Romans used it for making seals as a sign of ownership and as a stone of healing, while Egyptians believed the pink stone prevented aging and restored a youthful glow to the complexion.

Although it is known as another of the principal love stones, many people misunderstand the true nature of rose quartz energy.

Like all the crystals of the trigonal system, it produces constant energy, but it works more to the benefit of those who wear or carry it than it does (as was more traditionally believed) to attract love and lovers to you. Many people who work with this energy will even experience trauma or a surfacing of old pain. Rose quartz energy is healing in that respect, but it is very active and doesn't necessarily "let sleeping dogs lie."

Some who have worked with this stone insist that things may, indeed, get worse before they get better, especially in affairs of the heart, as rose quartz's energy works to remove old blockages and encourage the qualities of forgiveness, tolerance, patience, and understanding. So if you've been nurturing a secret grudge against your ex, harboring a rejection complex, or carrying around emotional baggage from old parental issues, expect to have to do some serious inner work when you use this stone.

Many contemporary practitioners have termed rose quartz a stone of "unconditional love," and in a sense that is very much true, for its principal long-term effect will be to reawaken the heart to a sense of the innocence and wonder of love and to remind us that, indeed, all true love is unconditional. But many people will find rose quartz energy a bit difficult at first, feeling perhaps that it asks more of us than it gives. In extreme cases it can even exacerbate feelings of unworthiness until we really begin to understand what self-love is all about, and that involves our ability to connect with others according to what Spirit wants for us, not what we want for ourselves.

At the physical level of love, rose quartz is used for the treatment of sexual dysfunction and in some cases to increase fertility. Not a stone associated with wild nights of passion, it nonetheless can be a great aid to those who are lacking physical self-confidence or who have body issues or doubts about their attractiveness.

Rose quartz can be of tremendous help in all matters of love, and working with this energy can be not unlike working with a really good personal therapist. But just like therapy, it can take time before you experience a real breakthrough, so if you choose to wear or carry this stone, it's best to be patient, don't push, and be ready to cultivate and expand your own capacity for love.

RUTILATED QUARTZ

Two stars once on their lonely way
Met in the heavenly height,
And they dreamed a dream they might shine always
With undivided light;
Melt into one with a breathless throe,
And beam as one in the night.
RICHARD LA GALLIENNE

■

QUARTZ STONES THAT contain mineral inclusions are known as *rutilated quartz* or *sagenite* by geologists, yet the various popular names for such stones, including *Venus-hair stone, Cupid's darts,* and *Fleches d'amour,* offer a better clue as to their uses in matters of the heart. Like others of the quartz family, this type belongs to the trigonal group of crystals and has a hardness on the Mohs scale of 7.0, although its rutile needles are somewhat softer, ranging from 6.0 to 6.5. Rutiles are needlelike crystals within quartz that may look red, silver, black, or brassy yellow and have a general appearance not unlike the crystals that form in an ice cube. Today, quartz with rutile inclusions is found in Madagascar, Brazil, South Africa, India, Sri Lanka, Germany, and Switzerland.

Pliny wrote nearly two thousand years ago that quartz crystals form from ice created by intense cold for long periods of time in dark clefts and caverns in the mountains. This theory held sway in cultures all over the world until the eighteenth century, which saw the dawn of modern geology. Rutilated quartz has been used as gemstones and other ornamental and religious objects for thousands of years.

The mineral rutile is said to intensify the metaphysical properties of its host quartz crystal, and, in matters of the heart, the golden variety is the best stone to wear or carry as an antidote to loneliness. Simply put, if you're looking for love, it will prove an invaluable aid in putting you in the right place at the right time. Also said to relieve depression and loneliness, the stone's energy will help you find a new direction in your personal life. Think of those needles as a kind of compass pointing the way to happiness.

Sharing some of the important healing properties of its cousins, rock crystal and smoky quartz, this is a stone that integrates energy on many levels and enhances your understanding of others. Thus, it's excellent to have around when you may be clinging to the past, torturing yourself with questions such as "But *why* did he leave me? What went wrong?" You can also say good-bye to guilt and other assorted hang-ups when working with this energy, because it is very useful in helping one to understand the root causes of problems and then learning to let go.

Above all, this quartz helps you to avoid self-pity and to focus on solutions rather than problems. Like all the love stones, it is an aid to removing the barriers to personal and spiritual growth. Offering relief from moodiness and the anxiety that so often interferes with the ability to love, it is said to be a balancing stone for the heavy of heart, as it cleanses and lightens your personal energy. Rutilated quartz is associated with the solar plexus chakra, sometimes considered a link between the root and crown chakras. This offers some explanation as to why it's also believed to be a terrific stone for getting your energy moving and getting you out of a rut.

Rutilated quartz also alleviates feelings of alienation, and isolation and helps to open one's eyes to the interconnectedness of all life. Believed also to have strong regenerative powers, this is the stone to use during the "change of life," both for males and females, as it reawakens desire, strengthens resolve, and renews a sense of adventure in relationships.

We are all born for love. It is the principle of existence, and its only end.
—Benjamin Disraeli

∎

Often called the "lover's stone," rubies are believed to enhance passion, imagination, and creativity. The name derives from *ruber*, which is Latin for "red," and this stone is the scarcest (and among the most expensive) of all gemstones. One of the hardest natural stones, rubies belong to the corundum class of minerals and the trigonal crystal group. Ruby is second only to diamond in its hardness, measuring 9.0 on the Mohs scale. Only red corundum is referred to as "ruby"—all other stones in the class are called "sapphire." Ruby's coveted red color ranges from medium red to dark orangey red to purplish red. Today, rubies are mined in Africa, Asia, Australia, and Greenland. They are most often found in Myanmar, Sri Lanka, Kenya, Madagascar, and Thailand, but they have also been found in the states of Montana, North Carolina, and South Carolina.

Because of the relative rarity of real rubies, they are not widely employed by contemporary New Age practitioners, yet few stones have as rich a history or are surrounded with as much myth, lore, and romance. Long believed to hold mystical power, many cultures associate the energy of rubies with the fires of passion and creativity. The reddest rubies most likely convinced ancient peoples of ruby's extraordinary powers. Rubies are mentioned in the Bible in both the Book of Proverbs and in the Book of Job. The Greeks and Romans ascribed to the ruby the power of emitting light in darkness, while some Hindu

THE MOST FAMOUS movie shoes of all time, Dorothy's ruby slippers in the *Wizard of Oz*, didn't start out as ruby at all. Frank Baum's original novel featured silver slippers, but a screenwriter made the change when it became obvious that silver slippers just wouldn't stand out on-screen. Symbolically, however, it was an excellent choice. Because rubies are traditionally associated with the heart center, the ruby slippers became a symbol of self-knowledge. Dorothy was able to master their magic and gained the ability to attain her heart's desire. If it's true that home is where the heart is, rubies can help remind us all to follow our hearts.

texts describe the abodes of their gods as being lighted with rubies. Thirteenth-century medical literature from India tells us that a ruby could cure digestive disorders, while both Burmese and Roman warriors put rubies under their skin to protect them in battle. The Romans associated the stone with the god Mars and considered it a talisman for virility, strength, courage, and physical prowess.

With a very heart-oriented energy, rubies impart a powerful boost for both the physical and emotional aspects of love. Most often associated with the heart chakra, ruby energy is sometimes associated with the second chakra as well and thought to raise Kundalini energy from the sexual organs to the heart center. In some traditions it is said that the ruby combines the powerful energy of erotic love with the equally powerful energy of romantic, unconditional love. What we do know is that ruby energy will dispel fear, eliminate any vestige of a "martyr syndrome," unblock emotions, heighten sexual desire, and renew both your appetite for love and your appetite for life.

All in all, the ruby is one very motivational stone.

■ BUYER BEWARE! ■

WHEN WE SAY a ruby is scarce, we mean it. So unless you've inherited it, stolen it, or could actually afford it without taking out a second mortgage, it probably isn't a real ruby, though there are reasonable examples of lab-grown gems becoming available. Like its cousins the emeralds, all natural rubies have imperfections in them, including color impurities and needlelike inclusions known as **silk.** Should a stone not show any sign of such inclusion, it's a sure sign it has been heat-treated to improve its color and clarity. Occasionally rubies show an optical phenomenon called "asterism," which has more to do with a stone's cut than its quality. Such stones are called "star rubies" and can be more valuable than normal rubies simply because the phenomenon is so rare.

SODALITE

(Also see chapter 8, Stones for Emotional Wellness and Healing)

LOVE IS ALL WE HAVE, THE ONLY WAY THAT EACH CAN HELP THE OTHER.
—EURIPIDES

■

SODALITE IS A key component in lapis lazuli, and the two are often confused. A stone that rarely forms crystals, sodalite belongs to the isometric crystal system and measures 5.5 to 6.0 on the Mohs scale. It is most commonly found in Canada, Italy, Brazil, British Columbia, and Maine.

As a mineral frequently mistaken for lapis lazuli, sodalite shares much of its appeal and history and carries much of the same kind of energy. It was not discovered in its solitary form until 1806, when it was found in Greenland. It would take another hundred years before this appealing dark blue stone would come into fashion or use on its own. When sodalite was found in Canada's Princess mine, it became instantly fashionable, and many pieces of jewelry dating from this period include the deep blue stones.

If you're the type of person who is frequently a fool for love, this is the stone to work with. Though its relatively short tradition says that sodalite is a stone of logic, rationality, and truth, its energies are not so easily dismissed.

This stone is also a powerful tool in developing all-around emotional health. It instills confidence and restores or renews a positive self-image. In love, as in any other area of life, we all make mistakes, but this stone will aid you in the simple art of getting over a broken relationship. Extraordinarily useful for those who are getting over a divorce, recovering from a lost love, or from just plain getting dumped, sodalite will put you back in the game.

Sodalite sculpture

Sodalite helps one heal from more serious issues of sexual abuse, but it can also help anyone with balancing all the issues that surround sexuality. Further, sodalite is a communicator, so if you've been having sexual troubles within a relationship and need to have one of those oh-so-delicate and sometimes uncomfortable conversations, keep a bit of sodalite nearby. It particularly helps to keep those who have shut down sexually to open up again to the experience. Equally, for people who have become imbalanced because so much of their energy is invested in their sex lives, it helps them to balance and connect with other aspects of life. And since good sex is ultimately all about how we communicate with one another, it aids our ability to be in touch both verbally and nonverbally.

Sodalite is particularly useful for getting honest about your emotions, and like its sister, the lapis, serves to unite head and heart and a few other physical organs as well. It helps to dispel what is irrelevant in your love life, and that includes past mistakes, emotional upsets, and insecurities.

Most important, in matters of the heart this stone promotes trust, enhances companionship, and steers a relationship toward common goals.

In this life we cannot do great things. We can only do small things with great love.
—MOTHER TERESA

■

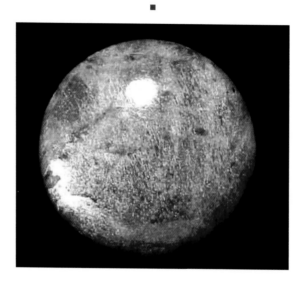

A VARIETY OF aventurine feldspar, sunstone belongs to the triclinic crystal group and has a hardness on the Mohs scale of 6.2 to 7.0. True sunstone is hardly a common stone, found only in Norway, Siberia, and several locations in the United States, including parts of New York State, Pennsylvania, and North Carolina. Oregon sunstone is a plagioclase feldspar and found in Oregon, parts of Arizona, New Mexico, and Utah. Distinguished by its unusual transparency, it was declared a gemstone by the U.S. government in the 1970s.

Ranging from translucent to transparent, when sunstones are viewed in just the right direction, shimmers flash from within the stone. This effect is called **aventurescence** and results from light reflecting from minute parallel metallic platelets suspended in the sunstone, caused by flat crystals of copper. It's interesting to note that its mineral other half, the moonstone, also displays a similar effect, known as *chatoyancy*.

One of the most positive energy-bearing stones you can wear or carry, sunstone is believed to strengthen the life force, bring luck, instill optimism, and increase strength and vitality.

Sometimes called *heliolite* (for the Greek god of the sun), ancient Greeks used sunstone to prevent poisoning and to increase prosperity. In India it is thought to bring luck and romance to the wearer. The Vikings are rumored to have used it for navigational purposes, while Canadian Indians employed it in medicine wheel rituals. It is thought to be especially good for men to increase their sexual powers and to stimulate arousal, stamina, and virility. For anyone, though, there is no better stone to wear or carry than the sunstone to increase your personal powers of attraction.

On the shy side? Need encouragement? Get a sunstone. It's like having your own personal life coach whispering in your ear, offering constant support. Looking to catch the eye of a special someone? Wear a sunstone necklace, or, gentlemen, place a stone in your shirt pocket, near your heart.

This happy and optimistic energy urges you to set fears aside and act from the radiance within you. In other words, sunstone gives *confidence*, and when you're looking for love, there is surely no more attractive quality in the world. Sunstone will help you also in getting over a lost love and creating a new space in your heart. Great for artists and creative people, it promotes positive self-expression, enthusiasm, self-esteem, sexual enjoyment, and playfulness. Symbolically linked to moonstone, the two can be carried or worn together by either sex as an aid to attaining perfect balance between masculine and feminine energies and what mystics call the "inner marriage."

3

STONES FOR MONEY AND PROSPERITY

Riches cover a multitude of woes.
—MENANDER

WHETHER YOU FEEL yourself drawn to the simple life or freely admit to being a hard-core materialist; whether money represents the security of a weekly paycheck and a 401K or the feast-or-famine fortunes of the entrepreneur, one thing is for certain when it comes to money: we all need it, if only because the coin of the realm is the currency we use to meet basic needs like food, clothing, and shelter.

When using crystal and gemstones as an aid to shore up your financial situation, however, it's important to keep in close touch with your real feelings about money—having it, saving it, spending it, and what and whom you're liable to spend it on. For a subject so rarely discussed in psychological terms, it seems we all carry an awful lot of baggage in our wallets and handbags along with the bills and the bling. Have you ever wondered why money seems to work so well in some people's lives and so destructively in others'? Why some people seem to truly be in control of their money while others allow money to control them?

For example, how closely is your sense of self-esteem tied to your bank balance? Are you an impulse buyer whose credit card interest is enough to make you hyperventilate? Does buying things you can't afford make you feel at first powerful, then mortified? Are you thrifty, even cheap? Do you refuse to allow your money to buy you even a little happiness? Is money a competitive issue for you, indicating a need for social affluence or to keep up with the Joneses?

The fact is, your worth as a person has nothing to do with how much money you have. Instead, research suggests that striving for affluence and absorbing the messages of a consumer culture does anything but buy happiness. Rather, the accumulation of wealth for its own sake tends to hurt social relationships and promote ecologically destructive behavior.

In order to work with crystals, minerals, and gemstones in matters of material well-being, we must also look at the intricate links to both the financial and psychological factors involved to make sense of why people do what they do with their money. The paradox is that for most of us, our feelings about money veer to extremes. We love money or we hate it, we fear it or we worship it—but we certainly never ignore it. As a result, we imbue the objective reality of dollars and cents with all sorts of completely subjective projections. Yet we know so little about why we experience these emotions toward money and the effects they have on our every day lives. Consider the CEO of a multibillion-dollar enterprise who makes disastrous decisions in his personal finances, or the couples who squabble constantly over issues of mine, yours, and ours.

For all of our spiritual seeking, most of us fail to realize how our feelings about money affect not merely our financial habits, but the degree of satisfaction we get from the money we have. The stones in this chapter have been chosen because their energies can assist you in developing a healthy relationship with the financial side of life and help you make significant changes in your relationship with money. Though we all have heard the maxim that it can't buy happiness, money can cer-tainly enhance happiness and an overall sense of prosperity, or it can just as certainly destroy them.

Again, because there no set rules in the very new area of working with specific kinds of crystal energy and structure, and because individual circumstances vary from person to person, you will find that the money and prosperity stones included here are drawn from a number of different crystal groups, though there is a marked preponderance of stones belonging to the orthorhombic group of crystals, with a somewhat smaller percentage of stones belonging to the hexagonal group. It is worth noting, however, that as we saw in chapter 1, it makes sense that the majority of money stones come from these two groups because (a) hexagonal energy is *reciprocal*, in much the same way financial transactions are reciprocal by nature; and (b) orthorhombic energy is a magnifier, in that it can help draw more resources into your life.

Whatever your personal financial situation or style, these stones will help you develop a healthier, more conscious concept of money. Working with specific stones for your particular situation will increase your understanding of how you affect money and how money affects you. Think about it—if you really know *why* you want money, you may just get all the money you want.

Use these stones for meditation, in ritual, or simply carry them in your purse or pocket. In doing so, you can increase your own will and clarify your intention to bring more money into your life.

Money? How did I lose it? I never did lose it. I just never knew where it went.
—EDITH PIAF

■

Named for the French mineralogists who supplied the first specimens, adamite has an orthorhombic crystal structure and is a secondary ore of zinc. Typically ranging from white to pale green in color, it will sometimes show trace amounts of purple and is fluorescent under ultraviolet light. Today adamite is found in Greece, Chile, France, England, and Death Valley, California, as well as in Durango, Mexico. Measuring only 3.5 on the Mohs scale, adamite is not typically used much as a gemstone but is a favorite of mineral collectors, because of its lime-green fluorescence.

■ GLOWING IN THE DARK ■

FLUORESCENT MINERALS ARE minerals that emit visible light or color when activated by ultraviolet light, x-rays, or electron beams. How does it happen? At the atomic level, when certain electrons within the crystal specimen are exposed to these kinds of beams, they absorb energy and jump to a higher energy state. The fluorescence is displayed when those same electrons jump down to a lower energy level and emit light of their own.

Specifically, adamite energy works to stabilize unconscious impulses and emotions. As with most crystals of orthorhombic structure, its energy works to bring forth the unconscious to the conscious, giving us first and foremost greater access to our inner riches, which in turn helps manifest in greater prosperity.

Used by many contemporary practitioners to stabilize emotions and aid self-expression, adamite is also thought to instill great courage. Of special use when seeking employment, it may very well attune you to career possibilities you didn't even know you had.

An important crystal for material gain, adamite works well with other money stones and can be used to augment or stabilize other energies. Particularly helpful with businesses and ventures, it will prove itself to be of great assistance in contract negotiation, resolving disputes, and generally keeping track of all those pesky financial details. Keep one with you for job interviews and employment reviews, or when asking for a raise. It will help you to respond to bosses and supervisors with clarity and composure.

Because it is one of the crystals that serves to unite heart and mind, most people generally find adamite to be a great stimulator in business dealings, enabling those who keep it close to successfully follow a hunch and at the same time use good common sense.

(Also see chapter 8, Stones for Emotional Wellness and Healing, and chapter 10, The Stones of Creativity)

Money is like a sixth sense without which you cannot make a complete use of the other five.

W. SOMERSET MAUGHAM

■

AMAZONITE IS A form of pale green feldspar found in Brazil, Russia, India, and parts of the United States. Often confused with jade, amazonite belongs to the triclinic group of crystals. Its intense color is caused by the presence of lead, and some of the best specimens in the world are found at Pike's Peak in Colorado. A relatively soft stone, amazonite ranges from 5.0 to 6.0 on the Mohs scale.

Some sources say the stone is named for the legendary Amazon women warriors, while others say it is named for the Amazon River, though no deposits have been found there. Historically, amazonite has been used in jewelry in India, Mesopotamia, and the Sudan. In Egypt amazonite was fashioned into tablets in parts of the Book of the Dead and was even found in King Tut's tomb.

As with any mineral that has a high lead content, amazonite should be kept out of reach of young children. It is further recommended that if you use the stone in jewelry, make sure you avoid prolonged exposure to the skin. Amazonite is best carried in a pouch or pocket, where you can derive all of its benefits with none of its side effects.

This is a stone whose energy can be instrumental in distilling raw information into useful expression. Especially good for entrepreneurial types and people in sales, it is also believed to improve your powers of communication, helping to get your ideas across. Work with amazonite as you embark on new business ventures. Sometimes called the "hope stone," it inspires confidence, hope, and increased feelings of self-worth. Believed by many contemporary practitioners to be a stone to aid artists on the path to success, amazonite is especially useful for anyone who is self-employed or self-representing. This particular energy works in a way that helps to filter information and increase intuition where matters of money and business are concerned.

For those who are battling credit card or other debt, it can help to carry amazonite to avoid dubious purchases and practice greater self-control because of its ability to temper impulsive spending.

In all respects this stone disperses negativity, increases confidence, and helps avoid mistakes and self-damaging behaviors. Like all the feldspars, its energy works well with other stones, and when used in combination with Aqua Aura or topaz, the improvements in your financial outlook may be very impressive indeed.

Money cannot purchase what the heart desires.
——CHINESE PROVERB

■

A POWERFUL COMBINATION stone, ametrine is a compound of amethyst and citrine. A rare and unusual stone sometimes called "golden amethyst" or "trystine," ametrine is a member of the quartz family and occurs when amethyst and citrine reside in the same crystal. Because the color combinations of purple and gold are entirely natural, no two ametrines will ever be exactly alike. Ametrine belongs to the hexagonal group of crystals and measures 7.0 on the Mohs scale. Today Bolivia is the foremost producer of these extraordinary stones.

The Anahi Mine in Bolivia is the major world producer of ametrine. The mine first became famous in the seventeenth century when a Spanish conquistador married a princess named Anahi from the Ayoreos tribe and received it as a dowry. The stone was introduced to Europe through the conquistador's gifts to the Spanish queen.

Bolivians proudly refer to the ametrine as *bolivianita*.

Despite its remote location, ametrine eventually made its way to Brazil, where it was sold as a Brazilian product. Economic instability and exploitation of the country's resources in turn led to a change in the government of Bolivia in 1989. In the early 1990s the new government offered tax incen-

■ NEW METHODS AT AN OLD MINE ■

PERHAPS ONE OF the best ways to understand how ametrine can help to transform your financial life is to consider the way it has transformed the Anahi Mine itself in recent years. Today, with the aid of pressurized hoses, miners spray the rock dumps of the mine's bygone years with water, enabling them to uncover lost deposits of ametrine in an environmentally sensible fashion and uncovering large amounts of the stone that might otherwise have been overlooked. Inside the mine workers use advanced equipment and software to reveal where old deposits might have been missed and are able to analyze the quality of those deposits by computer.

Such new techniques make the best of available resources, while at the same time increasing the mine's production at relatively low cost over more conventional mining methods, making it more prosperous than ever before. So if you want to uncover hidden assets, increase production, and become more prosperous than you've been before, ametrine energy is most definitely on your side.

tives to attract foreign investment in the mining industry. The rights to the mine were sold, and during the past decade these highly collectible gems became available on the domestic marketplace.

One of the principal stones of transformation, amethyst is said to bring serenity in the midst of change and to enhance a person's ability to assimilate new ideas. Long believed to make one shrewd in business matters, amethyst also improves mental acuity with regard to the practical realm.

Citrine is held to be especially useful in stimulating the mind, enhancing creativity, and strengthening one's self-confidence. Traditionally thought to be of assistance in acquiring and maintaining wealth, it can also serve as a kind of psychic antioxidant, removing negative influences in one's financial life.

Ametrine is definitely the stone to use if you're interested in building a secure financial base. Amethyst helps you visualize and clarify your goals, and citrine helps to manifest your vision into the physical world.

However, this is a slow empire-building sort of energy rather than the kind to get you out of a tight spot when the rent is due. Use it to make long-term changes, as an investment adviser, and in making critical financial decisions, such as closing on a mortgage or taking out a loan to expand your existing business.

Especially good for forming business partnerships of all kinds, ametrine can be of great use for those involved in mergers and acquisitions. It will help ensure your decisions are the right ones and will continue to keep those revenues flowing far into the future.

Above all, ametrine is a stone of abundance. Its unique energy, revealed in its unique crystal structure, will awaken you to the simple fact that opportunity, prosperity, and the ability to create good fortune are all too frequently right under our noses.

ANDALUSITE

Happy is he who has gained the wealth of divine thoughts;
wretched is he whose beliefs about the gods are dark.
—EMPEDOCLES

■

ANDALUSITE IS A **polymorph** with two other minerals: kyanite and sillimanite. A polymorph is a mineral that shares the same chemistry but a different crystal structure with one or more other minerals. Its transparency ranges from translucent to transparent, and colors include white, red, orange, green, and brown. Named for Andalusia, the province of Spain where it was first discovered, it measures 7.5 on the Mohs scale and belongs to the orthorhombic crystal system. The gem variety comes mainly from Brazil but is also found in Sri Lanka, Myanmar, Russia, the United States, and, of course, Andalusia.

In cut form the gem displays many colors in different directions. While similar stones, such as tanzanite, are cut to maximize the stone's color, andalusite is usually cut in such a way as to get a pleasing mix. The best color play is seen in fancy shapes, particularly rectangular and cushion cuts. It is mainly a collector's item and has not seen wide use in the jewelry trade.

Like all crystals of the orthorhombic system, the energy is slow-acting over longer periods of time. Thus, andalusite is not a stone to use for get-rich-quick endeavors.

It's often called the "seeing stone," because it enables those who wear or carry it to calmly see the various parts of one's character without bias. Used also to see the different sides of any situation, it is especially useful for people who are trying to resolve credit difficulties, pay down their debts, and come to a new understanding of themselves in relation to their financial issues. Andalusite is also believed to enhance memory and recall, so if you're a person who has trouble remembering whether or not you paid a particular obligation, it will help you quite literally to balance the books in that respect.

This is the stone to use if you're trying to simplify your financial life, for it encourages moderation in all things. It is also a stone that is said to be helpful for meditation and centering, enabling shoppers to stay focused on what they really came for instead of going for impulse purchases.

Although it is sometimes called "poor man's alexandrite," because it offers color play at a low price, andalusite encourages thrift, economy, and value. With patience and focus it will impart a sense of increased security and contentment, and will improve one's ability to use the resources at hand.

■ A MINERAL UGLY DUCKLING ■

IN ITS NATURAL state, andalusite is one of the great "ugly ducklings" of the gem world and even today is almost unknown in jewelry. When placed in the hands of a talented gem cutter, however, the swan within is revealed, and faceting and polishing will show off a beautiful array of colors ranging from brown to green to reddish gold.

The gratification of wealth is not found in mere possession
or in lavish expenditure, but in its wise application.
—MIGUEL DE CERVANTES

UNLIKE THE MAJORITY of stones included in this book, Aqua Aura is an artificially created crystal that combines the powerful energy properties of quartz crystal with that of gold. These very attractive crystals are created when rock quartz crystals are heat-treated at high temperatures in a vacuum, and gold vapor is added. The gold atoms fuse to the crystal's surface, giving the crystal an iridescent sheen. Though the base quartz used in the process belongs to the trigonal system, it is uncertain whether the atomic bonding with the gold alters that basic structure or augments it in ways we don't know. The process was awarded the United States Patent in February 2006. The resulting color is similar to that of fine aquamarine with an enhanced opalescence. Today Aqua Aura is becoming increasingly available the world over. Since Aqua Aura is a quartz, it has a hardness of 7.0 on the Mohs scale.

Wearing Aqua Aura is said to help one to shine with inner beauty and is thought to be a particular aid in attracting wealth and success. With a very high and intense energy vibration that combines the powers of gold and clear quartz, it seems to hold special abilities to create financial wellness. Aqua Aura is particularly helpful for drawing opportunities from a distance, so if you work in the global marketplace or wish to expand through channels such as foreign investment, this crystal will attune you to the multitude of possibilities available.

Though many New Age practitioners have attributed to this crystal powers so potent as to be almost magical, in money matters it is most helpful in serving to quite literally raise your consciousness with regard to your personal motivations and patterns regarding spending, saving, and sharing of financial resources.

As a stone of abundance, Aqua Aura offers

a self-revealing energy, whatever you choose to use it for. You may rest assured that it will help you to understand some of those all-important feelings you may be harboring about money and what it can and cannot do for you. While emotional truth is not always an easy thing to face at first, continued exposure to the energy of Aqua Aura will make for a healthier and more prosperous approach to life in the material world.

To understand just why Aqua Aura is so beneficial in money matters, it helps to understand the energizing qualities of its two components—clear quartz and gold. Clear quartz is a power stone. As with all the quartzes, it emits a constant energy. Clear quartz is a crystal that can be "programmed"—that is, infused with thoughts and intentions, which are also forms of energy. The quartz amplifies intention to the point of manifestation. So if you have the intention of improving your finances, the quartz works to help you attain that goal. Gold is a mineral of spirituality, understanding, and attunement to nature. It attracts positive energy, is a legendary symbol of wealth, and offers great healing. Further, gold can remove negative energy from the chakras and heighten the energy of other stones. It encourages happiness and good feelings about oneself and others.

With each of these elements working to amplify the energies of the other, Aqua Aura truly becomes a stone of mastery and material manifestation. Properly programmed with your most sincere intentions, prosperity and financial well-being are all but assured.

AVENTURINE

Luck affects everything. Let your hook always be cast;
in the stream where you least expect it there will be a fish.
—OVID

■

AVENTURINE BELONGS TO the quartz family and is characterized by the sparkling effect known as *aventurescence*, which is essentially the same thing as the "schiller effect."

Usually green in color, inclusions of mica will give a silvery sheen, while inclusions of hematite will give it a reddish or grayish sparkle. Found in India, Chile, Spain, Russia, Brazil, Austria, and Tanzania, it measures 6.5 on the Mohs scale of hardness. Aventurine belongs to the hexagonal group of crystals, and because it is a quartzite—formed by quartz crystals along with other minerals—it is technically a rock and not a separate mineral species. It can often be mistaken for amazonite, jade, or even malachite.

The name *aventurine* derives from the Italian *a ventura*, meaning "by chance." Most aventurine is carved into beads and figurines, but it is also used for vases, bowls, and other ornaments. Especially popular in India, it is widely used for beads and ornaments.

Historical records indicate that aventurine was being imported to the famous German gemstone center of Idar-Oberstein in the late 1800s. After World War I many of these lapidaries were importing aventurine from various locations. American dealers have been importing the stone since World War II, and today a good deal of aventurine quartz is sold in the form of beads.

Aventurine is the stone of opportunity and is said to open doors and increase luck in every endeavor. It is definitely a good stone to have with you when interviewing for a job, going to an audition, promoting a product, or playing the lottery. Traditionally the stone of gamblers,

■ IDAR-OBERSTEIN ■

THOUGH NOT FAMILIAR to many Americans, the gemstone region around the quaint German town of Idar-Oberstein, about ninety miles south of Frankfurt, is famous around the world. The Romans first discovered the city's treasures, finding many precious stones in the area more than two thousand years ago, and until recent years the spot continued to yield a variety of riches.

Today Idar-Oberstein is home to more than five hundred businesses in the gem and jewelry trade, including lapidaries, traders, and superior designers of every description. The city has been known as one of the best places to find unique and unusual gemstones—all of which are celebrated at the Intergem trade fair held there every October for the past two decades.

it is also said to be an aid in balancing emotions and helping you keep a poker face.

In any event, it is one of the best stones to wear or keep nearby during periods of financial stress, such as when you sit down to pay the monthly bills. If you're the type of person who is prone to lie awake nights worrying about the market, aventurine is equally effective in calming the spirit and restoring a sense of objectivity where financial matters are concerned.

Especially valuable for high rollers of all kinds, aventurine exerts a stabilizing effect for people in financial positions, or indeed any situation where the stakes are high; its energy can give you the confidence and objectivity needed to "play with the big boys."

Tradition tells us aventurine is best worn or carried on the left side of the body, and when worn near the heart, it will bring luck, a sense of overall well-being, and greater prosperity.

BARITE

There are three ingredients to the good life: learning, earning, and yearning.
—CHRISTOPHER MORLEY

■

BARITE'S NAME DERIVES from the Greek word for "heavy." Usually colorless or white, it is also found with blue, green, yellow, or red shadings. Another of the crystals with an orthorhombic structure, it measures 3.0 to 3.5 on the Mohs scale. Barite is the main ore of barium and is found in Australia, Belgium, England, Morocco, and Africa. In the United States barite is found in the West and parts of the Midwest.

Barite roses, which have been tinted with iron to a red-brown hue, are sometimes called "desert roses" and are popular among healers and New Age practitioners for a variety of healing uses. Native American lore says the rose formations of barite were gifts from those who had entered the spirit world and returned in the night to carve them.

Barite in any form is useful in dealing with matters of money and finance, simply because its energy works to clear obstacles in one's life path and to strengthen resolve. A crystal with a strong grounding energy, it has a way of bringing you down to earth and imparting the strength to deal with pressing material issues.

Barite is especially good for those who have strongly polarized feelings about money, as its energy works to balance one's feelings on the subject and "find the middle way." In addition, it imparts a strong sense of initiative to pursue one's goals—whether they lie in a tidy bundle for retirement, finding a way to pay for college, or establishing or reestablishing a sense of comfort and security.

Barite is used to add weight to oil-well drilling mud to keep oil in the drill hole and prevent oil from gushing out of the hole. This is just one way barite can be used to conserve valuable resources.

A crystal for people who indeed want to enjoy the good life, barite energy can also be used to augment the energy of other stones, while at the same time helping to remove those blockages—whether physical, mental, or emotional—that can stand in the way of lasting success.

(Also see chapter 7, Stones for Physical Healing, and chapter 10, The Stones of Creativity)

Better an ounce of luck than a pound of gold.
—YIDDISH PROVERB

■

CALCITE GETS ITS name from the Greek word *chalix*, which means "lime." It is found in almost any color, but for purposes of improving money matters and increasing prosperity it's best to work with the white or green variety. Calcite is one of the most common minerals in the world and can help you locate any number of easy-to-find treasures of the kind found right under your nose. Belonging to the trigonal crystal group, calcite measures a relatively soft 3.0 on the Mohs scale. Calcite is common in many locations all over the world, with notable deposits in the midwestern United States, Germany, Brazil, Mexico, and many parts of Africa.

White calcite can work its energy to eradicate any sense of purposeless. Too often those who fail to find financial success and stability are plagued by a sense of not quite knowing what they're doing here, and thus have trouble connecting to gainful employment. Equally useful for those who are stuck in dead-end jobs or consider themselves mere drones at their place of business, calcite will be of great aid in amplifying their deepest desires for what they really want out of life and can offer guidance and assistance for getting it. It clears you of negative energy and those behaviors that keep you clinging to a false sense of security or what you may have been conditioned to believe you must do in order to survive.

Thus, it's a terrific stone for artists, entrepreneurs, and creative types who may have deeply held fears about giving up their day jobs. It's also a helpful stone to work with when wanting to strike out on your own, make a career change, or become self-employed against the wishes of loved ones.

Since calcite has a strong receptive energy, it can help you attune to opportunities and make greater use of chance or lucky breaks that other people may not be aware of. An energy amplifier, it also works well with any of the other money stones to quicken results.

The green variety of calcite will not only heighten your awareness of the opportunities for success in your most immediate environment, but it may also have the world beating a path to your door. When used in conjunction with a financial activator, such as green aventurine or citrine, it is believed to be of great help for home-based businesses, cottage industries, or so-called mom-and-pop enterprises. Carry a green calcite crystal to ensure that even the most commonplace financial transactions go smoothly, and you may even discover that for once the bank has made an error in your favor.

CITRINE

A rich man is nothing but a poor man with money.
—W. C. FIELDS

■

THE NAME CITRINE comes from the old French word *citrin*, which means "yellow." A variety of quartz, the color results from small amounts of iron impurities in the crystal structure. A member of the trigonal group, natural citrine is found in Brazil, France, Madagascar, and Russia, as well as in North Carolina, Colorado, and California in the United States. With a hardness of 7.0 on the Mohs scale, it is a popular stone and affordable for jewelry.

Sometimes called the "success stone" or the "merchant's stone," citrine's energy promotes confidence, abundance, and an increased sense of possibility. History offers few references to this relatively rare stone, though the first occurrences seem to be the use of citrine by Romans in the first few centuries after the birth of Christ. During the Romantic period, citrine saw increased use as a gemstone. Historically, natural citrine has been found in Spain, Scotland, France, Hungary, and in several mines in South America, and it has been inevitably linked (and confused with) its gemstone counterpart, yellow topaz. Perhaps, though, no one would be talking about citrine at all if in the middle of the eighteenth century it had not been discovered that amethysts and smoky quartz can also be rendered yellow by heat treatment. In the course of the ensuing two hundred years, heat treating became so much a matter of course that most of the stones available are not natural citrine but are, in fact, either heat-treated amethyst or smoky quartz. If finding a true citrine is a cause of concern, a trained specialist can help tell the difference—heat-treated stones will display subtle stripes, while natural citrines will tend to be cloudy.

Though historically linked with topaz, citrine didn't really gain popular attention until the 1930s, when European artisans at Idar-Oberstein began to import it in large quantities from South America. Its appearance came at just the right moment to coincide with an upheaval in social conditions and an increasing demand by the bourgeoisie for fashionable and affordable gemstone jewelry. In America citrine and other semiprecious stones saw a huge rise in popularity as tightening of money and resources came with World War II.

A stone with powerful regenerative energy, citrine is particularly recommended for people experiencing a sense of burn-out in financial matters. So if you're in a period where you feel like you're working hard but getting nowhere fast, or if the ladder of success is feeling more like a treadmill, this is the stone for you. Often those who are experiencing financial troubles feel themselves at the mercy of a system beyond their control. In such instances, citrine energy will work to restore confidence and a sense of direction. Imparting what might best be called a sense of willful optimism, citrine will also help to mitigate depression and eradicate irrational attitudes toward financial dealings. With its fast-acting energy, it will put you back in touch with a sense of what you need to survive in the world and will further improve communication from the soul to the ego.

■ GEMSTONE FASHION ■

GEMSTONES, LIKE ANYTHING else, tend to enjoy periods of popularity and go in and out of fashion. In the case of these baubles, however, their popularity tends to be inextricably linked to world events, wars, and fluctuating economies.

As far back as the seventeenth century, gemstone fashion was determined by economic reality. In the heyday of European royalty, the gems themselves may have been awe-inspiring, but in a world where only a few were very rich and the rest were pretty darned poor, there simply wasn't that much jewelry available.

In the nineteenth century, with the rise of the industrial revolution, a whole class of newly affluent people began to take a serious interest in gems as more of them became available through advanced mining techniques, and more people were able to afford a bauble or two. While the wealthy continued to flaunt diamonds, rubies, and pearls, the up-and-coming classes created a fashion for less expensive gems. Turquoise, for example, became hugely popular in the 1850s. The burgeoning science of archaeology also gave rise to an interest in antiquities as people became conscious of the fact that the ancients regularly wore gold, pearls, carnelian, and a variety of other stones. As a consequence, jewelry fashion saw a resurgence of cameos, tiered necklaces, and rings of agate and other common stones.

By the turn of the century, flaunting one's wealth was de rigeur, and jewelry fashion reflected an over-the-top sensibility. If your family had money, you wore jewels—big, beautiful, and as ostentatious as possible. Opulence defined the Edwardian and art nouveau eras, and examples of gemstone "suites," or matching ensembles, became all the rage.

But the horrors of World War I changed not just the world economy, but also the world's outlook. Extravagance was out and modest was in. The Roaring Twenties brought back jewelry in force, however, with a resurgence of diamonds, rubies, emeralds, and pearls displayed in a wealth of bold art deco designs. Costume jewelry also saw a huge rise during the period, with readily affordable rhinestones, marcasite, and other semiprecious stones such as topaz and even tourmaline, made widely available.

The crash of the stock market ended all that, however, as markets tightened the world over and money dried up. What had previously been a lively trade in stones from the Far East ended, and, instead, imports from South America began to increase with the introduction of huge amounts of citrine, amethyst, and gem-variety quartzes and tourmalines. Coinciding with the advent of World War II and another worldwide reduction in resources, the jewelry of the 1940s and 1950s was entirely different from any period that had gone before.

The 1960s and 1970s saw jewelry of first the pop art era and then a trend toward the natural, which used seeds, beads, shells, and uncut stones and crystals. Meanwhile, though, the war in Vietnam was giving rise to a host of entirely new technologies—among them, new processes for heat-treating, lab-grown stones, and a variety of other techniques. As a result, today the average consumer has perhaps the widest array of jewelry choices available than at any other time in recorded history.

For business owners, some sources recommend keeping a citrine crystal in your cash drawer. For the rest of us, a bit of citrine carried in our wallets will help to keep the cash flowing. Said to enhance mental capacity and intuition, citrine will keep you alert to new opportunities and restore a sense of confidence in the future.

Even wisdom has to yield to self-interest.
—PINDAR

DUMORTIERITE IS AN aluminium silicate mineral, belonging to the orthorhombic crystal system. Usually denim-colored, there are rarer examples of violet and pink as well as green and browns. Named for French paleontologist Eugene Dumortier, it typically occurs in aluminium-rich metamorphic rocks. Dumortierite has a Mohs hardness of 8.5 and is found in Brazil, Canada, France, Italy, Madagascar, Namibia, Norway, Poland, Russia, Siberia, Sri Lanka, and several states in the western part of the United States. Sometimes it is mistaken for sodalite because of its similarity in appearance, and more often it is sold as fake lapis lazuli.

Essentially a very businesslike stone, dumortierite's energy will help you better prioritize, organize, and visualize your financial goals. Helping those who wear or carry it to become more clear-eyed and realistic, dumortierite enhances organizational abilities, self-discipline, and orderliness. Those who use this stone seem to be instantly blessed with a very healthy interest in the bottom line. It's definitely the stone to use when it's time to get organized. After all, thinking you need to be better organized or wishing you were better organized is one thing; settling down to do it is ultimately what gets the job done.

Also reported by some sources to be a great stone to have when you need to sell yourself, dumortierite's energy will encourage you to see and accept reality and react to circumstances in your own best interests. So if looking out for number one is a concept you have difficulty with, this stone can enhance your ability to perceive just where those best interests lie.

Especially good for people who can't keep track of their receipts or remember if they removed their bank card from the ATM, who tend to tell fibs about their credit card balance or once claimed that the dog ate their taxes, dumortierite will be very useful for anyone who has experienced the issues of avoidance that so often enter into the subject of personal finance.

Riches are not an end of life, but an instrument of life.
—HENRY WARD BEECHER

■

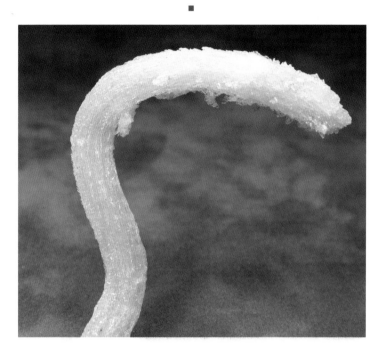

GYPSUM'S NAME DERIVES from the Greek word meaning "burned." Usually white, colorless, or gray, it may also contain shades of red, brown, and yellow. Gypsum is a common mineral and is quite soft, measuring 2.0 on the Mohs scale. It has a monoclinic crystal structure, which means its energy is quite easy to direct. Other forms of gypsum include selenite, a clear, transparent form of the mineral, and alabaster, which has been used since ancient times in carvings and ornaments. Found in deposits all over the world, major locations of gypsum include Mexico, Italy, and the United States.

Sometimes called the "good luck" stone, gypsum in any form is the stone to use when you want to make money with a specific idea. Its energy is receptive in nature and must be directed toward a specific goal. It's a good stone to use if you're looking to get a patent on your latest invention, sell your software idea to Microsoft, or want to draw people to a Web site promoting your latest product. The point is that gypsum energy can bring you prosperity, but it needs to be directed and consciously attached to a specific goal. Just using it to bring you more money, without having something specific to sell or promote, is too vague a goal for it to work effectively.

Basically, gypsum is a master facilitator, which means it has a wide variety of uses in crystal work and can be used very successfully with other stones. It adds both flexibility and resolve to your endeavors, and is a great stone to keep at your workspace. In any of its many forms this is a stone of mental clarity that promotes sound business practice and ensures honesty and honor in business dealings. A great mover of energy, it will prove of invaluable assistance in business situations where finalizing a deal has been delayed or other obstacles stand in the path of your success. Use it in combination with aventurine to create new opportunities, or with tiger's eye to improve timing of financial decisions, avoid procrastination, and increase progress.

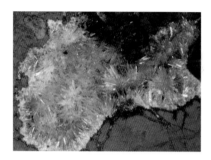

LAZULITE

There are people who have money and people who are rich.
—COCO CHANEL

■

THE NAME *lazulite* comes from the Arabic word for "heaven." A phosphate-based mineral, it may also contain magnesium, iron, and aluminum. Ranging in color from dark azure blue to bright blue, lazulite belongs to the monoclinic crystal group and measures from 5.5 to 6.0 on the Mohs scale. Today this mineral is found in locations all over the world, including Austria, Switzerland, Mexico, and Brazil, while North American locations include Georgia, California, and the Yukon Territory in Canada.

Lazulite has been traditionally used as a worry stone, and when it comes to financial matters, who hasn't done their share of worrying? Contemporary practitioners know, however, that lazulite energy is not only very good for soothing worries, but it is also very useful in breaking the compulsive spending habits that tend to create our financial worries in the first place!

A stone with strong grounding energy, lazulite is the stone to use if you're ready to have that conversation with yourself about where all the money goes. With energy that helps penetrate deep to the heart of any matter, lazulite is best to use when, for example, you find you just can't say no to your children, no matter how expensive the toy, or if you suddenly discover how much your addiction to triple mocha lattes is cutting into your monthly budget. It's terrific for ending bad habits of all kinds, but since so many of our financial habits and compulsions have deeper psychological roots, it's principally valuable when working with money issues.

If you're a "shop 'til you drop" type who can't pass a shoe store without going in, a kleptomaniac, or even an out-of-control eBay addict, lazulite is the stone to keep with you, simply because it will help you to better understand the sometimes-intricate relationships between our spending and our hidden anxieties.

■ BUYER BEWARE! ■

LAZULITE IS A relatively rare stone and is not to be confused with its close cousin, lazurite, or the mineral azurite. The best indicator in buying lazulite in rough form is that the crystals may appear rather dull and unimpressive. Otherwise, location or country of origin is your best indicator that your lazulite specimen is "true blue."

Try not to become a man of success, but rather try to become a man of value.
—ALBERT EINSTEIN

■

MAGNETITE IS A form of iron oxide with an isometric crystal structure and measures anywhere from 5.5 to 6.5 on the Mohs scale. Magnetite comes from many locations around the world, with large deposits in the United States, South Africa, Germany, and Russia.

Known as the "stone of stability," the lodestone variety of magnetite has the ability to indicate direction by aligning itself with the earth's magnetic field, acting in much the same way as a compass. The direction-pointing nature of lodestone was known as far back as fourth-century China, and by the twelfth century the Chinese were known to use lodestone for navigation. In the Middle Ages lodestones were a favorite of the Crusaders, who believed them to be powerful protectors. Mankind's ongoing fascination with this mineral's magnetic qualities over the ensuing centuries has played a significant part in the development of our understanding of the earth sciences, electromagnetic fields, and quantum physics.

■ A MAGNETIC BED? ■

PIONEER HYPNOTIST ANTON Mesmer used magnetite and lodestone elixirs to advocate the idea that human energy could be manipulated and attracted through the use of the stones. A contemporary of Mesmer's was Dr. James Graham, inventor of the "Royal Patagonian Magnetic Bed." He installed the bed in a fashionable London townhouse in the late 1700s and rented it out for fifty guineas a night, claiming that the streams of magnetic effluvia from the quartz crystals and lodestones used in its construction would ensure the exceptional quality of any offspring lucky enough to be conceived there.

Whether you use an actual lodestone or the more common form of magnetite, it will impart an energy that is sure to stabilize your financial life. This stone is an excellent choice for those feast-or-famine types of personalities whose financial lives seem to be in perpetual flux. It exerts a grounding and centering influence and, as its physical characteristics indicate, is a strong attractor of money and good fortune.

Used as amulets and in talismans for centuries, magnetite's energy adds purpose, stamina, and strength. In business, use it to attract customers; it's also good to have as you try to collect on your invoices. If you have conflicts about money, magnetite will help to resolve them, as it works to allay fears and confusion in this area. Equally, if you tend to be rather overly attached to your material goods, magnetite will be useful in helping you to become more generous with resources. It's great for people who struggle with the perennial issues of yours, mine, and ours and will help those who have difficulty accepting their financial responsibilities.

For more ambitious types, magnetite will be of great aid in helping to attract those in positions of power. Use it when you want to take out a loan, close on a mortgage, or make other long-term financial commitments.

Finally, magnetite will help protect you from those who may be dishonest in business, and it can be a protective force in dubious financial ventures. It's not for gamblers, by any means, but will help protect the innocent from being deceived in all money-related matters.

■ WHAT'S THE DIFFERENCE? ■

WHILE ALL MAGNETITE will display magnetic properties, the true difference between an ordinary piece of magnetite and the legendary lodestone is that the lodestone is magnetite that has been struck by lightning (or exposed to its electronic equivalent).

When it is a question of money, everybody is of the same religion.
—Voltaire

■

TIGER'S EYE, OR tigereye, is a member of the chalcedony quartz group and belongs to the trigonal group of crystals. One of the chatoyant gemstones, it exhibits a changeable silky luster as light is reflected within its thin, parallel bands. Ranging in tone from browns to red and yellows, it measures 7.0 on the Mohs scale. Today tiger's eye is mined in western Australia, South Africa, the United States, Canada, India, Namibia, and Myanmar.

Named for its similarity in appearance to the eye of the tiger, in ancient times the stone was thought to be all-seeing. The Romans wore it as a protection against enemies, while ancient Egyptians believed the beautiful tiger's eye would bring good fortune and protect its bearer. They related the

■ **TIGER'S EYE**
SUPPLY AND DEMAND ■

NEVER UNDERESTIMATE THE effect of mine finds on the price of gems and minerals. Tiger's eye, for example, once sold for $6 or more per carat (approximately $11,200 a pound), but when it was found in great quantity on the Orange River in South Africa, two speculators simultaneously sent large cargoes of the stones from South Africa to London, and the price immediately fell to twenty-five cents a pound.

stone's golden glow to the sun, which they worshiped as a god.

Because of its grounding yet powerful energy, carrying or wearing tiger's eye enhances integrity, willpower, the willingness to cope with matters of a practical nature, and the correct use of power. Long believed to be a lucky stone, it's especially good at bringing in money when you need it most and can give a much-needed boost to a flagging bank account.

Specifically, tiger's-eye energy works to improve your timing in all financial matters. It helps to strip away any illusions you may harbor about your financial dealings and has the ability to create order out of chaos. It's great for tax time, straightening out matters of estate, and the general integration of worldly energy.

A stone of what might best be called practical wisdom, tiger's eye will be of tremendous assistance in making financial decisions. It imparts the necessary energy to see you through complex negotiations, helping you to get things in their proper perspective without excess drama, worry, or denial about the bottom line.

With its truly transformative energy, tiger's eye can transform your financial future simply because of its ability to change worries, anxieties, and fears into a logical, practical, and confident approach to all matters material.

■ TIGER'S EYE VARIATIONS ■

SOME VARIATIONS OF this stone carry much the same energies but can be used in more specific instances. Red tiger's eye will impart the strength and stamina to take a more energetic approach to financial affairs and is good to use when certain reforms in spending habits or changes in the way you do business are indicated.

Yellow tiger's eye, while not emitting as strong a vibration as citrine or topaz, is especially useful for physically manifesting money and material success. It will help to amplify or expand your plans and bring your visions into reality.

'Tis money that begets money.
—ENGLISH PROVERB

■

TOPAZ IS NAMED for the island of Topasos in the Red Sea. Known since ancient times, topaz is a fairly common gemstone worldwide. The best variety to use for financial purposes is so-called "Imperial" topaz which displays orange, pink, red, or violet tones. These colors result from chromium impurities in the topaz crystal structure that are believed to come from exposure to natural forms of radiation. Topaz belongs to the orthorhombic crystal group and measures 8.0 on the Mohs scale. Today most imperial topaz comes from Brazil.

Another theory regarding the origin of the name *topaz* is that it derives from the ancient Sanskrit word *tapas*, meaning "fire." Similarly, two theories exist as to the origin of the name "imperial" topaz. The first says the word "imperial" was first attached to a golden variety of topaz as an honor to the Brazilian royal family, while another states that the term originated in Russia in the nineteenth century, when topazes with pink tones were discovered in the Urals and proclaimed by the czar to belong only to himself and the royal family. Today, most natural, untreated topaz comes from Brazil.

The Ouro Preto mine in Brazil is an area so rich in topaz that one mineral dealer tells of an area monastery with a staircase paved with topaz crystals.

We do know that topaz has been widely recognized since the Middle Ages, when Germany was a principal source of the stone. It was popular among Europeans as a talisman and, like citrine, was imbued with any number of magical properties. It was also thought to prevent nightmares, calm tempers, and to cure asthma.

Long associated with the accumulation of wealth, imperial topaz is also thought to offer powerful protection against financial loss, robbery, or other emergencies. A slow-acting stone, its energy nevertheless is highly useful for those concerned with contemporary issues such as identity or credit card theft.

Thought to enhance potential and increase what is commonly known as "street smarts," topaz is especially good for people who are at the beginning of or at a turning point in their careers. A great aid to the physical manifestation of goals and ideas, this stone will serve as an aid in career direction, wise use of financial resources, and finding new professional enthusiasm.

Since its energy emphasizes the acquisition of wealth, topaz is an excellent stone to have when choosing investments for long-term, rather than short-term, rewards. For that reason, it's terrific to have it close to you when scrounging around flea markets or yard sales, looking for a special find, shopping for antiques, art collecting, or similar activities. However, if you're a thrifty sort, topaz is not the stone to use, as its principal vibration is of a nature that will encourage you to spend money in order to make money.

■ BUYER BEWARE! ■

NATURAL OR HEAT-treated, all topaz may change color or fade with exposure to heat and light. Keep in mind when shopping for topaz that 99 percent of all blue topaz, for example, has already been heat treated, and such practice is becoming more commonplace every day. In any event, the best natural topaz will almost surely come from Brazil, but whether in cut stones or crystal form, its original colors may alter significantly with exposure to sunlight or high temperatures.

Money can move the gods.
—CHINESE PROVERB

■

TOURMALINE IS THE name given to a group of eleven minerals all having essentially the same crystal structure but varying considerably in chemical composition. What we think of as gemstone tourmaline is actually the mineral elbaite. Green tourmaline is also known as *verdite*, and sometimes as *Brazilian emerald*. The name *tourmaline* derives from the Sinhalese *turmali*, which was originally applied to an assortment of colored stones. Tourmaline has a trigonal crystal structure and is found in a variety of different areas, including Brazil, Italy, Sri Lanka, Pakistan, Russia, as well as the states of California and Maine.

All the tourmalines contain a wide scope of healing effects, but green tourmaline is the one to use in financial affairs. Thought to bring money and stimulate creative abilities, this stone has powerful—even aggressive—energy. Want to swim with sharks? This is the stone for you. In fact, tourmaline's energy is believed by some healers to be best suited to males, and it is sometimes recommended that women don't use it at all but choose aventurine instead. Only experimentation with this energy will let you know if tourmaline is right for you, but the good news is that you'll know that in very short order. The energy of a green tourmaline doesn't fool around.

The first tourmaline recognized in Europe was found in 1703 among a package of Ceylonese stones discarded by a Dutch lapidary.

Long believed to foster prosperity and financial success, tourmaline is about getting to the top of the heap in any endeavor. It's for those who aren't afraid to work hard, or play hard, either. If you're harboring any ambivalent feelings about money, have a fear of success, or just aren't certain what your feelings really are when it comes to dollars and cents, green tourmaline is sure to clear up any mysteries in pretty short order. Tourmaline will break up energy blockages that cause stress and confusion, but you may well find yourself too busy making money to have much time for confusion anyway.

More specifically, green tourmaline provides the kind of energy that will help you think outside the box when it comes to money matters. It will certainly assist you in a more creative approach to solving any financial troubles, but it is also sure to greatly expand your previous conception of what is possible for you to attain. Using tourmaline may not make you a millionaire by any means, but its powerful energy is dedicated to manifestation. For that reason, it's considered a valuable tool for creative types, writers, artists, and those who sometimes have difficulty making ends meet.

Just be clear with your intentions when working with tourmaline's energy, or you may well find yourself with a real embarrassment of riches, or a wealth of obligations you may find difficult to fulfill.

■ PINK POWER? ■

FINE DEPOSITS OF pink tourmaline were discovered in San Diego County, California, in the 1890s. The discovery caught the eye of a woman who was probably the biggest fan of pink tourmaline in history: Tzu Hsi, the notorious Dowager Empress, who ruled China from 1860 to 1908.

Known for her eccentricities as much as her tyranny, the Dowager Empress started a fashion for the stone in China's royal circles. Tiffany gemologists took orders for several tons of pink tourmaline at a time, and when one shipment had been carved by Chinese artisans and jewelers in a wide variety of trinkets and ornaments, an order for the next shipment would immediately arrive. Historian Peter Bancroft, in his book *Gem and Crystal Treasures,* wrote that 120 tons of gem-grade tourmaline valued at eight hundred thousand dollars was mined between 1902 and 1910, much to the empress's delight.

But it is a pretty thing to see what money will do!
—LUCIUS ANNAEUS SENECA

AGATE IS A variety of chalcedony quartz that occurs in nodular masses in volcanic lava rocks. These quartzes form in concentric layers and fill cavities in a host rock. The results are round nodules or bands similar to tree trunks and may appear as eyes, scallops, or as miniature landscapes with dendrites that look like trees. This last type is called "tree agate" or "moss agate," which is the common name for **dendritic** agate. Agates are microcrystalline quartzes, but most people believe they are classified in the trigonal group of crystals. Measuring from 6.5 to 7.0 on the Mohs scale, agate is found all over the world, including Brazil, Uruguay, Mexico, California, Colorado, and Montana.

The word *agate* comes from the Greek name for a stone originally found in the Achates River in Sicily. Agate has been found with the remains of Stone Age man in France from as early as 20,000 BC to 16,000 BC. Historically, we know that Egyptians used agates before 3000 BC for talismans, amulets, seals, rings, and vessels.

More than any other type of stone, how well you work with a particular tree agate will depend entirely on your reaction to the pictures, branches, and formations in a specific example. It's particularly recommended to look at a variety of tree agates, especially when they are cut in slab form in order to better reveal their beauty. Like beautiful miniature paintings, these little works of nature's art will speak best to only one person at a time.

Tree agate is traditionally known as a stone of plenitude and abundance. Offering a grounding energy, it deepens your connection to the earth and can serve to heighten awareness of practical matters. Not to be used for quick financial fixes, it's important to be patient when using agate as a personal talisman, though the closer it is kept to you, the faster it will work.

As with all the agates, tree agate is essentially a grounding stone and is especially good for those who want or need to better manage their money and conserve resources. If you're saving up for something special, this is the stone to carry to avoid unnecessary spending and grow that nest egg.

Long considered a stone of prosperity, agate helps people to better see the big picture in their financial relationships and, indeed, illuminate their views of money, especially as it relates to issues of sharing, diversification, and the all-important maxim for success: pay yourself first.

ULEXITE (TV STONE)

Many people take no care of their money till they come nearly to the end of it, and others do just the same with their time.
—JOHANN WOLFGANG VON GOETHE

■

ULEXITE IS A secondary mineral of borax and is directly deposited in arid regions from the evaporation of water in intermittent lakes called "playas." Playas get their water from the rainwater runoff of nearby mountains. This runoff is rich in the element boron and is highly concentrated by evaporation. Eventually the concentration is so great that crystals of ulexite, borax, and other boron minerals form and accumulate to considerable thickness. Structurally complex, ulexite is generally considered to be of the triclinic crystal group. The stones are usually white or colorless, and their hardness measures 2.0 on the Mohs scale. Ulexite is found in many locations around the world, including California and Nevada; Tarapaca, Chile; and Kazakhstan.

This mineral gets the name *TV stone* from its ability to magnify anything placed beneath it in a distinct optical effect that does not distort the magnification. For that reason, some sources recommend placing a piece of ulexite on a dollar bill or other piece of currency when experiencing financial need.

More specifically, however, this stone's most unusual energy helps those who use it to go beyond an immediate solution or quick fix to a financial problem and actually implement a cure. Thus, ulexite is excellent for people who seem to have chronic money troubles, as it works to neutralize conflicting energies and set things to rights. Its atomic structure is rather chainlike, so working with this stone helps you make those all-important connections between your financial state and your spiritual life and vice versa.

Basically a very clearing stone, it helps you to see the true meaning of your behavior and intentions. If you're the sort of person who is either an easy touch when it comes to others, or perhaps the kind who is chronically hitting up friends or relatives for a loan, ulexite will help you to better see into your motivations.

Thanks to its fiber-optic qualities, this stone has a very direct energy, and some heal-ers claim it can even be addictive. We do know that this is a relevatory, "a-ha!" sort of vibration, which is of great use in gaining insight into the previously mysterious. In financial matters it takes you to the core of your problems, points the way to resolution, and activates a solution. If you pause to consider its chainlike structure, you'll have a clearer idea of how the events of our lives are linked with our material well-being.

Finally, ulexite has been known to stimulate creativity and imagination, especially in business matters, and it is an excellent stone to use when things gets out of proportion or when there is an ongoing struggle for control.

■ SHOPPING ■ FOR VALUE?

A LOT OF people never pause to ponder, *What's more valuable? Mineral specimens or cut gemstones?* The answer may surprise you.

Semiprecious minerals, such as garnet, tourmaline, and amethyst—as well as precious gems, such as diamonds, emerald, and rubies—are important because of their cutting value, or, how much of the stone can be used for faceting and cutting into gemstones. Cutting value is measured by size, clarity, and color. But when a crystal exhibits the same properties in its natural state, its value can rise to more than twenty times its cutting value.

4

THE STONES
OF PROTECTION

Do not protect yourself by a fence, but rather by your friends.
—CZECH PROVERB

WHEN WE BEGIN to talk about using crystal energy for protection, we need to first become conscious of just what we feel we need protection from. Illness? Enemies? Unexpected twists of fate? Maybe, but just as often the things we struggle to protect ourselves from are projections of our own deepest fears onto external situations and people.

Now, no one would disagree that the world can, indeed, be a dangerous place and that as human beings we are vulnerable. The crystals in this chapter have been used for thousands of years, and, indeed, our ancestors were just as interested in using stones for protection as we are. Much of the information you will find here is drawn from literature regarding the protective powers of these stones, though it is worth noting that the majority of those included here belong to the hexagonal or

trigonal crystal structure, just as many of the love stones belong to that same group.

The trick—if there can be said to be one—in using these crystals effectively is to do your best to identify the true source of the negative influence that supposedly has the capability to do you harm, and to recognize that love is, indeed, a powerful antidote to fear. The goal is to use these stones to restore your inner sense of security and the sense that you are already protected. In essence, these are stones that can be said to be great enhancers of faith and harmony—with yourself, with others, and with what has been called, for lack of a better term, God's plan for your life.

No one is entirely immune from fear, and as human beings we are geared for survival. But sometimes fears or external stressors create a sense of foreboding that is difficult to shake. Too, we are exposed to a phenomenal amount of negative messages every day. They make up not just the headlines, but the prime-time television lineup as well. One doesn't have to live in denial of such factors at play in our lives, but it is important to identify them as sources of negative influence.

Physical injury, disease, or long-term illness can also contribute to fears and feelings of weakness or vulnerability. In such instances, it can prove beneficial to work with stones and crystals to strengthen the physical body in combination with protection stones.

Finally, some people really are their own worst enemies. They require protection not from external forces, but from inner negative influences, attitudes, and habits of mind. Those with a history of obsession, depression, addiction, or phobia will find enormous benefit from working with some of crystals included here, simply because they require protection from themselves. Such personalities too often feel themselves at the mercy of external forces and carry a sense of being victims of fate. Thus, they require certain kinds of energy to achieve not just a greater sense of security, but an increased sense of all-around emotional wellness, too.

On life's journey faith is nourishment, virtuous deeds are a shelter,
wisdom is the light by day, and right mindfulness is the protection by night.
If a man lives a pure life, nothing can destroy him.
—BUDDHA

AMBER IS A fossil resin. Although not technically a mineral, it is sometimes used as a gemstone. Ornaments, beads, and talismans of amber have been excavated that date from the Neolithic period. Most of the world's amber is in the range of thirty million to ninety million years old. Semifossilized resin or subfossil amber is called "copal." Amber's name probably derives from the Arabic word *anbar*, a word that originally referred to ambergris, which is a different substance entirely. Sometime called "succinite," true amber has a hardness of between 2.0 and 3.0 on the Mohs scale and is generally found along the shores of the Baltic and North Seas and parts of Russia. Another type of amber found in the Dominican Republic is somewhat softer and is known as *blue amber*.

Known for its inclusions of insects, fossilized leaves, and other materials, amber seems to offer us a window into history itself. Amber was much valued as an ornamental material in very early times, and took on great value and significance to, among others, the Assyrians, Egyptians, Etruscans, Phoenicians, and Greeks. It is one stone that has never gone completely out of fashion since the Stone Age. It has been found in Mycenaean tombs; it is known from excavations in Switzerland; and amber beads have been found among Anglo-Saxon relics. Several world cultures, including the Turks, believed this stone was important for physical protection, as objects made of amber could not pass on infections among those who handled it. The Greeks first discovered amber's electromagnetic qualities; when rubbed with a cloth, the stone will attract other particles.

Russian royalty were fond of elaborate amber necklaces and chokers and believed wearing the stone protected people against throat and respiratory infections. Ancient Romans, on the other hand, carried balls of amber to help cool them during the torrid summer months.

It's likely both methods of using amber were helpful to some degree. Because of amber's piezoelectric qualities, it will heat up by drawing energy to a cold area and cool down when it is too warm, as when it is placed in contact with the skin.

A great all-around healer, amber is good for body and soul and is of particular merit when its owner is under physical or emotional stress. Exuding a gentle calming influence upon the mind, it's an excellent stone to wear or carry if you're facing a number of self-imposed obstacles and feel the need to get out of your own way. While some traditions use amber as a love stone, its greatest power is in its ability to impart optimism, confidence, and a renewed sense of hope in the future.

A powerful drawing stone, amber will draw out negativity from the body and the mind. Because of this ability, some practitioners say it's important to cleanse these stones after use and not to wear or carry them all the time, but only until you feel a change in your personal energy field.

■ BUYER BEWARE! ■

AMBER IS AN easy stone to fake, and a variety of imitations made of plastic, polymers, and other materials are all too readily available. The best indicators for finding the real stones are color, streak, hardness, and country of origin. So-called Prussian amber is the best bet, though amber from the Dominican Republic is widely available in inexpensive jewelry. Dominican amber is quite soft; it is easily scratched and is likely to lose its luster with exposure to body heat.

How to Tell if It's Real Amber

Here are a few basic tests you can perform at home, or even at the dealer's if they'll let you, in order to determine whether or not your stone is real amber or a clever impostor.

Heat Test: Take an ordinary needle, and heat the tip with a match or lighter until it is glowing red. Push the point of the needle into the sample in an inconspicuous spot. So-called copal amber or plastic will melt faster than the genuine article.

Acetone Test: Ordinary nail polish remover with acetone can be used to test your amber. Using an eyedropper, drop a bit onto the clean surface of your stone, and allow it to evaporate. Repeat. The surface of an inferior specimen will be sticky—real amber won't be affected.

Friction Test: Rub the stone vigorously with a soft cloth. Real amber will become heavily charged with static electricity and will easily pick up small pieces of paper or lint.

ANGELITE

(Also see chapter 9, The Psychic Stones)

Though I speak with the tongues of men and angels and have not charity,
I am become as sounding brass, or as tinkling cymbal.
—I Corinthians 13:1–3

■

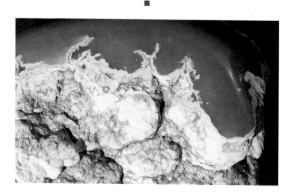

Angelite is a trade name for a form of anhydrite gypsum that has been compressed for many millions of years. Anhydrite is normally grayish, colorless, or this lilac-blue variety, named for the angels. Though really good specimens are relatively rare, recent discoveries in Mexico and Peru are characterized by fine crystals, an internal play of light, and the characteristic heavenly blue color. Angelite belongs to the orthorhombic group of crystals and has a hardness of 3.5 on the Mohs scale. Some specimens will display fluorescence under light.

Because of its scarcity until recent times, not much is known of the history of angelite. Said by many contemporary healers to put one in closer touch with the angels themselves, its most obvious energy is that it helps those who use it to develop compassion and remove emotional blockages that stand in the way of their spiritual development. Also offering protection in a person's immediate environment, it contributes to a sense of safety and security in the home. Other information indicates that it may exert a protective influence on the natural environment, so it is especially good to have if you are in an area where things such as weather and wildlife may be showing signs of imbalance.

Carry a piece of angelite with you when it becomes necessary to speak the truth in a difficult situation or negotiation of any kind. Associated with the throat chakra, it can work to open up your powers of self-expression. Ultimately, angelite is a stone that helps one let go of past mistakes, develop a greater sense of compassion and empathy, and contribute to the quality of grace that enables us to forgive one another.

Especially useful for those who are experiencing deep psychological pain from some type of loss, angelite can be a great aid for people who are in a grieving process or in recovery from post-traumatic stress, as it works to alleviate feelings of powerlessness, pessimism, or loss of purpose in the world.

(Also see chapter 6, The Stones of Transformation)

The ways of the world are weird and much more unpredictable than either scientists or theologians generally make things look.

—WALTER KAUFMANN

■

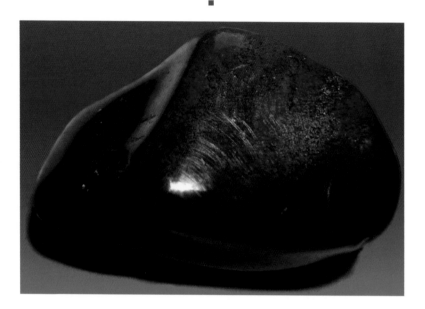

BLOODSTONE IS A form of green jasper dotted with bright red spots of iron oxide. Known as *heliotrope* by the ancient Greeks and Romans, this jasper belongs to the trigonal crystal system and measures 6.5 on the Mohs scale. Major deposits can be found in Russia, the United States, Germany, France, and Egypt.

The Greeks revered bloodstone as a harbinger of change. In the Bible this was the last stone of the twelve tribes of Israel and the first stone for the founding of the New Jerusalem. Legend also tells us that bloodstone—or the "martyr's stone," as it is sometimes called—was formed when drops of Christ's blood fell upon green jasper. An important stone in much medieval literature, Christians often used bloodstone to carve scenes of the crucifixion and martyrs to the faith.

Long believed to be endowed with highly protective qualities, bloodstone has been used as an amulet to protect against the evil eye.

Like its cousin, the red jasper, it is associated with justice and carried as a protection against the lack of it. Endowed with special healing characteristics, bloodstone is used today as an aid in helping one become more knowledgeable in the ways of the world.

If you suffer from a fear of the unknown or a kind of free-form anxiety, bloodstone's powerful protective qualities will expand your knowledge of worldly affairs without rocking your boat of stability. It is also very effective in aiding those who carry the psychological baggage of a martyr complex, and serves to enable them to understand the nature of sacrifice without the emotional pain associated with a more self-centered worldview.

Bloodstone can also be useful as a kind of all-around antioxidant, protecting you from negative environmental influences and emotional upsets. It's good for controlling types, as it helps them release fears for the future and gain a more relaxed and accepting perspective of the here and now.

Above all, bloodstone is a powerful stone for self-actualization. If you're currently experiencing a period of difficulty, with no idea of how to "get there from here," and are experiencing frustration, depression, or anxiety as a result, it will help bring forth your dreams into worldly manifestation, while easing transitions along the way.

■ CAN IT MAKE YOU INVISIBLE? ■

BLOODSTONE WAS USED by certain members of the Borgia family, who thought it made them invisible. This was thought to be true in the early colonies of Massachusetts as well, and the stone undoubtedly played a part in protecting early settlers against witchcraft.

(Also see chapter 2, Love Stones)

He that will not apply new remedies must expect new evils;
for time is the greatest innovator.
—FRANCIS BACON

■

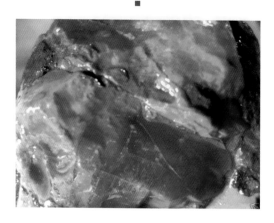

A CLEAR RED to brownish-red member of the chalcedony family, carnelian, or sard, is actually a variety of cryptocrystalline quartz, meaning their crystals are too small to discern, even under a microscope. Having a hardness of 7.0 on the Mohs scale, these stones may contain small amounts of iron and can be streaked or banded with white. Sometimes called the "Mecca stone," most carnelians are heat-treated today to enhance their color. Carnelian is found in many locations throughout the world, including India, Australia, Brazil, Madagascar, Russia, South Africa, and the United States.

The ancient Egyptians so revered the carnelian that it was one of three stones used most often in jewelry and ornaments, along with turquoise and lapis lazuli. In the Bible it is one of the twelve stones used to represent the tribes of Israel. Ancient Greeks and Romans called it *sardius* and used the stone for signets, seals, and cameos. In more modern times, Goethe attributed to it the powers of protection against evil, of continuation of hope and comfort, and of good luck. Rich in providing motivation, some have called it the "stone of self-esteem."

In addition to its powers in the area of love and sexual attraction, carnelian may be used to impart its specific energies for protection, especially in dangerous or dubious situations where you need all your senses working at optimum. It gives the confidence to see you through circumstances that might otherwise make you timid, and offers the simple physical energy to carry on.

Especially beneficial for traveling, it's good to keep a piece of carnelian in your pocket or backpack to protect against mishaps such as pickpockets, vehicle break-downs, and accidents of all kinds. It's good for jet lag, too.

A rock that is formed from a colorful mix of clay, quartz, and cinnabar is referred to in China as "chicken-blood stone."

CHRYSOPRASE

He that is down needs fear no fall,
He that is low, no pride;
He that is humble ever shall
Have God to be his guide.
—JOHN BUNYAN

■

A HIGHLY VALUED member of the chalcedony quartz group, chrysoprase is a highly translucent, apple-green stone that is often mistaken for jade. Measuring 7.0 on the Mohs scale, chrysoprase belongs to the trigonal group of crystals and usually forms in the cavities of volcanic lavas. Today there are major deposits of the mineral found in Brazil, Australia, India, and Poland.

Chrysoprase derives its name from the Greek for "golden leek," and in antiquity it was prized for its gold-tinged green color. Historically, chrysoprase was believed to protect the wearer from all manner of negative influences. The Egyptians, for example, believed it could cure the bite of an asp, while the mystic Hildegard von Bingen wrote that it had been created after sunset and had powers against the forces of darkness. It was also said to be a favorite of Alexander the Great.

Today we may rely on chrysoprase to help make conscious what has been unconscious. Its particular energies prove very beneficial for phobias and fears of all kinds, because it offers new insights into what lies at their root. More specifically, it emits a tranquilizing effect while serving as a shield against negative influences. Many people keep chrysoprase near the front entrance of their homes to protect against intruders and as a shield against possible robbery. Others keep it near their bedside as a protection against disturbing dreams. It's particularly useful to keep by the beds of young children who are afflicted with night terrors, or who are afraid of the dark, though do take care to keep it out of their reach, as young children and toddlers have a special fondness for any object that might be mistaken for a piece of candy.

This is the stone to carry with you if you harbor a fear of flying or other forms of travel. On the physical level, it is also said to speed healing of wounds and protect against infection, so if everyone at school or work is coming down with the flu, it's a good idea to have chrysoprase close if you don't want to catch whatever's going around.

Used as a gemstone, chrysoprase is said to have its powers considerably enhanced when set in silver. A great stabilizer and powerful protective influence, it will serve to calm the nerves of more unstable personalities, while for more rigid or obsessive types it will encourage letting go of fears and phobias by encouraging greater spontaneity.

(Also see chapter 7, Stones for Physical Healing)

One had to take some action against fear when once it laid hold of one.
—RAINER MARIA RILKE

■

HEMATITE IS A mineral form of iron oxide that may even look more like a metal than a mineral. The name *hematite* originates from the Greek word for blood, *haima,* which refers to the red color of the mineral's streak. When crushed, hematite will turn water red, and slices of the stone display a reddish tint. A member of the trigonal group of crystals, a subdivision of the hexagonal group, it measures 5.5 to 6.5 on the Mohs scale of hardness. Today the finest mineral specimens come from England, Mexico, Brazil, Australia, and the Lake Superior region.

Ancient Egyptians used hematite in the creation of magical amulets to protect them against madness. The Romans associated the stone with Mars, the Roman god of war, and believed that carrying the stone into battle would make them invincible. Considering the Roman military history of conquest, it apparently worked pretty well, too. Native Americans used the red ochre form of powdered hematite in various ceremonies and rituals, including war paint.

For more modern spiritual warriors, hematite retains its powers of protection. Its energy works specifically to absorb negativity and protect one against the darker forces.

Especially useful as a worry stone, hematite has a strongly grounding energy that clears the mind of distraction, stress, and excesses of nervous energy.

Hematite is so high in iron that if left in an environment with high humidity, it will actually rust.

Some sources say that hematite is a lawyer's stone that brings positive judgments in legal matters. While it may not make you invincible, it is a mineral that nevertheless will help you remain true to yourself, even in times of great turmoil.

■ SMILE WHEN YOU SAY THAT! ■

USING PRECIOUS GEMS and metals for cosmetic dentistry isn't the invention of "gangstas" or hip-hop celebrities. In fact, there's a great deal of archeological evidence indicating that elaborate dental inlays of metals and precious stones were quite a trend in pre-Columbian times. The legendary Mayas appear to have favored jade inlay work, while in Mexico, Ecuador, and other parts of Central America there have been discovered human teeth with inlays of hematite and turquoise, as well as examples of those adorned with gold, rock crystal, and obsidian.

These early dentists cut or rubbed away a section of tooth enamel from the tooth to be decorated and then used carefully carved inlays. While some experts have suggested such practices were the antecedent to how modern dentists fill cavities, there is also evidence to indicate that false teeth made of gemstones sometimes served as replacements for missing or decayed teeth. In any event, we do know that such elaborate inlay work was very highly developed. These fascinating examples of inlay have survived with no visible decay of the surrounding material, indicating they were so well fitted that the tooth itself was effectively protected against moisture or food matter.

Do not fear mistakes. You will know failure. Continue to reach out.
—BENJAMIN FRANKLIN

HEULANDITE IS IN the mineral family of **zeolites.** Typically forming in the cavities, or vesicles, of volcanic rocks, zeolites are the result of very low grade metamorphism and exert an energy connected with gentle, long-lasting change. Named after the mineral collector Henry Heuland, these crystals belong to the monoclinic crystal system. They have a pearly luster and may be pink, white, yellow, gray, green, or brown. Relatively soft, heulandite measures 3.0 to 3.5 on the Mohs scale.

Heulandite is sometimes known as *Australian jade,* and contemporary sources say that heulandite brings one ancient mystical knowledge. In matters of protection, however, it is the crystal to use when you feel yourself beset with small worries, small problems, and a host of troublesome details that are all seemingly beyond your control.

The beautiful, transformative character of heulandite's energy reminds us to keep an open mind even in difficult situations. It exerts a calming, steadying influence and encourages us to keep in mind the bigger picture and the larger plan at work in our lives.

An excellent healer of the emotions, heulandite is a stone to work with when dealing with a sense of loss or grief. It will help to neutralize distressing thoughts and the sense that one is being patronized or condescended to. Other sources advocate its use when you are feeling threatened by those you envy, or suffer from insecurities based on jealousy of another's accomplishments.

Associated with the crown chakra, heulandite's energy will serve to remind you that all limits exist only in the mind. Its crystal habits are unique—no two specimens are the same—and thus it reminds each person of their own uniqueness and purpose in the universe and that their lives and circumstances are not accidental. On the physical level, it can prove of great assistance in weight loss and problems of balance.

RED JASPER

(Also see chapter 7, Stones for Physical Healing)

Even a paranoid can have enemies.
—Henry Kissinger

■

JASPER IS FOUND in many different varieties in locations all over the world. Usually marked by interesting inclusions and patterns, these varieties are often known by their

■ QUICK TIPS FOR USE OF JASPER ■

JASPERS BRING JOY and are useful in many types of healing and therapy and for general use. Below are some of the types of jasper you may encounter and their use in specific situations.

Flower Jasper—Eases tensions and soothes heartache. Helps the troubled lighten up.

Picasso Jasper—Reminds us to celebrate and live a little. Especially good for the elderly or those who are worried about growing old. It reminds us that it's never too late to live life to the fullest.

Picture Jasper—a meditation stone said to be of help in receiving messages from the past. Improves grounding and creativity and strengthens ties with nature. Great for cooped-up city dwellers.

Poppy Jasper—enhances physical strength and stamina; creates a happy and positive outlook. Especially good for postpartum depression.

Rainbow Jasper—helps one to focus on essential information without being too analytical. Great for students and for silencing the "inner critic."

"picture names," including *picture jasper, Picasso jasper,* and *rainbow jasper.* Red jasper is also known as *imperial red jasper* and *silex.* Belonging to the trigonal crystal system, it measures 6.5 on the Mohs scale. Major deposits can be found in Russia, the United States, Germany, France, and Egypt.

The tradition of using red jasper as a powerful protection stone dates from ancient times. The Egyptians enhanced its power by cutting glyphs into it for protection against sorcery, while the Greeks and Romans carried it as amulets or used it in seals. It was believed by many different cultures, including Native Americans, to be a bringer of rain and a protector against attacks by wild animals.

Today we understand the stone to be especially effective as defensive energy. Carry it to keep you out of danger and away from dubious situations and people. It has the ability to balance aggressive energies, or to create them when necessary. It can prepare you for conflict and protect you from harm. Excellent for spiritual and actual warriors, red jasper is also said to order the spiritual life of those who use it, imparting the qualities of strength, willpower, and confidence in their course of action.

Above all, red jasper is very helpful in imparting the ability to confront and resolve a sense of injustice. It can be very useful in helping to gain added insight into any difficult situation, especially those where the facts are in question or the playing field isn't quite level because of differences in hierarchy, social, or economic status.

A must-have stone to carry to court or to guide in any legal conflicts, red jasper is especially essential for lawyers and those involved in any kind of law enforcement. Athletes, too, will love this stone and its competitive spirit that protects at the same time. You may not have to lead an army when you wear or carry red jasper, but you will feel as though you can because of its energetic and courageous vibration.

In essence, the energy of red jasper can be characterized by one word—progress. It will keep your project, yourself, and all the members of your team—whether at work or at play—moving in the right direction, without giving into the temptations of procrastination, digression, or staying stuck in the interest of maintaining security.

JET

He who is not everyday conquering some fear has not learned the secret of life.
—Ralph Waldo Emerson

■

Jet is a geological material that is not considered a mineral in the true sense of the word, but rather a *mineraloid* derived from decaying wood. Actually a variety of coal called "lignite," jet is sometimes known as *black amber*, and, like amber, it has an electric charge when rubbed that attracts other particles. Produced by the compression of decaying vegetable matter for millennia, jet has been used in jewelry and amulets since ancient times. Jet is black or dark brown but may contain pyrite inclusions, which have a brassy color or metallic luster. Measuring a relatively soft 2.5 on the Mohs scale, the best specimens come from England, but jet is also found in the United States, Poland, France, Germany, Spain, India, and Russia.

The name *jet* is derived from the French *jaiet*. Many of us know the adjective *jet-black* perhaps better than we know the material itself. Popular in Victorian times and for its use in mourning jewelry, it has also been made into rosaries. Long strings of jet beads were very popular during the 1920s, when they were considered haute couture.

Perhaps because of its popularity among the Victorians, jet is today considered a stone for alleviating and bringing grief to the surface so that its owner may be healed. Historically, however, its tradition as a stone of protection is far more ancient. Many have attested to its ability to ward off evil, negativity, and psychic attack.

It's definitely good to have jet with you as protection against bad vibes or in circumstances when you know something is amiss but can't quite identify what it might be. Also said to protect finances and against depression, jet can be very useful if you're worried about money or as an augment to antidepressant medication.

Many modern-day practitioners of witchcraft use jet in rituals to draw and channel energy, so if you're troubled by a seeming lack of direction in life, jet may help you find your way. Jet also has the ability to calm, to absorb negative energy from body and mind, and to release stress. On the physical level, it's great for those affected by tension headaches or migraines.

Finally, many healers use jet in combination with other stones, such as tourmaline, to heal grief and gain sympathy and increased understanding and empathy from others. Used with smoky quartz, its effects are also intensified with a purifying and strengthening effect.

Good jet is hard to find, and imitations abound. Your best clue to identifying an authentic sample is touch. If it feels warm, it may be the genuine article. Common fakes like glass or substitute stones are cool to the touch.

(Also see chapter 6, The Stones of Transformation)

Enemies and lovers are destined to meet.
—CHINESE PROVERB

OBSIDIAN IS A type of naturally occurring volcanic glass of igneous origin. Produced when lava cools rapidly and freezes without time for crystal growth, it is not a true mineral because of the lack of crystalline structure. Its color ranges from dark green to brown or black. Obsidian is relatively soft, with a typical hardness of 5.0 to 5.5. Principal varieties include snowflake obsidian, sheen obsidian, rainbow sheen, and Apache tear. Found all over the world, Yellowstone National Park in the United States, has a mountainside containing great quantities of this material.

Considered valuable by many cultures as far back as the Stone Age, obsidian was used by primitive people for arrowheads, blades, and swords. Because of its lack of crystalline structure, it can be honed to remarkable thinness; it was also polished for use as mirrors. Pre-Columbians used it extensively for tools and decorative objects. Today obsidian is used in cardiac and eye surgery, as blades made of this material have a cutting edge up to five times sharper than high-quality surgical steel scalpels, resulting in a cleaner cut and less tissue trauma.

Long believed to be a stone of protection, obsidian's ancient uses in cutting tools offer a clue to the true nature of this energy, for it works to help one "cut the crap" in daily life. It discourages the tendency to beat yourself or others up emotionally and holds a mirror-like energy that will assist you in coming to terms with problems.

Obsidian is very grounding and will help you to better see your own shortcomings. It encourages the special kind of strength we need to release the pain of memory and summon the courage to face a new era in our lives. It is particularly useful for people who are trying to change addictive behaviors, such as overeating, smoking, or other problems, and can be especially helpful as a protection against the temptation to indulge in self-destructive patterns of any kind.

Sometimes those who are working with obsidian will find long-lost talents, or creative impulses will surface from the deepest parts of the self, demanding attention. Ultimately, this is a stone that helps you to reclaim lost parts of yourself and bring them into the here and now. While other stones in this chapter, such as selenite, involve outward-directed energy, obsidian energy is all about the inner work necessary to make real progress in our lives. As such, it is the perfect choice for those times when we are indeed our own worst enemy.

(Also see chapter 9, The Psychic Stones)

We should take care not to make the intellect our god;
it has, of course, powerful muscles, but no personality.
—ALBERT EINSTEIN

■

ONYX IS A member of the chalcedony quartz family. Usually black, gray, or brown with straight white bands, it differs from banded agates, which generally display curved lines. Sardonyx is a type of onyx with bands of sard, or carnelian, alternating with the stone's white or black layers. Found worldwide, important locations include Mexico, Brazil, Madagascar, India, Algeria, and Pakistan. Onyx measures 6.5 to 7.0 on the Mohs scale.

The name *onyx* (the Greek word for "fingernail") originates in an ancient Greek myth. The story goes that Eros (Cupid) clipped the goddess Venus's fingernails while she was sleeping and scattered them over the beaches of the earth. Seeing what Eros had done, and knowing the goddess would be displeased, the Fates intervened and turned the fingernails to the stones, which the Greeks called onyx.

In ancient times, the stone was believed to protect one against all manner of evils, including snakebite and venomous insects, and against a number of contagious diseases as well. Associated with what might best be termed "defensive magic," onyx is said to be impossible to program with individual intention—a quality that doubtless earned it at least part of its reputation as a shield against the darker powers.

In any event, onyx energy is indeed quite protective by nature, but don't expect a warm, fuzzy, feel-good vibration. It has been said to help its owners to achieve their destiny, to dispel nightmares, and to be of great aid in developing the powers of self-control and personal discipline.

A stone of uncompromising standards, onyx will either work well for you or it won't. If it does work, you can rest assured that you are in possession of a powerful protective force and are sure to find greater insight, an improved sense of confidence, and a sharpened sense of the inner truths of any situation.

■ BUYER BEWARE! ■

ONYX IS EASILY dyed and has been for centuries, though the process was a well-kept secret for hundreds of years. When shopping for onyx, beware of the more unnatural-looking colors, such as bright blue. The black variety, however, is sure to show at least some areas of translucence in its natural state. The dyeing or staining process for this stone was supposedly a secret until it was first published in 1903, though Pliny the Elder noted the process eighteen hundred years earlier. Red onyx was the result of heating carnelian, black onyx resulted from a thick solution of sugar and water followed by a treatment of sulfuric acid and heat.

But I say to you that listen, love your enemies, do good to those who hate you, bless those who curse you, pray for those who abuse you.
—LUKE 6:27–28.

PETRIFIED, OR FOSSILIZED, wood is formed when organic materials are replaced by agate and other minerals bit by bit as they decompose. Most often it is brown, but it can also be gray or green. The Petrified National Forest in Arizona is perhaps the most famous source of wood agate, but it can be found in Argentina, Egypt, and the Czech Republic as well. Very heavy and dense, it has a hardness of 7.0 on the Mohs scale and is widely used in jewelry, ornaments, decorative objects, and even furniture.

Some legends insist that wearing or carrying a piece of petrified wood will make you invisible, thus protecting you from danger. Romans wore it to please the gods that would

bring an abundant harvest, while ancient Persian magicians used it to divert dangerous storms. Native Americans said that sucking on a piece of petrified wood would relieve thirst. Other sources say that those who look upon these fossils cannot remain secretive, as they will force you and others to share the truth.

Since petrified wood has been used since prehistoric times, it has been imbued with hundreds of magical properties over the centuries. Today we understand its ability to impart clarity and a broader perspective.

If you find yourself in a situation where you're beset by seemingly insurmountable obstacles, petrified wood will prove a powerful force in helping to remove them. Because we so often perceive our circumstances to be somehow impossible to overcome and, as a result, tend to fear the worst, this stone's energy will work not only to allay fears, but also to smooth the path to genuine progress. When things go wrong, as they sometimes do, petrified wood will serve to remove negative influences and any sense that you are a victim of bad luck.

Petrified wood is also of great assistance for those times when anxiety about the future keeps us from taking necessary steps in the right direction. If you're the type of personality prone to an excess of "what if's?" it will help stabilize and direct your energy in a more constructive fashion.

An excellent choice when your dreams seem out of reach, use petrified wood or wood agate to assist you in achieving goals that you are having trouble attaining. Its gentle yet powerful influence will work to stabilize your immediate environment, and at the same time will keep you focused on the longer term.

Fear has its use but cowardice has none.
—MOHANDAS GANDHI

■

ANOTHER FORM OF gypsum, selenite crystals take many different forms: long wands, so-called desert roses, and ulexite, or TV stone, and others. A common mineral, selenite is quite soft, measuring 2.0 on the Mohs scale. It has a monoclinic crystal structure, which means its energy is quite easy to direct. Selenite is the clear, transparent form of the mineral and is found in deposits all over the world, with major deposits in Mexico, Italy, and the United States.

The name *selenite* comes from the Greek word for "moon" and can be translated as "moon rock." Sometimes referred to as "satin **spar**," it is easy to scratch and somewhat flexible. Exceptional individual crystals measuring up to seven inches long have been found,

along with complex combinations weighing as much as forty pounds.

The clearer forms of selenite, especially in wand form, may strongly resemble quartz wands. To make sure you're getting one or the other, be sure to hold it for a few seconds. A selenite crystal of gypsum will feel noticeably warmer to the touch than a quartz crystal.

Selenite, like all gypsum, is a master facilitator, which means it has a wide variety of uses in crystal work and can be used very successfully with other stones. Although any number of attributes have been assigned to selenite, it is especially useful for cleansing quartz and other minerals. Psychologically and materially, it has cleansing effects as well, and is said to remove negative influences of all kinds.

Place any crystal, specimen, or pocket stone you have been working with on top of your selenite. The crystal will both clean any energies present and help to recharge your other crystals and stones. You can greatly increase any other crystal or stone energy by pointing your selenite at the other stone, visualizing just how you want that stone to perform.

In addition to removing negative energies, selenite enables one to more readily access unconscious impulses and patterns of behavior, so it's important to be mindful when working with it. Its energy is best directed outward rather than inward as a protective influence.

Especially useful in helping to clarify issues, as well as your own mental processes, selenite can sometimes operate beyond your plans for it, so if you suddenly start to experience visions of the future or past lives, don't say I didn't warn you. Selenite is associated with the crown chakra and has certain powers to amplify circumstances, so if you're feeling especially vulnerable, use another stone until you're on a more even keel.

These crystals can be especially useful for people who are suffering from chronic illness such as chronic pain syndrome, skin disorders, back or other chronic pain, or syndromes such as chronic fatigue. It restores balance and can help you to gain considerable insight as to the root cause of a specific condition.

Finally, some sources claim that selenite energy operates like no other, working rather like a radio that tunes into areas of difficulty or static. Our problems may not always be what we believe them to be, but selenite energy can be very illuminating, whether we agree with its diagnosis or not.

He who prays five times a day is in the protection of God,
and he who is protected by God cannot be harmed by anyone.
—ABU BAKR

■

SERPENTINE IS A group of common rock-forming silicate minerals; it may contain minor amounts of other elements, including chromium, manganese, cobalt, and nickel. The term *serpentine* may refer to any of twenty varieties belonging to the serpentine group, and the stone is said to owe its name either to its serpentlike colors or from an old belief that the stones were effective protection from snakebites. Most serpentines have a hardness ranging from 2.5 to 4.0 on the Mohs scale, and colors range from white to gray, yellow to green, and brown to black. The various kinds of serpentine fall within the orthorhombic, monoclinic, or trigonal groups of crystals. Found all over the world, major deposits occur in Canada, the United States, China, France, Norway, Italy, and Cornwall, England.

The Maori of New Zealand once carved beautiful objects from local serpentine, which they called *tangiwai,* meaning "tears." The Romans used it as a decorative facing stone. In classical times, serpentine marbles were mined in Greece. The ancients carried serpentine seals for blessings, and the Egyptians used it in amulets. In America the Zuni people use serpentine for fetish carving, and it was prized by the Aztecs as well. In more recent times, Nicholas the II, the last czar, was said to have an entire dinner service made of serpentine as a tribute to Rasputin for saving the life of his son.

Having a magnetic energy, serpentine has been used to draw out toxins from the body. As a stone of protection, it is particularly useful for those who are burdened by accumulated stress. Long-term caregivers and other medical personnel, for example, will find it especially helpful in preventing a drain on their own energies. Schoolteachers will find it serves them equally well in preventing constant colds and infection. It can also help you access reserves of strength and energy you didn't know you had, and to get a second wind in trying times.

Psychologically, wearing or carrying serpentine also works to draw out and eliminate toxic mental attitudes and clear the mind. Good for meditation, this is an energy that teaches us the kind of strength that comes through consistent, gentle, and patient action. For that reason, it will be of special use to those with quick tempers or the kind of personality prone to "act in haste and repent at leisure."

> ■ BUYER BEWARE! ■
>
> SERPENTINE IS OFTEN dyed and sometimes used to imitate jade. Such varieties are usually sold under the trade names *Korean jade*, *Suzhou jade*, *Styrian jade*, and *new jade*.

SUGILITE

He is able who thinks he is able.
—BUDDHA

■

NAMED FOR THE Japanese geologist who discovered the first specimens in 1944, Ken-ichi Sugi, sugilite forms in masses and ranges from deep red to purple in color. A member of the hexagonal group of crystals, it measures 6.0 to 6.5 on the Mohs scale. Important deposits of the stone can be found in Japan, Canada, and South Africa.

Though the first sugilite find occurred in 1944, the first deposits suitable for jewelry and gemstone use weren't recovered until 1979 from a South African manganese mine near Botswana. The sugilite was revealed when the roof of the mineshaft caved in, but recovery of the stone was delayed because miners were far more interested in other deposits.

Because of its relatively recent discovery, little is known about the historical uses of sugilite, but it has become very popular in jewelry making and with contemporary crystal practitioners. Like many of the hexagonal crystals, it possesses an energy of integration. A fine balancer of mind, body, and spirit, it has been suggested by some who work with it that it protects against spiritual shock or trauma, clears lingering disappointments, and encourages forgiveness.

A great stress reducer, this stone has a highly spiritual vibration that is akin to a light in the darkness. Its energy is not one of simple reassurance or comfort but instead conveys the qualities of real protection, even against the darkest forces, and even amid the most trying of circumstances, enabling those who use it to be a "light unto themselves."

Sugilite has a way of mitigating hostility and long-term conflict, and is a great instructor to those who yearn to live their own truth. With this stone, you will find yourself able to face even the most unpleasant conditions without fear. It encourages positive thinking, banishes depression and emotional turmoil, and conveys a sense of forgiveness and real mercy toward one's fellows, opening those who use it to higher forms of love.

5

THE STONES
OF POWER

Power! Did you ever hear of men being asked whether
other souls should have power or not? It is born in them.
—OLIVE SCHREINER

IN THIS AGE of political correctness, any discussion of power tends to make people a little nervous. We're not supposed to really want power, because it smacks of ambition, greed, and manipulation. Everyone has heard the expression "Absolute power corrupts absolutely." And although it is true that much of the world's miseries have been caused by those who abused and corrupted power—especially political power—it's equally true that just as much of civilization's progress has been the result of those who attained and administered power wisely and well. Too often we tend to think of power as an instrument of domination—something we hold over others, or something they hold over us. But for purposes of this chapter, let's return to nature and think about what power really is.

If you consider electricity, for example, you know that it is a form of energy than can be directed. Properly directed, it can illuminate your house, warm your oven, and cook food for yourself and others. The electrical power of lightning, on the other hand, can start wildfires, destroy buildings, and even kill. Electricity is neutral, as is all energy, and yet it is unquestionably a form of power available to us all. If you consider power as a form of energy, then, it is both active and passive. The ability to harness and direct electricity is active use of power; capacity, on the other hand, is passive power.

What we think of as personal power operates in exactly the same fashion. When our own power as individuals is consciously directed, we are able to accomplish miracles. Unconsciously, personal power can be as destructive as a wild lightning strike. Those who profess to have no power are avoiding the truth, for each of us has been blessed with the capacity for power and, whether actively or passively expressed, will be asked at some point to call this gift forth from within us.

Chances are, if you've turned to this chapter, you've already heard that call to bring forth your truest potential, to share with others your own unique form of energy, and to connect that energy with a higher sense of purpose for your life. Do keep in mind that these gemstones and crystals have not been chosen for those who are interested in world domination, but they will be of great assistance in empowering you—the user—steering you toward a clearer sense of your own destiny.

These stones belong primarily to the monoclinic crystal group, which tells us something about how their energy operates; it inspires us to action and growth and helps us to realize our fullest potential, whatever the circumstances or situation. Physicists have recently found in energy experiments with the monoclinic crystals that their energy patterns fluctuate along the crystal's axes, contributing to what scientists call a state of "metastability." Many regions of the human brain are also described as metastable, meaning they move easily between autonomous function and interdependent function. With metastability, neural patterns can be coherent and focused without becoming fixed or stuck. It's the kind of flexibility that is adaptive, and it contributes to our overall strength in rapidly changing circumstances and environments.

Ultimately, whether the call to greater power comes to you in the form of a still, small inner voice, or a flash of inspiration, a burst of energy, a full-blown vision, or the voice of God himself, pay attention. It's time to get in touch with the energy that makes your life run—your own power. How you use it is up to you.

When power becomes gracious and descends into the visible—
such descent I call beauty.
—Friedrich Nietzsche

■

One of the most beautiful of the agates, the blue lace variety comes from South Africa and is identified by its delicate colors and blue-and-white banding. Agate is of the chalcedony family and has a cryptocrystalline structure with a hardness on the Mohs scale of 7.0.

Blue lace deposits remained hidden for more than fifty million years in the isolation of the African desert and were first uncovered in the early 1960s by an American prospector named George Swanson. The stone is believed to have a special significance because there is only one known deposit in the world, and its particular coloration has been identified with earth itself. The Tyler Ecology Award, administered by Pepperdine University, has adopted the stone as a symbol of world ecology—a visual symbol of our own blue earth in the vastness of space.

Obviously, then, there is no historical record of blue lace agate, but modern healers tend to associate the stone's energy with peace and happiness. My own view is that this particular stone offers those who wear or carry it that particular quality known as grace. The ability to receive grace, or divine direction, is something most, if not all, of us have struggled with at one time or another. Grace is not always comfortable, however, and having it does not imply that the spiritual path is necessarily strewn with rose petals, but can get quite thorny indeed.

Like all the agates, blue lace agate is a grounding stone that aids in calming the emotions, cooling the temper, easing tension, and facilitating communication, particularly in difficult situations. A stone that offers great poise, it helps you keep your head while all about you others are losing theirs. With it, you will find your thinking much improved and your ability to see the patterns of behavior in your own and others' lives greatly amplified. In a very significant way, this energy enables you to connect the dots of circumstances and experience to see the bigger picture and to convey that breadth of vision to others.

With its gentle power at work for you, blue lace agate is also said to foster love, loyalty, abundance, longevity, courage, and acceptance, while at the same time offering protection from negative forces. The kind of stone that Mother Teresa might have chosen as an amulet, blue lace agate's indefatigable power will do much to convince you and those around you that heaven is, indeed, on your side.

■ BUYER BEWARE! ■

BLUE LACE AGATE has been steadily increasing in popularity and in use as a gemstone. While dyed agates exist, there are relatively very few fakes of the stone itself because of its intricate lacy inclusions. Natural variations in color do occur, though, depending upon the depth of the vein from which the stone was mined. But because there is only one known deposit of this stone in the world, sharp-eyed investors might want to consider buying blue lace agate today, as prices could appreciate considerably in coming years.

The power of hope upon human exertion, and happiness, is wonderful.
—ABRAHAM LINCOLN

LIKE PEARLS, CORALS are formed from organic matter. It's an interesting phenomenon that both are products of the element water, and in fact, they are chemically related, as both consist of more than 90 percent carbonic lime. It is a virtual miracle that nature uses the same dull material to create fiery red coral and to grow beautiful pearls. Corals are not necessarily red and can be found in a wide range of colors ranging from red, white, and blue to brown and black. Having a hardness of 3.5 on the Mohs scale, high-quality coral is expensive, and most bargain pieces have been filled with plastics or wax.

Blessed with a long history, the origins of coral's name remain mysterious. Some say the word comes from the Greek *koraillon*, while others say it comes from the Hebrew, *goral*, which is the name for the stones used to cast an oracle.

Many ancient cultures have been fond of the stone and used it for a variety of jewelry and ornaments. The Greek myth surrounding coral is contained in the story of Perseus. Having petrified a sea monster, Perseus placed Medusa's head on the riverbank while he washed his hands. When he recovered her head, he saw that her blood had hardened the seaweed and turned it into coral. In other myths, Poseidon resided in a palace made of coral and gems, and Hephaestus first crafted his work from coral. The Romans believed coral could protect children and cure the stings of snakes and scorpions. Pliny the Elder, in his *Natural History*, has recorded the trade of coral between the Mediterranean and India in the first century AD.

Modern practitioners hold a variety of opinions about the powers of coral and recommend it for a wide variety of uses, such as attracting lovers, improving self-expression, and easing depression. They do tend to concur, however, that its powers are much enhanced when it is set in gold. Having a strong, sunny yang energy, perhaps coral's best use can be described in a single sentence: It makes you popular.

Coral jewelry became hugely popular in the 1940s and was a favorite of American jewelry designers. As soldiers shipped coral trinkets, jewelry, and souvenirs back to their wives and girlfriends from the South Pacific, designers were captured by coral's appeal and began to incorporate it into a wide variety of pieces.

Whether your goal is to win hearts or win an election, coral energy will add a certain oomph to your cause. Essentially a stone of passion, it attracts prosperity, while at the same time increasing your own creativity and optimism. It imparts what might best be called "charisma," yet at the same time its energy tends to be community-focused, in that it works on the kinds of initiatives that aren't so much tied to individual goals as they are to group effort of all kinds.

Imparting strong qualities of leadership, coral can be used to reconnect with nature and its wonders, or to gain a greater sense of your purpose in the world and what we call self-actualization. In general terms, though, it's best for people who feel called to lead, manage, or administrate large projects or enterprises, and whose ultimate goal is the good of all.

AUSTRALIAN SCIENTISTS ARE seeing larger rates of coral die-offs in the world's oceans than they've seen in the past eleven thousand years, which is giving some cause for concern; yet at the same time, the news may not be as alarming as it might immediately appear. In past instances of such die-offs, coral reefs appear to recover quite rapidly and to maintain steady coral levels over time.

I repeat . . . that all power is a trust; that we are accountable for its exercise;
that from the people and for the people all springs, and all must exist.
—BENJAMIN DISRAELI

■

CROCOITE IS A rather unusual lead mineral and can be a beautiful and colorful specimen that is well-known for its distinctive orange-red color. The main sources of quality specimens come from Tasmania, Australia, Russia, and California. A member of the monoclinic crystal group, it measures 2.5 to 3.0 on the Mohs scale and is usually identified by extremely colorful red, orange, or yellow crystals on a brown rock matrix.

Traditionally believed to be a very feminine stone, legend says if worn by a single female, crocoite will heighten her chances of finding a partner, because it advertises her fertility and readiness to bear children, thus exalting her sense of feminine power. Male or female, however, this is a crystal that is all but

guaranteed to make others sit up and take notice. Not recommended for nervous types, it is nevertheless an excellent choice to place on your desk at work when you're trying to gain attention, a raise, or a promotion for a

job well-done. Carry a piece in your pocket when it's time to give that critical presentation or close the deal. Crocoite relates to the navel chakra and will serve to stimulate and enhance intuition, creativity, and sexuality. It's one of the breakthrough stones that is an essential choice for jump-starting a venture, a project, or a particular area of your life.

Some practitioners say crocoite stimulates recovery from illness or addiction. It definitely possesses an energy to assist you in making transitions from one state of being to another and is a real breakthrough stone to use in every area of your life. Like all crystals of the monoclinic group, it emits the constant pulsating energy that spurs one to growth and action. It encourages self-possession; cogent, think-on-your-feet assessments of situations and people; and, above all, focus and clarity in the pursuit of your personal goals.

CUPRITE

(Also see chapter 7, Stones for Physical Healing)

He who has great power should use it lightly.
—LUCIUS ANNAEUS SENECA

∎

A MINERAL WITH a high copper content, cuprite shows fine examples of well-developed cubic crystal forms that reveal internal reflections of the true deep red inside the almost

CUPRITE IS ONE of the copper-based mineral ores that suffers from prolonged exposure to light. If you have a fine cuprite specimen, keep it out of direct light, as prolonged exposure will cause it to form a dull film.

black crystal. Other varieties of this mineral, such as chalcotrichite, show tufts of needlelike crystals that have a beautiful red color and a special sparkle that make them popular display cabinet specimens. Measuring 3.5 to 4.0 on the Mohs scale, cuprite belongs to the isometric crystal group and is found in Arizona, Africa, Australia, Chile, and several locations throughout Europe.

Cuprite shares many of its energy properties with copper, and metaphysical lore says that it is helpful for reducing worries about situations one has no control over. Associated with opening the flow of Kundalini energy at the root chakra, it is also said to raise awareness and assist in teaching and delivering spiritual messages.

Very grounding and stabilizing, cuprite is associated with imparting the will to get things done. Historically, it was believed to heal one's relationship with one's father, so if you've experienced problems in your own quest for success because of either a weak or overly dominating father, it will help set you on a more productive path.

Cuprite imparts the kind of security that comes only with real confidence in oneself and one's abilities, so it will prove useful for more introverted types whose abilities and dedication are often overlooked. It's a crystal of self-discipline and has proven especially helpful for those who have a tendency to fritter away their time and resources on nonessentials.

In a more personal sense, some sources insist cuprite can help gain sexual power over another, so some people may find it useful for purposes of seduction. A stone with strong masculine energy, it can be helpful to women in male-dominated professions as well.

This is not a capricious energy, however. Cuprite's effects tend to be long-term and long-lasting. And although it does help those who have issues with authority become more comfortable with that aspect of power, it also teaches that with power comes sometimes-awesome responsibility.

DIOPSIDE

The power of Thought, the magic of the Mind!
—LORD BYRON

■

ANOTHER EXAMPLE FROM the monoclinic group of crystals, diopside includes a number of varieties such as *cat's eye, black star,* and the much rarer *violan.* With a hardness of 5.0 to 6.0 on the Mohs scale, crystal varieties can be found all over the world, with major deposits in Upstate New York, Russia's Ural Mountains, Italy, Austria, Germany, Sri Lanka, Brazil, Mogok, Myanmar, Madagascar, South Africa, and Finland.

Diopside was named in 1800 from the Greek words *dis,* meaning "double," and *opsis,* meaning "vision," probably in reference to the fact that different colors are displayed when the stone is viewed from different angles when in crystal form. Contemporary healers use diopside according to its color, associating the darker varieties with the lower chakras and the lighter specimens with the throat, brow, and crown chakras. In any instance, however, the energy properties and associations remain essentially the same, contributing to the powers of logic, organization, and material manifestation.

■ THE BLACK STAR ■ OF INDIA

BLACK STAR DIOPSIDE is also known as the *black star of India*. In the Vedic tradition, it is believed the stone's chatoyancy may act as a gateway for spirits to see inside of our world or our hearts. Black star diopside is said to stimulate the intellect while promoting a balance between art and science.

More specifically, it sharpens the intellect and encourages the powers of expression, making it an excellent choice for writers, teachers, and those who seek to strengthen their verbal skills. Some say it's also of particular merit when used by mathematicians and those in the sciences, as it can aid in making the kinds of quantum leaps we associate with new discoveries and inventions.

Whatever your situation, diopside helps you to gain objectivity, awareness, and understanding, which are important qualities for people who want to increase their own power. So if fears or suspicions are standing in the way of your success, this energy will keep you from getting too hung up on your own or anyone else's feelings. A great guilt reliever, it's the perfect choice for those who handle administrative matters on a daily basis, particularly those who face decisions regarding human or other resources. It helps you make decisions calmly and without guilt or worry as to the consequences.

With an energy that encourages commitment, objectivity, and analysis, diopside will work to improve the quality of your timing when it comes to the presentation of your innovations and ideas, especially in an academic or administrative environment. Its pulsing energy can be of great assistance in situations where it's necessary to jump through the hoops or negotiate the red tape of the corporate or bureaucratic structure, such as writing a business plan, applying for a grant, or getting a much-needed loan.

■ FAMOUS HEIST ■

IN 1964 THE Black Star of India—which was not diopside (or black star) at all, but a famous sapphire—was, along with the Delong star ruby, the object of an infamous burglary, carried out by the mobster popularly known as Murph the Surf and two other men. The jewels were ransomed for a trifling twenty-five thousand dollars and recovered. Both stones were found at a designated drop-off site—a phone booth in Florida.

Knowledge and human power are synonymous.
—FRANCIS BACON

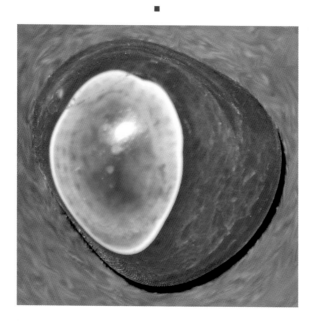

AGATES ARE NOT a distinct mineral species, but a group name for stones formed from silicates, chiefly chalcedony quartz. In any event, they are nearly identical to quartz in composition, have a cryptocrystalline structure, and measure 7.0 on the Mohs scale. Most agates occur in cavities created by cooling lava. Thus, agates have a banded structure, with their layers being approximately parallel to the sides of the cavity. Today important sources of agate are the Ural Mountains of Russia, Brazil, Eygpt, Germany, India, Italy, Madagascar, Mexico, Uruguay, and the western United States.

The name *agate* derives either from the river Achates, now known as the Drillo, in Sicily, where the stone was supposedly first found, or from the Greek word for "happy." Eye agates (also known as *Mexican, cyclops, Botswana,* and *ring agates*) display a colorful concentric banding, and when cut crosswise, the stone will appear to have a center, or eye.

Traditionally, these agates were thought to protect one from the evil eye, harmful magic, and other misfortunes. Thus protected, those who wore or carried agate were thought to be "agreeable, persuasive, prudent yet bold." It was believed agate brought God's favor and bestowed the power to vanquish enemies and to acquire riches in addition to rendering one invisible.

Islam in particular reveres the stone. According to tradition, whoever wears an agate ring is believed to be protected from various mishaps and will enjoy longevity, among other benefits. In the Shia book of prayers, we are offered a glimpse of magical benefits associated with the agate:

Whosoever endures the night 'til sunrise wearing an agate ring on his/her right hand, before seeing or being seen by any human that morning, turns the agate ring toward the palm side of his/her hand, and while looking at the gem recites the 97th chapter of the Qur'an followed by this prayer [specified], then the God of the Universe shall grant him/her immunity on that day from any danger that falls from the sky, or rises up to it, or which disappears into the earth, or rises out of it, and he/she shall remain protected by the power of God and the agents of God until dusk.

—Mafatih Al-janan

As a personal stone or amulet, eye agate specifically enhances the powers of concentration and manifestation. Meditation with these stones will serve to return you to a true sense of self and restore a sense of the divine within.

Typically referred to as having "grounding" energy, eye agates offer a more soul-based centering, a point from which you can then direct your energy and power outward into the universe. As with any of the power stones, how you use that power is up to you, but eye agate will nevertheless prove a powerful ally in your quest for what you truly desire.

Power is, in nature, the essential measure of right.
—RALPH WALDO EMERSON

■

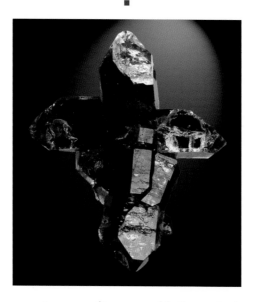

THE HERKIMER DIAMOND is not a diamond at all, but a double-pointed, or **double-terminated,** quartz crystal that has already been faceted by nature. Though popularly thought to be found in only one location, in Herkimer, New York, similar doubly terminated quartz crystals have been found in a few other locations, including Arizona, Afghanistan, Norway, Ukraine, and China, though these cannot rightly be called "Herkimer." Herkimer diamonds have a trigonal crystal structure and measure 7.5 on the Mohs scale.

Though most of us think of Herkimer diamonds as relatively recent entries into the world of crystals, these stones are by no means a recent discovery. The Mohawk Indians and early settlers knew about the crystals and prospected for them in nearby streambeds, stream sediments, and newly plowed fields.

They are naturally faceted, each having eighteen facets and two points. The double termination means these crystals have almost no contact with their host rock, which is dolostone—a combination of limestone and dolomite. Most are very clear, though some will contain inclusions of decayed vegetation or anthracite—that is, coal. Usually ranging in the area of one-half inch long, much larger specimens have been found.

As with any doubly terminated crystals, these can truly be said to belong to the master class of crystals, and, as such, one should approach their use with caution and intention.

As they exert a very strong frequency, some say Herkimer diamonds assist in communication with other planes and dimensions of reality. Many users report that this crystal assists with activation of the so-called third eye and imparts extraordinary powers of perception. Wearing or carrying a Herkimer diamond may give you extraordinary influence over others, too, and endow you with an almost visionary capacity.

A stone that imparts greater access to your own inner voice and guidance system,

it might be best called the "wisdom stone," for people who use this energy wisely will almost surely realize exceptional benefit. Those who use it unwisely, however, will just as surely come to know the real value of wisdom in all respects. Double-terminated crystals are like the proverbial two-edged sword and offer an energy that, indeed, can cut both ways.

Through the practice of meditation, it is said that these stones can be programmed by the user to enhance whatever emotional and mental states he or she may desire. They work especially well to complement the energy of other quartzes for specific intentions and will serve to further amplify the specific qualities and purposes of a great variety of stones and minerals.

A Herkimer diamond will not render you a magician or a superhero, but they do offer extraordinary insight, real vision, great creativity, and greater access to the realms of that thing we call "power" in every area of life.

■ ARKIMER DIAMOND ■

SHORT, STOUT, DOUBLE-TERMINATED crystals that come from Arkansas have a shape similar to the Herkimer diamond from New York, but usually have a hardness of 7.0, as opposed to the Herkimer's 7.5, on the Mohs scale. Sharing many of the same healing properties of Herkimer diamonds, they can also be utilized in any situation that is appropriate for clear quartz crystals.

What it lies in our power to do, it lies in our power not to do.
—ARISTOTLE

■

KUNZITE IS ANOTHER of the stones that has been with us for millions of years, yet it was only "discovered" less than a hundred years ago by gemstone specialist George Kunz, from whom it got its name, when pale pink kunzite was found in 1902 in San Diego County in California. Belonging to the monoclinic group of crystals, it is today mainly found in Afghanistan, Madagascar, Brazil, and the United States. Ranging from pale pink to lavender, some kunzite crystals display a red-orange fluorescence under light. It measures a 6.5 on the Mohs scale, but is more frequently found in crystal form than in jewelry, as it is difficult to cut without fracturing the stones.

Since kunzite is a relatively new designation, there is little historical tradition associated with it. Many contemporary healers advocate its use in alleviating depression and mood disorders, but as with all the monoclinic crystals, its best use is as a transformative and power-enhancing energy.

A strong balancing stone, kunzite offers great energy for reconciling strong emotions with physical reality. If you're a person prone to scatter your forces or subject to getting knocked off course in emotional storms, kunzite is the stone to carry. It will be a great aid in helping you become less erratic in your thinking and more devoted to your goals.

Increasing the powers of self-discipline, concentration, and focus, kunzite exerts a more subtle influence upon the environment and has a way of simply clearing the path to success. Not a stone for more rigid, power-hungry types, kunzite is nevertheless very useful for people afflicted with the "Hamlet syndrome," who feel themselves unduly subject to those slings and arrows of outrageous fortune. It conveys the ability to emotionally distance oneself from problems, instills a sense of security, and offers comfort on the sometimes-rocky road to worldly accomplishment.

I love power. But it is as an artist that I love it. I love it as a musician loves his violin.
—NAPOLEON BONAPARTE

KYANITE HAS SEVERAL alternative names, including *disthene, munkrudite,* and *cyanite.* Unlike many other crystals included in this chapter, it belongs to the triclinic group, displaying elongated, columnar crystals. Kyanite is most unusual in that different degrees of hardness can be measured in the same crystal. Along the perpendicular axis it will measure 6.5 on the Mohs scale, while if measured parallel to the axis, it is only a 4.5.

Its name derives from the Greek word *kyanos,* meaning "blue." This mineral has in former times been used in the manufacture of porcelain and spark plugs. In the metaphysical lore, it is frequently recommended for realigning the chakras and is one of the three stones believed never to need cleansing, the other two being amethyst and citrine.

Kyanite is never heat-treated to improve its color. One of its more interesting properties is that it undergoes an irreversible expansion when fired at high temperature.

Several advocates of this stone insist that it's a stone for channeling, astral travel, and past life and dream recall. Place a wand on your bedside table, and expect vivid and compelling messages from your unconscious.

This energy is powerful stuff. Think of it

as a tonic, brain food, a shot in the arm, a kick in the butt, and an all-around morale booster. It can also be used to give added energy to other crystals and charge them with specific purposes. Kyanite will work to remove blockages in your personal energy field, often quite suddenly, and will have all the natural force of a lightning strike, so if you're not adequately prepared to make some sweeping changes in the way you deal with others and the world, you may be in for a surprise.

Like its natural color, kyanite's energy can feel very much like the proverbial bolt from the blue, bringing a rush of energy, inspiration, and even brilliance. It requires a certain openness, however, and is best not used by stodgier personalities or those who are typically devoted to more controlled and orderly states of being.

Yet if you really do want to be a "player," this powerful energy is a good bet. On the physical level, it improves brain function and is also useful for people with memory problems. In any event, it promotes complete honesty, sometimes with unexpected results.

A variety of black kyanite is known to be a boost to meditation and will serve to deflect negativity in all of its forms.

LEPIDOLITE

(Also see chapter 8, Stones for Emotional Wellness and Healing)

To control others is to have power, to control yourself is to know the way.
—LAO MA

LEPIDOLITE IS A form of mica and has only in the past decade become available on the mineral market in any quantity. An ore of lithium, it forms in masses that contain a substantial amount of lithium. Typically ranging from pink to lilac, color is the best field test for its authenticity. A member of the monoclinic group of crystals, it measures 2.5 on the Mohs scale of hardness, and it is found in Brazil, Russia, the state of California, and several locations in Africa.

Sometimes known as the "peace stone," lepidolite was originally called "lilalite" when first discovered in the eighteenth century. Variously thought to be associated with a calming influence, because of the small amounts of lithium present in the stone, it nevertheless emits a peculiarly transformative energy that is highly recommended for those whose plans are carried out in secret, or who prefer to exert their power behind the scenes.

Lepidolite allows events to unfold without challenge, and it is a very helpful stone to offer rivals as a gift. It promotes a general feeling of well-being among all those who carry it, and exerts a helpful energy that has a way of turning challenges into triumphs.

Above all, lepidolite reminds us not to take ourselves too seriously, so if you feel yourself caught up in the sense that life is somehow a contest to be won, this stone will prove of great assistance in removing the element of anxiety from your sense of ambition. It reminds us all that ultimately we are right where we need to be at any given moment.

Long held to be of great aid in business and financial affairs, lepidolite is thought to draw prosperity, and at the same time serves to release the guilt that can occur along with material aspirations. It encourages honesty with yourself at the deepest levels and beckons you to greater heights of achievement. Best of all, it aids in strengthening and promoting the kind of power that need not climb on the backs of others in order to reach the heights of achievement and success.

Lepidolite is one of the stones of power that exerts a subtle strength. It encourages graceful changes and harmonious transitions. In a way, it may be described as an elegant sort of energy, enabling you to get what you want without becoming embroiled in the nastier tactics of dog-eat-dog psychology.

The way to have power is to take it.
—William Marcy Tweed

■

Moldavite is an olive-green or dull-greenish vitreous substance formed by a meteorite impact. It is one kind of tektite, or material that is derived from meteorites. For a long time it was believed to be a variety of obsidian, but today most sources agree it is of extraterrestrial origin. The total amount of moldavite scattered around the world is estimated at 275 tons. There are now only four moldavite mines that are in full operation, all of them in the Czech Republic. It has been predicted that within ten years there will be virtually no appreciable amount of gem-grade moldavite left in the ground. A natural form of amorphous crystal, or glass, moldavite measures a hardness of 5.5 to 6.0 on the Mohs scale.

In Eastern Europe, ancient peoples regarded the dark green crystal as a spiritual talisman as early as twenty-five thousand years ago. The excavated site of the famed Venus of Willendorf uncovered a number of crystal moldavite amulets, arrowheads, and cutting implements. Perhaps moldavite's greatest role in crystal history is that it is, in some versions, the substance used to create the Holy Grail of Arthurian legend, which in some versions of the tale, was fashioned from an emerald that fell from the sky. Because history tells us that many ancient peoples tended to refer to all green gemstones as "emerald," the implications are clear.

Modern practitioners favor this stone for a variety of uses, but all seem to agree on its powerful energies. The conventional wisdom seems to be that moldavite is capable of effecting great change in short periods of time. Some view this stone as a catalyst for inner evolution, a way to access the powers of the higher self to more properly align yourself with the will of the divine.

Make no mistake, this is intense energy, and its effects are quite direct. Some recommend its use in healing when no other form of treatment seems to be effective, while others say its highest use is in healing environmental issues.

For personal use, proceed carefully and with a sense of the mystery and adventure of life itself. The power of moldavite may strip away your illusions, but it will almost surely reveal the more beautiful truths of existence.

Today moldavite is often polished and sold as *chrysolite,* or *pseudochrysolite,* when set in jewelry or sold as beads. Mineral specimens, too, are highly prized among collectors, having a distinct inclusion pattern very much like a dendritic fern and being much more "gemmy" or translucent. Lower-quality examples of moldavite are much darker green and more opaque, and there is usually a big price difference between the two.

■ ABOUT METEORITES ■

FROM EARLIEST ACCOUNTS we know that meteorites are nothing new and may even have played a significant factor in developing civilizations, both from a spiritual and a material standpoint. The ancients believed the heavens to be homes of the gods, so falling stars (meteorites) signified the descent of a god or its image to earth. It's also believed that meteorites played an important part in the development of the earliest iron tools and weapons before the art of treating iron ores had been invented.

Babylonian astrologers said the passage of a meteor across the heavens was always a good omen, especially if it was bright and had a tail. Just such an event is recorded as taking place in about 1150 BC. The Old Testament implies the ancient belief that certain stones were animated by a divine spirit. In the Book of Jacob his dream is attributed to a divinity that dwells within the stone. In the Book of Joshua we read the account of a battle where "the Lord cast down great stones from heaven."

Early in the sixteenth century, another shower of stones fell on Crema, east of Milan, Italy. One of the finest treasures of the Vatican, the painting known as the *Madonna di Foligno* shows one of these Crema meteorites in the form of a fireball.

Creativity is the power to connect the seemingly unconnected.
—WILLIAM PLOMER

SPINEL IS THE great impostor of gemstone history. Long a substitute for the ruby, many famous historical examples are actually spinels. Today spinel is rarer than it once was and highly prized by collectors. Belonging to the isometric crystal group, it comes in a variety of colors and measures 7.5 to 8.0 on the Mohs scale. Most spinel is mined in Myanmar, formerly Burma, where the stone was recognized as a separate mineral species as early as the sixteenth century. Other important deposits are found in Sri Lanka, Tanzania, and parts of Russia.

Part of the reason spinel has been frequently confused with ruby is not just a matter of color, but of location. Often found in the same deposits as rubies, the significant difference is that spinel is magnesium aluminum oxide, and ruby corundum is an aluminum oxide. In the earth, rubies crystallize only when magnesium is exhausted.

Though the gem cutters of bygone days could undoubtedly tell the difference between rubies and spinel, it's unlikely that they would let on, especially when hired for such important tasks as fitting a set of crown jewels. As a result, spinel graces any number of royal examples, including the Black Prince's ruby, a 170-carat spinel that adorns the imperial state crown of England. The Timur ruby, a 361-carat example, now owned by Queen Elizabeth, has the names of some of the Moghul emperors engraved upon its face, attesting to its pedigree.

Interestingly enough, today spinels are still substituted for rubies, by owners who prefer not to display the real thing in public. Though spinels certainly aren't inexpensive by themselves, some feel it's better to lose a one-hundred-thousand-dollar spinel than a one-million-dollar ruby.

Metaphysically, spinel is a stone of power,

because of its long association with revital-ization and rebirth. It is said to have the power to awaken Kundalini energy—the pri-mal energy force within us. Called the "immortality stone" by many, red spinel is a supreme booster for self-confidence and transfers its encouraging energy to all with whom you come in contact. Particularly rec-ommended for people who suffer from a fear of success or who feel guilty about going after what they truly desire in this life, spinel will work to remove any inner blockages or resistance to attaining a greater level of self-actualization and achievement.

A great stone to use when it's important to gain support from others for your cause or idea, red spinel's energizing effects will serve to raise your own awareness to new levels of personal best. Not having an egotistic energy by any means, spinel simply facilitates the

THE COLORS OF SPINEL

SPINEL IS AVAILABLE in a range of col-ors from across the spectrum. As such, many healers and crystal practitioners associate different colors of spinel with the chakra centers and assign the various stones significance accordingly. Below is a list of other spinel colors and how they can be used in a variety of circumstances.

Black: offers insights into material issues and imparts increased stam-ina. The color adds an earthiness to spinel's core qualities and grounds them in real-world effort.

Blue or Cobalt: exceptionally beau-tiful and very rare; stimulates com-munication, channeling, and creative expression.

Brown: said to improve health and your connection to the physical body; a very grounding stone.

Colorless or Clear: stimulates interest in mysticism; facilitates wider vision and spiritual enlightenment.

Green or Yellow: awakens the heart center and deepens connectedness to others through kindness and compas-sion; can increase intellectual power.

Orange: promotes creativity, intu-ition, and emotional balance, and clarifies sexuality.

Violet: leads you to the higher forms of intuition; stimulates spiritual development.

way a sense of universal power moves through each one of us in order to find individual expression. Guaranteed to brighten your point of view, it will definitely sharpen your perception, uplift your outlook, and bring others around to your new attitude.

■ THE POWER OF PLACE ■

THE CRYSTAL BALLROOM in Portland, Oregon, enjoys a national reputation for a reason. For ninety years this elegant establishment has been a destination for live music, dance, and making memories. The hall has witnessed first loves unfold, police raids, stars of silent movies, Beat poets, psychedelic light shows, and a number of narrow escapes from fire, neglect, and the wrecking ball before being listed in the National Register of Historic Places. Today it hosts everything from rock 'n' roll and country to hip-hop and big band swing.

The Crystal opened in 1914 as World War I began, in the days when people could still get arrested for dancing the tango. During the Depression, dance revivals raised spirits, and the Crystal Ballroom was also one of the few places in the country to host formal dances for African Americans in the days of segregation.

In the 1960s the Crystal was transformed into the ultimate rock palace, featuring artists such as Little Richard, the Grateful Dead, Ike and Tina Turner, Country Joe and the Fish, and Buffalo Springfield, along with many others.

While the action on the stage has always thrilled, one thing everyone remembers about the Crystal is its astounding "floating" revolving dance floor. The Crystal's mechanical dance floor (now fully restored,) may be the only one left in the United States.

Whether or not the Crystal Ballroom's astonishing history has anything to do with its namesake is uncertain, but those who come to the Crystal seem to be inspired by an energy emanating from the site itself, a phenomenon social scientists call "the power of place."

6

The Stones of Transformation

The cosmos is interesting rather than perfect, and everything is not part of some greater plan, nor is all necessarily under control.
—Starhawk

Transformation, according to a Webster's dictionary definition, is: "Any change in an organism which alters its general character and mode of life, as in the development of the germ into the embryo, the egg into the animal, the larva into the insect (metamorphosis), etc.; also, the change which the histological units of a tissue are prone to undergo." The late 1990s, however, saw the term introduced into the vernacular, especially as it applied to states of being. Transformation became synonymous with psychologically related words such as *breakthrough, awakening,* and *realization.* Instead of being confined to a concept of metamorphosis as an organic condition—as when a caterpillar becomes a butterfly—it came to be equated with all manner of psychospiritual states, up to and including what we have come to call "enlightenment." For purposes of this

chapter, however, I'm going to suggest that we return to a more organically based definition of transformation, specifically as it relates to the use of gems, mineral and crystals.

The stones in this chapter, in some form or aspect, convey, either through their appearance, their energies, or their traditions, the dual aspect of nature itself. There is no light without darkness, no good without evil, no day without night. There is positive and negative, expansion and contraction. Nature, then, can be seen to be in a continual process of what we typically call "transformation," just as we are.

For some people, periods of transformation can be very difficult, heralding major life changes of the kind where you feel as though the ground is literally shifting beneath your feet. For others, outward circumstance stays pretty much the same and a transformation takes place on a profound inner level. We may not understand initially just what needs to change, or even why it needs changing, but as a popular bumper sticker points out, "Shift Happens," and when it does, it helps to have tools to ease you through the changes.

On a more personal level, it's impossible for me to predict just why you, the reader, might be interested in the stones included here. A major move or change in lifestyle? A rebirth? Revelation? Are you looking for a whole new you? All of those things can be said to be transformational in nature, and all are equally valid. Whether the transformation you need involves a metamorphosis of your circumstances, your perceptions, or your physical or emotional state of being, you will find the stones included here have one thing in common: they work to absorb negative energy or influence and transmute it into positive energy.

In terms of crystal structure, many of them fall into the tetragonal group. They give and receive. As such, these energies can be thought of as part of an organic process that is going on all around us, all the time. In a way, the energy of this crystal group can be thought of as the constant inhalation and exhalation of nature itself. Breath is vital to life; our breathing makes the rest of the body's systems function smoothly. Thus, the transformational energy of the tetragonal group will be of great aid in facilitating the metamorphoses of your own, constantly evolving being by drawing in and giving out the energy to keep your processes running smoothly.

Successful transformation, in whatever area of life, comes down to a few essential qualities: a willingness to change, the ability to let go of outworn attitudes or conditioning, the patience to endure the process of change, and, finally, the openness necessary to face the unknown. In working with these stones, you will find the process of change itself easier to accept. They will assist you in removing blockages of energy, emotion, and thought that sometimes impede progress. They will help steady you in the midst of change. Above all, they will help you become less resistant to your own process of evolution—whatever the future brings.

(Also see chapter 9, The Psychic Stones)

Wisdom is a sacred communion.
—Victor Hugo

■

AMETHYST BELONGS TO the quartz family and the tetragonal group of crystals, but it differs from the rest of the quartzes because of that crystal structure. As one of the so-called master crystals, amethyst, whether in the form of clusters, points, tumbled rocks, or cut gemstones, is available throughout the world. Though availability contributes to its affordability, the quality of amethyst differs by locale. Measuring 7.0 on the Mohs scale, amethyst from the Americas can be found in large sizes, while stones from Africa and Australia are smaller but have a higher color saturation.

The purple color of amethyst is a result of small amounts (approximately forty parts per million) of iron impurities at specific sites in its crystal structure. The difference between amethyst and others of the quartz family, such as citrine, is simply the oxidation state of the iron impurities present in the quartz. In natural form it can be found in **geodes** or in crystal form. A variety of amethyst discovered in South Africa is noted for its periwinkle to lilac color and has been called "spirit quartz."

As one of the principal stones of transformation, amethyst's particular properties have been recognized in several diverse cultures, beginning with the Greeks. The word *amethyst* is from the Greek *amethystus* and is translated as meaning "not intoxicated." The Greeks attributed the origin of amethyst to the gods and mention the stone in a myth about the god Dionysus, who tended to revelry and excess, being gifted with the stone by the goddess Diana, who ruled wisdom. In Tibet amethyst is considered to be sacred to Buddha, and in the rest of the world, prayer beads, worry stones, and rosaries are often fashioned from it. Amethyst has also been found in ancient Egyptian tombs as an aid for one's journey to the afterlife.

During the Renaissance, amethyst became a symbol of modesty and service to God. It was believed the color represented a unification of conflicting influences that signified the joining of the spirit, represented by blue, with the physical body, represented by red. At one time amethyst was thought to encourage celibacy among the devout—a symbol that their physical lusts had been transformed and conquered by higher, more spiritual energies. Because of that, amethyst was prominent in the ornamentation of churches in the Middle Ages, and bishops still often wear amethyst rings. Amethyst's association with transformation has its roots in these traditions.

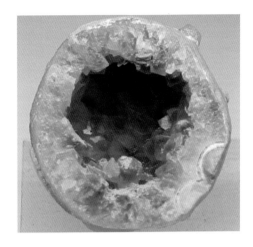

In India and Asia the color of amethyst is associated with the crown chakra, the highest level of enlightenment and the point at which the physical body meets the infinite spiritual energy of the universe. In healing, the stone helps to ease any difficulties in transition in any circumstance because of its transformational properties.

Amethyst works not only to aid the spiritual journey but also to help those who yearn to achieve higher levels of understanding. Because the crystal is said to transform energies from a lower vibration to a higher energy, it also transforms energy from an ordinary to a higher level of consciousness and awareness. Amethyst has the capacity to awaken spirituality at any level of social, emotional, intellectual, and physical interaction, and is thought to offer particular comfort to those who are experiencing grief, the loss of a loved one, or change itself as representative of loss. On the cellular level, it imparts its transformational aspects to physical functions, such

---

Some lore insists that amethyst will prevent baldness and improve the complexion, while other stories have traditionally linked the stone with universal love. The amethyst ring worn by Saint Valentine was engraved with the image of Cupid.

as helping to regulate metabolism and improve immunity.

Amethyst aids those who wear or keep it close to them in a variety of ways. It is especially useful in clarifying difficult decisions and helping opposing factions in finding a common ground. It has further been said to protect against manipulative situations by allowing the wearer to have a more in-depth perspective on their circumstances and opening the spirit's eye to higher connection, beyond our capacity to reason.

Said to also have a relieving effect on stress, grief, depression, emotional despair, and ineffective communication, amethyst encourages inner peace in difficult circumstances, deepens intuitive powers, and increases communication between right- and left-brain functions. Especially useful for those times when you can't see the forest for the trees, amethyst lends its transformational powers to increased unity among body, mind, and spirit and eases the process of necessary change, even in the most trying of circumstances.

APOPHYLLITE

The way of the Creative works through change and transformation,
so that each thing receives its true nature and destiny and comes into permanent accord
with the Great Harmony: this is what furthers and what perseveres.
—ALEXANDER POPE

■

APOPHYLLITE, WHOSE NAME roughly means "to leaf apart" in Greek, is a classic among mineral collectors. Technically, however, *apophyllite* is a general term for three minerals that are similar in their chemistry and physical properties and usually produce a rectangular prism capped by a pyramid shape. Also belonging to the tetragonal group of crystals, apophyllite specimens are usually colorless or white, though more colorful samples are available. Measuring 4.5 to 5.0 on the Mohs scale, these crystals are found in ancient lava and basalt flows, and apophyllite specimens come from all over the world. Occasionally they can be found in double-terminated forms, usually with the mineral stilbite (see pg. 167).

It's been written any number of times that what we call "consciousness" is like peeling away the layers of an onion. Thus the layers, or leaves, that form an apophyllite crystal provide an energy that can help you to both peel back those layers to arrive at a deeper sense of truth and to "crystallize" your own consciousness in such a way that each layer is in better communication with the whole.

Very useful for self-analysis, apophyllite encourages us to be as accurate as possible and helps us to access the "witnessing self," particularly in times of turmoil. Especially good for those times when you simply don't know which end is up, these crystals will help you get in touch with your own faults, failings, and deficiencies in an objective fashion, and keep you focused on solutions rather than problems.

Encouraging resourcefulness and the energy to make productive changes, this stone offers a sense of refreshment and rejuvenation for the senses. Apophyllite is very useful for breaking down complex ideas or problems into their component parts.

Said by many modern practitioners to strengthen a sense of connection between the spiritual and material realms, apophyllite can boost intuition and even increase clairvoyant powers. Associated primarily with the crown chakra, you can fully expect an "aha!" moment or two when working with the energies of this crystal. More important than revelation, however, it also imparts the energy to act, even when you may otherwise be confused or hesitant to move on.

With its essentially mystical vibration, apophyllite will serve to renew your sense of confidence in the natural perfection of things, no matter where you are in your transformational process, and to assure you of your place in the grander scheme.

BLOODSTONE

(Also see chapter 4, The Stones of Protection)

Change alone is eternal, perpetual, immortal.
—ARTHUR SCHOPENHAUER

■

BLOODSTONE IS A form of green jasper dotted with bright red spots of iron oxide. Sometimes known as *heliotrope* by the ancients, this jasper belongs to the trigonal crystal system and measures 6.5 on the Mohs scale. Major deposits can be found in Russia, the United States, Germany, France, and Egypt.

The Greeks revered bloodstone as a harbinger of change. In the Bible this stone was the last stone of the twelve tribes of Israel and the first stone for the founding of the New Jerusalem. Legend also tells us that bloodstone—or the "martyr's stone," as it is sometimes called—was formed when drops of Christ's blood fell upon green jasper. An important stone in much medieval literature, Christians often used bloodstone to carve scenes of the crucifixion and martyrs to the faith.

To understand bloodstone as a stone of transformation in addition to its legendary powers to protect, it's necessary to return to its more ancient history than is brought to mind by its nickname. The Babylonians revered it for its divinatory power, and the Leyden Papyrus, an Egyptian manuscript on ancient chemistry, declares, "The world has no greater thing than bloodstone," attributing to it the power to open all avenues, dissolve prison walls, and avert any number of potential disasters. Its ancient history points to bloodstone's use in magic rites and alchemy, where the red and green of the stone symbolized the union of opposites.

In the transformational sense, bloodstone will help reconcile you to upheaval or turmoil as a necessary stage of the process. With its strong associations with the Mother goddess, it attunes you more fully to the energies of the whole and keeps you grounded in the "real" no matter how arduous your spiritual journey.

If you are on a spiritual path, bloodstone keeps you centered on truth and provides the great courage necessary to continue on a spiritual quest. Steadying, protective, and imbued with a certain magic, suffice it to say that you may never know just how much help you have in a bloodstone as long as it serves to render you impervious to harm.

(Also see chapter 9, The Psychic Stones)

Things do not change; we change.
—HENRY DAVID THOREAU

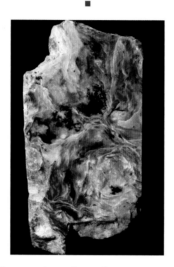

CHAROITE IS AN unusual and rare mineral that to date has been found in only one location: along the Chara River in Russia. A colorful mix of white, lavender, lilac, violet, or purple, it has a pearly luster and is rapidly gaining in popularity as it becomes more widely known. Belonging to the monoclinic crystal group, charoite has a hardness of 5.0 on the Mohs scale.

Almost immediately dubbed "the stone of transformation" or the "stone of the spirit" by modern practitioners upon its entry into the record books in 1978, this stone imparts powerful energy. Celebrated for its ability to release negative influences and transform them into positive impulses and actions, charoite provides for a clearer connection between the head and the heart.

The notion that charoite was named after the Chara River in Yakutia (part of the Russian Federation) may be wrong. The nearest bends of the Chara River are located about seventy kilometers from where deposits of charoite have been found. It's more likely charoite was named because of the way people respond to it. The word *chary* in Russian means "charms" or "magic."

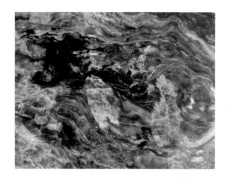

In periods of personal transformation charoite is especially useful for helping people come to certain realizations about those uncomfortable self-inflicted lessons of life.

Restoring a sense of universal love, it can also be of great aid when it becomes necessary to transform certain relationships, such as remaining friends after a divorce.

Truly a stone that works for the best possible outcome in any circumstance or difficulty, charoite is an excellent choice for those moments that require a deep "let go." In a sense, it helps you better understand the nature of change itself. If it is true that as one door closes, another opens, its powerful energy will make sure that you make it over the next threshold with your confidence in life fully restored.

▪ A WISE BUY ▪

THE PRICE OF charoite depends strongly on its quality. The most precious charoite, of deep violet color and few inclusions, is now very difficult to find. Even lower-quality stones, with a lot of inclusions, are becoming rare today. As one of the stones found in only one locale in the world, though, buying any charoite can be considered a very wise investment.

CHRYSOCOLLA

Chrysocolla is a beautiful, blue-green "crust" that forms in areas where there is a high copper content. "Drusy chrysocolla" is a form of the stone that contains enough quartz or chalcedony to make it useable for jewelry. The stone's crystal structure is difficult to identify, but it is thought to fall in either the orthorhombic or monoclinic group. Measuring only 2.5 to 3.0 on the Mohs scale, so called stabilized forms of chrysocolla are frequently marketed as turquoise. Chrysocolla is found today in parts of Africa, Chile, and Peru, as well as in Mexico, Arizona, Utah, and New Mexico.

Its name originally comes from the Greek words for gold and glue. Ancient Egyptians called chrysocolla the "wise stone," and legend has it that Cleopatra carried the stone with her wherever she went. Native American cultures revered the stone for its power to strengthen the body and restore a sense of calm in troubled circumstances.

Thought to be especially useful for people known to fly off the handle, chrysocolla increases a sense of tolerance and patience. Believed also to strengthen intuition, it makes a wonderful personal amulet during periods of transition and transformation, simply because it has a way of restoring one's faith in the spiritual process and in the idea of a larger plan. On the physical level, it will help with hormonal fluctuations at any stage from puberty onward.

Chrysocolla's special grace will help you to become more conciliatory and can lessen your resistance to change. Its particular transformational qualities impart discretion, clarity, and willingness. An especially good choice for highly emotional, irritable, or overly sensitive people, it helps those who wear or carry it to maintain a measure of emotional detachment and serve to open the channels to the higher wisdom that comes from the certainty that everything really does happen for a reason.

■ BUYER BEWARE! ■

BEAUTIFUL AS IT is, gemstone-quality chrysocolla is relatively rare and is often stabilized with resins to improve its durability. As it is frequently passed off as turquoise, the best bet for jewelry buyers is to confine themselves to likely looking cabochons or wire-wrapped tumbled stones. When set in or worn with copper, chrysocolla's powers will significantly increase.

FIRE OPAL

Any idiot can face a crisis—it's day-to-day living that wears you out.
ANTON CHEKHOV

■

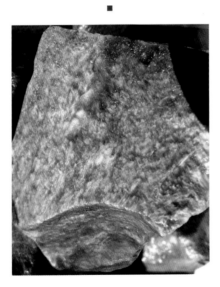

THERE ARE TWO categories of opals—common and precious. The precious opals are composed of three groups: white, black, and fire opal. A solidified silica that has no

---

■ OPALS—GOOD LUCK OR BAD? ■

OPALS AS TOKENS of deep love and high esteem have figured prominently in world history. Legend has it that the real reason Marc Antony won the heart of Cleopatra was that he gave her a magnificent opal, and Shakespeare called the stone "The Miracle and Queen of Gems."

Napoleon presented his Josephine with "The Burning of Troy," a magnificent opal with brilliant red flashes, and opals have been incorporated in many pieces of royal jewelry. Queen Victoria contributed enormously to the popularity of opals throughout her reign, and the stone became highly prized by many members of England's fashionable set in the late nineteenth century. Yet curiously enough, many people think of the stone as unlucky or only compatible with certain signs of the zodiac. Alternatively, some people believe you can only wear them if they were given to you as a gift. The bad luck associated with opals seems to have its origins in a tale involving Sir Walter Scott. At the time when the queen started importing and purchasing opals from Australia, Sir Scott was of the opinion that she should be supporting the economy at home and not buying from Australia. When he wrote *Anne of Geierstein,* he included one particular character to make his point: Anne, an evil baroness, wore an opal that changed with her mood. At the end of the book, after an especially evil period of time, her opal flared bright red and "swallowed" Anne. When the opal's fire cooled, she was nowhere to be found. After this story came into circulation, opals got the reputation of being lucky only if they were your birthstone or if they were received as a gift.

Legends aside, however, it's likely that diamond dealers of the time contributed to the opal's bad reputation, as the popularity of opals during the Victorian era threatened to surpass even that of the more expensive and valuable diamond.

crystal structure, precious opals are translucent to transparent and are distinguished by a combination of milky to pearly opalescence and an attractive play of many colors. Fire opal is characterized by its yellow, orange, or red body color. Used extensively as a gemstone, most quality opal is found in southern Australia, Brazil, Mexico, Czechoslovakia, and the western United States.

The name *opal* is derived from the Latin word *opalus,* meaning "seeing stone," and it has been a gemstone since the heyday of the Roman empire. Ranked second only to emerald by the Romans, one beautiful example was set in the crown of the emperor. Opals are also set in the crown jewels of France. Described in medieval literature as a cure for diseases of the eye, through the ages opal has been popular in gem elixirs or ground up as medicine and used in a variety of healing potions. At one time these stones supposedly carried the power to render a person invisible.

As a stone of transformation, it is said that fire opals can be charged with every type of energy. That means they are a powerful aid in helping to control not so much the reality of change—but *how* things change. A stone that can be said to be extremely useful in helping you to take charge of your own life, fire opal will encourage you to spontaneous and inspired action, even when under duress. The stone's energy is unique in that it provides both stability and drive. It also offers great confidence, and it is said to draw opportunities for change and to increase your awareness of the options available to you. If stress has left you feeling apathetic or lethargic, fire opal will assist in renewing your energy reserves and jump-start your creative imagination.

▪ BUYER BEWARE! ▪

OPALS DEVELOP *CRAZING*, or a network of fine lines, both on the surface and within the stone, if they are exposed to the sun or allowed to dry out. In addition to making them vulnerable to cracking, the resultant loss of water leads to loss of the stone's characteristic iridescence. Oil your stone regularly to help it retain its water content. It's also important to protect it from alcohol or detergents that could dry the gem.

Life moves on, whether we act as cowards or heroes.
Life has no other discipline to impose, if we would but realize it, than to accept life
unquestioningly. Everything we shut our eyes to, everything we run away from, everything
we deny, denigrate or despise, serves to defeat us in the end. What seems nasty, painful,
evil, can become a source of beauty, joy, and strength, if faced with an open mind.
Every moment is a golden one for him who has the vision to recognize it as such.

—HENRY MILLER

IDOCRASE, OR AS it is sometimes called, "vesuvianite," usually forms in masses and can be difficult to distinguish from some garnet forms. Another crystal of the tetragonal system, it is found in colors ranging from white to yellow, red, blue, brown, green, and pink. Measuring 3.5 on the Mohs scale, it is more popularly found in tumbled rocks and mineral specimens than in jewelry. Notable deposits in the United States occur in California and some parts of New England, as well as in Canada, Italy, Russia, and Switzerland.

Another stone with considerable abilities to ease you through a period of transformation, it's a particularly effective choice to give as a gift to loved ones who are somehow part of your transformational journey. Like many stones in this chapter, its principal energy involves absorbing negative influences and transforming them into positive output.

Traditionally thought to be a stone that promotes loyalty and patriotism, idocrase has a way of keeping the peace among close associates, even through times of upheaval. Thus, if you are in a period of metamorphosis but would like to retain the loyalty of a spouse, a good friend, or a business associate, use this stone to keep those relationships on a more or less even keel.

Very often we are kept from making much-needed or significant changes in our lives by the unspoken wishes or habits of others. This stone will be of great aid in instilling the courage of your convictions, while at the same time clearing your path of any obstacles to transformation that may be unconsciously holding you back.

Having a very reciprocal sort of energy, idocrase can do much to heal long-standing problems with parents, or unfortunate habits in relationships. A great choice for negotiating the sometimes-treacherous territory of codependency, it delves deep into the roots of our needs, provides stimulus for change, encourages independence, and allows you to move on and grow.

■ A GEM BY ANY OTHER NAME . . . ■

MINERAL NAMES CAN change over the years or be grandfathered into popular usage, while its official mineralogical designation changes. The result is confusing, to say the least, as in the case of idocrase, formerly (and sometimes still) known as *vesuvianite*.

Labradorite, another example, is only known as *labradorite* if it comes from the coast of Labrador. When found elsewhere, it is officially (but not necessarily popularly) known as *spectrolite*.

(Also see chapter 8, Stones for Emotional Wellness and Healing)

Every mind was made for growth, for knowledge, and its nature is sinned against
when it is doomed to ignorance.
—WILLIAM ELLERY CHANNING

■

THIS MINERAL IS a plagioclase feldspar that belongs to the triclinic group of crystals. Fine specimens of labradorite are characterized by a high degree of iridescence containing blue, yellow, gold, and green. A great deal of labradorite is subject to **twinning,** where the crystals appear to be growing into or out of each other, a phenomenon caused by an error in the crystal structure. Measuring 6.0 to 6.5 on the Mohs scale, labradorite is named for the coast of Labrador, where it was first dis-

covered. Today it comes from Canada, Madagascar, India, Finland, and Russia.

As a stone of transformation, the twinned crystals of some labradorite serve as a reminder of our own transformational power. What can sometimes appear as an error in our psychic structure or personality is simply part of a process that allows further growth and change.

Specifically, labradorite provides us with greater access to the subconscious mind and its stores of creative energy, knowledge, and wisdom. It enhances the intuition and makes those who fear change better able to play a hunch. A stone that builds self-esteem, labradorite can open your eyes to the person you really are, as opposed to the one the world wants you to be. Offering a multitude of healing qualities, it also encourages the kind of self-compassion that reminds us, even in difficult periods, that there really are no mistakes, simply opportunities to learn and grow.

SCAPOLITE

Man is a microcosm, or a little world, because he is an extract from
all the stars and planets of the whole firmament, from the earth and the elements;
and so he is their quintessence.

—PARACELSUS

SCAPOLITE IS ITS own mineral species and belongs to the tetragonal crystal system. Though not well known, scapolite can range in color from yellow to orange to pink and violet, though it is most often white or colorless. Measuring 5.5 to 6.0 on the Mohs scale, this mineral is found all over the world, with notable deposits coming from Canada and the northeastern United States, Norway, Italy, Brazil, Mexico, and Germany. While gemstone-quality pieces of scapolite are rare, mineral specimens are popular, and some samples will display a fluorescence under ultraviolet light.

Named for the Greek word for "shaft," scapolite is known as the "problem solver's stone" and is said to be of great assistance not just in finding solutions, but also in discovering truly *elegant* solutions to even the most mind-boggling dilemmas.

Scapolite offers us both inspiration and strength, so if you're in the process of effecting changes in your life, use it to dissolve old energy patterns, ego resistance, and other forms of self-sabotage in order to open the path to success.

Said to work a calming influence on debilitating emotions, some intuitives have used the stone to block interference and static from electronic equipment, and those who are sensitive have found it useful for mitigating other undesirable environmental factors, such as noise pollution or too much information.

In a more spiritual sense, scapolite can be used to draw out pain and repressed emotions in order to release them. It enhances clear thinking, and some claim that it conveys knowledge of the future—a sort of ability to see what's around the next corner—in order to align one's actions more effectively with what's coming up.

Finally, scapolite is especially useful if you have a lifelong dream that has yet to be realized. It can add its own unique energy to the sense of "now or never" and will motivate you to do all that is necessary to bring your dream to manifestation.

SCHEELITE

Life belongs to the living, and he who lives must be prepared for changes.
—Johann Wolfgang von Goethe

■

THE MINERAL SCHEELITE is an ore of tungsten. Belonging to the tetragonal group, it is popular with collectors as a specimen, because it forms perfect tetragonal dipyramidal crystals. Measuring 4.5 to 5.0 on the Mohs scale, it is found in many locations throughout the world, including China, Australia, Canada, and the western and southwestern United States.

These crystals are important to keep with you during periods of personal transformation, because they have a very refined energy that works to integrate the spiritual self with your worldly self. An exceptional choice for poorly grounded people who, on an unconscious level, tend to yearn to "slip the surly bonds of earth and touch the face of God," scheelite energy works to stabilize the spirit in such a way that life is likely to seem less of a trial. It helps you cope with the practical, but more important, it works to infuse the practical with a sense of magic, just as it works in reverse—to infuse the spiritual with a sense of the practical.

Scheelite has been called a "stone of balance," but in fact its energy is more complex, making for increased clarity, insight, and coping ability. If you are inclined to be addicted to meditation, have neglected more immediate relationships, or have fallen into a spiritually informed holier-than-thou attitude, scheelite will correct any escapist aspect of your spiritual work and better align it with your personality. Also said to be helpful in correcting imbalances in yang energy, it is extremely useful for reconciling the realities of ego with the requirements of soul.

(Also see chapter 4, The Stones of Protection)

Through twelve pieces of obsidian, he can see everywhere. He can see everywhere, he can see everywhere, he can see everywhere.

—Navajo song

■

Obsidian is a type of naturally occurring volcanic glass of igneous origin. Produced when lava cools rapidly and freezes without adequate time for crystal growth, it is not a true mineral, because it lacks a crystalline structure. Its color ranges from dark green to brown or black. Obsidian is relatively soft, with a typical hardness of 5.0 to 5.5. Snowflake obsidian is characterized by inclusions of small, white, clustered crystals of cristobalite in the black glass that produce a blotchy or snowflake pattern.

Considered valuable by many cultures as far back as the Stone Age, obsidian was used by primitive peoples for arrowheads, blades, and swords. Because of its lack of crystalline structure, it can be honed to remarkable thinness; it was also polished for use as mirrors.

Pre-Columbians used it extensively for tools and decorative objects.

Today obsidian is used in cardiac and eye surgery, as blades made of this material have a cutting edge up to five times sharper than high-quality surgical steel scalpels, resulting in a cleaner cut and less tissue trauma.

Obviously, the snowflake variety shares many important properties of obsidian, but with some subtle yet significant differences in energy. One of the earliest stones used for *scrying,* or seeing visions, it has long been considered a powerful stone for warding off negative energy.

Snowflake obsidian also helps to clear unconscious blocks and helps one find necessary detachment from life through increased wisdom. It possesses a gentle energy that is of special benefit to sensitive, soft-hearted folks, and many have likened a session with snowflake obsidian to be very much like the chance to sit down and a talk with an old friend or elder.

Attributed with the power to bring unconscious thoughts and emotions to the surface, its energy nevertheless operates in a subtle fashion. Realizations made under this influence are likely to be less painful and come to the surface more gently than might happen otherwise, and secrets that are revealed have more the character of dawn than of darkness.

Obsidian will be very useful in helping you to better understand your own patterns and how to adjust them in order to live more fully, and it will provide much-needed balance in times of change. Offering protection from both physical and emotional harm, it is especially useful for those who are going through intense forms of therapy in order to heal the wounds of the past.

In a way, the energy of snowflake obsidian is very purifying, offering those who work with it the comfortable distance of detachment while at the same time enabling them to plumb the depths of experience.

STILBITE

They must often change, who would be constant in happiness or wisdom.
—CONFUCIUS

■

STILBITE BELONGS WITH a larger group of minerals called "zeolites," each with their own unique energy properties. Usually found in shades of pink or white, specimens can also

---

display yellow and red tints with transparent to translucent crystals. Unlike many of the stones of transformation, stilbite has a monoclinic crystal structure. It is found in India, Scotland, Iceland, the eastern United States, and Nova Scotia.

Characterized by thin crystals that combine into a sheaflike structure, stilbite's powerful energies can help you to gather your own forces, even in the midst of turmoil. So if you really need to get in touch with your inner guidance system, stilbite is for you. Some contemporary sources say meditation with stilbite will put you in touch with your spirit guides or guardian angels. In any event, it will help you regain a sense of direction for your life and a renewed sense of purpose.

This mineral also has a strong power to manifest things on the material plane, so if you're suddenly overcome by a wealth of synchronicities or unusual coincidences in your environment, use them as evidence of stilbite's power to get you where you need to go. Expect, too, a heightening of all the senses when working with this energy, along with the feeling of being more awake and alive. Because it promotes creative energy, stilbite can be a very inspiring tool for many, yet those who are extraordinarily sensitive or seek better grounding may find they would do well to make another choice in easing their particular transformation.

Nevertheless, many people report extraordinary success with stilbite, especially with regard to a general raising of their levels of awareness.

ZIRCON

Everything we hear is an opinion, not a fact. Everything we see is a perspective, not the truth.
—MARCUS AURELIUS

■

ZIRCON IS A silicate belonging to the tetragonal groups of crystals. Found in clear, transparent red, orange, and yellow, there is also a blue variety commonly known as *Siam zircon.*

Zircon has been much disparaged as a fake diamond, but it should not be confused with the artificial gem cubic zirconia. Having a hardness of 7.5 on the Mohs scale, zircon is typically found in beach sands in many parts of the world, particularly Australia, India, Brazil, and Florida.

Its name is derived from the Persian *Zargun*, which means "gold color." Ancient people considered zircon an important gemstone for travelers and a powerful stone of protection, especially against the plague. Making the sign of the cross with a zircon over food before eating it was said to expel demons, so it was sometimes associated with repelling witchcraft.

Hindu poets tell of the Kalpa tree, the ultimate gift of the gods, which was a glowing tree covered with gemstone fruit with leaves fashioned of zircon.

As a stone of transformation, zircon enables you to do spiritual exploration on a very deep level while at the same time protecting you from undesirable influences and intrusions. It facilitates change and eases transition. Some people believe that zircon is associated with purification and what mystics refer to as initiation to higher realms of consciousness.

For personal use, this is a good stone to have for those times when you feel yourself doing battle with your own inner demons or enduring the proverbial "baptism of fire."

It will aid you in confronting the shadow portions of the personality in yourself and others, and make it easier to assimilate their meaning. A stone that will be useful in transmuting even the direst of negative influence, zircon can be relied upon to help you rise above immediate circumstances in a quest for higher truth.

■ PAINITE ■

A CONGLOMORATE OF calcium zirconium and boron, the little-known mineral *painite* is named for mineralogist A. C. D. Pain. Extremely rare and with a hardness of 8.0 on the Mohs scale, up until the turn of the millennia there were only three known samples in the world. More has been discovered in the years since, in Mogok, Myanmar, but it is still among the rarest of the rare.

7

STONES FOR PHYSICAL HEALING

Healing is a matter of time, but it is sometimes also a matter of opportunity.
—HIPPOCRATES

BEFORE BEGINNING ANY discussion of how crystals can be used for physical healing, it's important to keep in mind that crystals are not a substitute for conventional medical treatment or even alternative medical treatment. In many instances they can be used to augment other treatments, but in no instance should they be used to treat a serious medical problem unless it's with the okay of your personal physician. People who have existing medical conditions, such as epilepsy, pacemakers, or other devices that could be affected by changes in their electromagnetic field, would be advised to approach any use of crystals for therapeutic purposes with extreme caution—if at all.

The energies of crystals resonate with what we call the biocrystalline systems of the body. Simply put, some of our cellular systems have liquid crystal or quartzlike proper-ties. These include the lymphatic systems, some fatty tissues, our arrangement of red and white blood cells, and the pineal gland. Depending on a crystal's individual energy patterns, vital energies can be transferred to areas where they are lacking and in some cases move energies that are "stuck."

Most of the crystals chosen for this chapter belong to the hexagonal group simply because they impart an encompassing type of energy that can work to heal a variety of ills. Hexagonal crystals have four axes and are capable of resonating to the major systems of the body to correct any number of imbalances. There are some exceptions, of course, but if you're in search of a stone to ensure overall wellness, crystals of the hexagonal group, or its subdivision, the trigonal group, are a good place to look.

Since each cell in the body vibrates with

its own life force, and each type of cell that forms an organ or system vibrates at a certain frequency, crystal energy works to harmonize those vibrations and restore cells to health. If we see illness as a disturbance in energy patterns, augmenting depleted energies restores balance to the system. Adding crystal energy when you are suffering physical ailments won't harm you, but it can help your body's systems operate more efficiently—to heal, to strengthen the immune system, and to mitigate factors such as stress, which leads to that run-down feeling that often leads to increased susceptibility to infection.

■ CRYSTALS AND CHAKRA HEALING ■

CHAKRA HEALERS WORK with the seven main energy centers of the body. Think of the chakras as spirals of energy, with each one connected to the next. It is essential to wellness that energy flows through the chakras in order to nourish the systems of the body. Traditionally, the seven chakras are connected to specific organs and systems and therefore have certain colors and crystals ascribed to them.

Below is a brief summary of some of the stones associated with the seven chakras.

- The *crown* chakra is located at the top of the head. Some corresponding crystals include amethyst, selenite, and clear quartz.

- The *brow* chakra (third eye) is in the center of the forehead. Healing crystals for this area include fluorite, lapis lazuli, sapphire, and sodalite.

- The *throat* chakra crystals most often used are aquamarine, blue lace agate, blue topaz, and turquoise.

- The *heart* chakra stones include jade, apophyllite, tourmaline, dioptase, and rose quartz.

- The *solar plexus* chakra is situated just below the ribs. Associated crystals are malachite, gold tiger's eye, and citrine.

- The *sacral* chakra is in the abdomen. Corresponding crystals include moonstone, red jasper, sunstone, and carnelian.

- The *base* or *root* chakra is located at the base of the spine. Associated crystals include bloodstone, obsidian, smoky quartz, and hematite.

Much of chakra healing is associated with color rather than crystal structure. The healer's choice of crystal will depend on whether the chakra is overactive or underactive. In general, the paler the color, the less intense and more gentle the energy within a given crystal, while the darker colors will provide a more dynamic energy.

The art of healing comes from nature, not from the physician.
Therefore the physician must start from nature, with an open mind.
—PARACELSUS

■

DISTINGUISHED BY A pale blue color reminiscent of the seawater for which it is named, aquamarine belongs to the beryl family and has a hexagonal crystal structure. The Mohs scale measures its hardness from 7.5 to 8.0, making it very popular for use as a gemstone.

The state stone of Colorado, aquamarines are also found in Brazil and parts of Africa. Today most aquamarine is heat-treated to improve the color. The deeper the blue, the more valuable the gem.

Because of its tint, aquamarine has long been associated with the seas. The Romans believed the stones were sacred to the god Neptune and were washed up on shore as gifts of the sirens. Ancient sailors traveled with aquamarine crystals, believing these talismans would ensure a safe passage and protect them against the sirens' song. In the Middle Ages aquamarine was thought to magically overcome the effects of poison.

Aquamarine is closely related to the emerald and is a member of the beryl family. Beryl was used as far back as two thousand years ago to correct vision, and it continues to be used today in the manufacture of eyeglasses.

The color of aquamarine is most closely related in physical healing to the throat chakra. It is of particular use when you have a respiratory infection, as it improves breathing. Some sources indicate aquamarine can also be used for disorders of the upper digestive tract and in cases of chronic heartburn. Thought to be especially useful for people afflicted with allergies, wearing aquamarine regularly will lessen sensitivity to environmental irritants, pollens, and other allergens.

A gift of aquamarine symbolizes both safety and security, especially within long-standing relationships. Some people even say that the aquamarine reawakens love when love has grown cold.

■ PARACELSUS: ALCHEMIST AND HEALER ■

THE LIFE OF Paracelsus, the famous physician and healer of the sixteenth century, was fraught with stories of controversy, exile, and charges of heresy by the established medical minds of his day. Educated in alchemy, medicine, mineralogy, and surgery, he is reputed to have been hot-tempered, rebellious, and generally irascible, thus being constantly in trouble with the authorities.

Nevertheless, today we find echoes of his remarkable work evident in alternative medical practices the world over. A pioneer thinker, Paracelsus held the greatest respect for the energies of minerals in preventing infection and curing disease, and he believed man to be an integral part of nature rather than an intruder upon it. Much of his work was based on the notion of man as a microcosm of the macrocosm. He held, as do many current practitioners, to the idea that physical maladies stem from being out of harmony with the universe. Thought by many to be nothing short of a magician, Paracelsus had tremendous faith in the body's ability to heal itself once its systems were brought back into balance with the use of herbal medicines, gem elixirs, crystal therapies, and homeopathic treatments.

Only strength can cooperate. Weakness can only beg.
—DWIGHT D. EISENHOWER

∎

A MEMBER OF the phosphate group of minerals with a hexagonal crystal structure, apatite is a major component of teeth and bones. Usually green, it can also be found in yellow, blue, reddish brown, and purple and has a measurement of 5.0 on the Mohs scale. Notable deposits of apatite have been found in Mexico, Canada, Germany, and Russia.

The name apatite comes from the Greek word meaning "to deceive," probably for its resemblance to other, more valuable crystals. For obvious reasons, because of its chemical composition, apatite is associated with the healing of bones. Purported to aid in the absorption of calcium, it also helps those with arthritis, joint problems, and osteoporosis. Some sources say that carrying a piece of apatite is a good way to help regulate blood pressure, as its metaphysical energy works to reduce irritability.

For equally obvious reasons, the stone is also frequently used in obesity treatment, but that's probably more because of the name than anything else. Associated with the sixth chakra, or third eye, however, it is an excellent all-around stress reducer and is especially useful for those who are suffering from burnout and the kind of physical fatigue associated with that condition. Regular use of apatite will contribute to overall strength and increased physical energy, acceptance, balance, healing, and helping us to see the truth about ourselves.

motes greater self-acceptance and is especially useful in resolving issues of body image. Some find this a very potent stone to work with, while others don't give it such good reviews. Generally speaking, if you choose apatite, it's best to keep a piece with you at all times as a means of increasing its potency. Alternatively, you might consider augmenting its energy with other stones, such as clear quartz, to increase its healing power. Essentially a great stabilizer and balancer, apatite works more slowly than many would desire, but its long-term effects are highly beneficial.

Many people believe that on both the physical and emotional planes, apatite pro-

CALCITE

(Also see chapter 3, Stones for Money and Prosperity, and chapter 10, The Stones of Creativity)

It is health that is real wealth and not pieces of gold.
—MOHANDAS GANDHI

CALCITE IS A form of limestone. Though calcite belongs to the trigonal group of crys-

tals, there are more than three hundred crystal forms identified in calcite, and these

CALCITES FOR PHYSICAL healing can be further specified through the use of particular colors for particular systems of the body and related ailments. The best way to use calcite is simply to lie in a comfortable position while placing calcite crystals along specified energy paths, or simply on areas that are experiencing discomfort. Direct contact with the skin is important, but for people with chronic conditions, carrying a piece in your pocket will have beneficial effects overall.

Green calcites are especially good for correcting any problems of the endocrine system and are useful for relieving pain.

Blue calcite is particularly good for an overall energy boost, and is used in treating sore throats, bronchitis, tonsillitis, thyroid problems, and high blood pressure.

Yellow calcite benefits the upper digestive tract and lower back.

Orange calcites reduce the symptoms of chronic fatigue. It is also used as an appetite stimulant and aids in the treatment of sexual dysfunction.

Honey or *yellow* calcites improve overall energy and have been used to mitigate the symptoms associated with diabetes.

forms can combine to produce a thousand different variations. Generally speaking, the hardness of calcite is 3.0 on the Mohs scale. Calcite is found in many locations throughout the world, including the midwestern United States, Germany, Brazil, Mexico, and many parts of Africa.

Its name derives from the Greek word *chalix*, which means "lime." Making up approximately 4 percent of the earth's crust, calcite takes many different forms, including stalactites, stalagmites, and marble. One of the best all-purpose healing crystals around, the various forms and colors of calcites are associated with color forms of chakra healing, Reiki, and

other disciplines. It is recommended that those who work in the healing arts keep a calcite crystal in their offices to offer protection, to transform negative energy, and to diffuse the possibilities of contagion. As a protecting, grounding, and centering stone, calcite is especially helpful in lessening the fear and stress associated with health problems. Thought to be the number one cleanser of stored negative energies in the human system, its purifying energy works on all levels of the body, mind, and spirit.

Physically, calcites are especially useful in healing chronic back pain, tooth problems, and joint disorders. Clear calcite can be used for treating all physical conditions. It can also be used for detoxifying and as an antiseptic agent.

CHALCEDONY

Wisdom is nothing more than healed pain.
—Robert Gary Lee

■

CHALCEDONY IS THE name for a group of stones made up of the cryptocrystalline variety of quartz, which means the crystals themselves are too small to be seen unless under high magnification. Generally believed to belong to the tetrahedral group of crystals, there are many forms of chalcedony in a wide variety of colors. The stones have a hardness of 7.0 on the Mohs scale and are found all over the world, including the United States, Austria, the Czech Republic, Iceland, Mexico, Britain, New Zealand, Turkey, Russia, and Brazil.

The name *chalcedony* comes from the name of the ancient Greek town Chalkedon in Asia Minor. Generally speaking, the term is usually applied to stones of the blue or lavender color range, while others of the group are known by more familiar designations, such as *bloodstone, onyx, carnelian,* or *mocha stone,* to name just a few.

Native Americans held the stone sacred and

used it in a wide variety of ceremonies and medicine rituals. In ancient times, cups and chalices were carved from chalcedony and lined with silver, as it was believed to prevent the effects of poison. Blue chalcedony is said to have been used in weather magic and for clearing illnesses associated with changes in the weather.

In physical healing chalcedony is a powerful cleanser because of its antiseptic properties. It increases overall physical energy and is believed to increase vitality, stamina, and endurance. Some healers use it as a memory aid in cases of senility, Alzheimer's disease, and dementia.

For general purposes, chalcedony can be used to improve the assimilation of vitamins and minerals and to help combat the buildup of cholesterol and plaque in the veins and arteries. Most effective when worn in direct contact with the skin, it enhances the immune system and has been said to aid in the regeneration of mucus membranes, healing the lungs, and helping to mitigate the effects of smoking on the respiratory system. Said also to prevent the buildup of fluids, it can be useful in instances of edema or where water retention is a problem.

Materia Medica, **authored by the Greek physician Dioscorides in the second century** AD, **was a premiere textbook of pharmacy for more than sixteen hundred years. Volume 5 of the work was almost exclusively devoted to the medicinal use of more than two hundred stones.**

I'm touched by the idea that when we do things that are useful and helpful—collecting
these shards of spirituality—that we may be helping to bring about a healing.
—LEONARD NIMOY

COPPER IS AN element that appears in any number of compounds to form minerals such as malachite and azurite, as well as existing in its own crystal form. With a hardness of 2.5 to 3.0 on the Mohs scale, it belongs to the isometric crystal group and is found in Michigan and Arizona, in the United States, as well as in Germany, Russia, and Australia.

Probably humankind's first metal, copper played a huge role in the development of a number of ancient cultures. As early as 3900 BC the Egyptians were developing common household items made of copper, and by 2500 BC Egyptian jewelry makers had developed copper work into high art. In Asia and the Middle East, religions such as Buddhism and Hinduism employed it in inlays, temples, and ceremonial vessels. In pre-Columbian America metalworking was highly advanced before the Europeans arrived, and indigenous peoples used copper for bells, ornaments, weapons, jewelry, and armor.

Copper's power to heal is traditionally based on its ability to conduct energy. Copper stimulates the flow of energy, helping those who wear it to overcome lethargy and regain vitality. Since the flow of energy is another form of communication, copper is thought to assist in the process of channeling, cleansing, and overall purification. Physically, copper healing saw a great revival in the early 1970s. It improves circulation of the blood, increases energy, and helps to stabilize metabolic problems. A fine detoxifier, copper is also thought to exert a powerful influence over debilitating problems such as arthritis or other rheumatic diseases. Those who wear a copper bracelet have reported decreased discomfort from conditions such as carpal tunnel syndrome. Good for athletes and for relieving the pain of old injuries, some modern therapists also say copper assists with increased oxygen intake and can help to reduce swelling and inflammations of all kinds.

Researchers at the Centers for Disease Control reported in July 2006 that the bacteria *Staphylococcus aureus* (MRSA) cannot survive on a copper surface more than forty-five minutes, although when it is placed on a surface of stainless steel, the same bacteria remains viable for more than three days.

CUPRITE

(Also see chapter 5, The Power Stones)

To keep the heart unwrinkled, to be hopeful, kindly, cheerful, reverent, that is to triumph over old age.
—AMOS BRONSON ALCOTT

■

A MINERAL WITH a high copper content, cuprite shows fine examples of well-developed cubic crystal forms that reveal internal reflections of deep red inside an almost black crystal. Other varieties, such as chalcotrichite, show tufts of needlelike crystals that have a beautiful red color and a special sparkle that make them popular display cabinet specimens. Measuring 3.5 to 4.0 on the Mohs scale, cuprite is found in Arizona, Africa, Australia, Chile, and several locations in Europe.

Sharing many energy properties with copper, cuprite has been used to heal metabolic imbalances. Although our bodies require only a small amount of copper (U.S. RDA is 0.9 mg for adults), its contribution to human health is undeniable and as essential as calcium, iron, and zinc.

From conception, cuprite is present in our bodies, and carrying a piece of cuprite is thought to be good for pregnant women as an aid to the development of an infant's heart, skeletal, and nervous systems, as well as arteries and blood vessels. Copper and related minerals, such as cuprite, continue to play a vital role in good health as we age—keeping our hair and skin in good condition while repairing and maintaining connective tissue in our hearts and arteries.

Associated with the root chakra, cuprite aids in oxygenation of the blood, builds muscle and stamina, and helps to restore healthy kidney function. Many therapists purport that it also assists in better absorption of nutrients and vitamins, and can be an aid in regulating disorders of the thymus. For women afflicted with menstrual cramps and bloating, cuprite can be used to relieve discomfort, and a piece of cuprite dropped in a warm bath can be especially effective. Finally, there are those who have found it useful in conquering addictions to alcohol and other drugs by correcting chemical imbalances in the system.

Some say cuprite is a very grounding and stabilizing stone that assists in the rise of Kundalini energy through the chakra centers. Others attribute to cuprite strong masculine energy and associate it with willpower, confidence, and overall physical strength. Recently, as more information regarding the physical and emotional states involved in the masculine version of menopause comes to light, an increasing number of therapists recommend cuprite for men who are experiencing loss of sex drive and other issues associated with midlife.

(Also see chapter 4, The Stones of Protection)

Physical strength can never permanently withstand the impact of spiritual force.
—FRANKLIN D. ROOSEVELT

HEMATITE IS A mineral form of iron oxide that may even look more like a metal than a mineral. The name *hematite* originates from the Greek word for blood, *haima,* which refers to the red color of the mineral's streak. When crushed, hematite will turn water red, and slices of hematite display a reddish tint. A member of the trigonal group of crystals, a subdivision of the hexagonal group, it measures 5.5 to 6.5 on the Mohs scale of hardness. Today the finest mineral specimens come from England, Mexico, Brazil, Australia, and the Lake Superior region.

Ancient Egyptians used hematite in the creation of magical amulets to protect them against madness. The Romans associated the stone with Mars, the Roman god of war, and believed that carrying the stone into battle would make them invincible. Considering the Roman military history of conquest, it apparently worked pretty well, too. Native Americans used the red ochre form of powdered hematite in various ceremonies and rituals, including war paint. They also used it as a remedy for dental problems, acne, and alcohol abuse.

The key to physical healing with hematite is to remember it has a chemical composition that is very high in iron, hence its long association with healing the blood—that vital life

HEMATITE CAN BE found in several different varieties, each with their own unique names and appearance.

Hematite rose is a circular arrangement of bladed crystals that looks like a rose blossom.

Tiger iron consists of alternating layers of silver-gray hematite and red jasper, chert, (a flint like quartz) and sometimes tiger's eye quartz.

Kidney ore is a form of hematite that is found in lumpy, kidneylike masses.

Oolitic hematite has a reddish-brown color and an earthy luster.

Specularite is sparkling silver gray and sometimes used as an ornamental stone.

force within the physical body. Almost by intuitive association, many cultures have also associated hematite with blood because of the deep red color of its streak. Beyond its use as an ore, it has been long appreciated for its shiny luster and its use in objects and jewelry.

Today, mineral and crystal healers use hematite for treating blood-related illnesses, such as hemophilia; anemia; heart, kidney, and liver diseases; cardiac issues; menstrual problems; and nosebleeds. Metaphysically, it works to draw out negative energy and works to balance and integrate the body, mind, and spirit. Physically, it is thought to keep the body cool and to decrease blood disorders, nervous problems, and insomnia. Hematite is associated with the root chakra and is popular for use as a grounding and protective stone.

IOLITE

(Also see chapter 9, The Psychic Stones)

I think your whole life shows in your face and you should be proud of that.
—LAUREN BACALL

■

IOLITE IS A blue silicate mineral that forms as crystals or grains in igneous rocks as a result of contamination by aluminum sediment. Ranging in color from blue to violet, the gemstone changes colors depending on the angle from which it is viewed. Typically known as the gemstone variety cordierite, it has an orthorhombic crystal structure and a hardness of 7.5 on the Mohs scale. Today most iolite comes from Sri Lanka, Myanmar, India, Madagascar, and Brazil, as well as large deposits in the state of Wyoming.

The name *iolite* is derived from the Greek *los*, meaning "violet." The legendary Viking sailors made use of iolite for a type of filter to determine the position of the sun on overcast days. Looking through an iolite lens, they could determine the exact position of the sun and thus navigate successfully.

In physical healing, iolite is believed to protect and improve the health of the liver. Some sources indicate that its energy is especially useful in lessening fatty deposits and as an all-around antioxidant that will help to

PLEOCHROIC IS A term used to describe minerals that show different colors depending on the direction from which you are viewing the crystal. The effect is sometimes quite dramatic, though some minerals will display a color change so small that optical instruments are required to detect it. Other minerals, such as iolite, show a truly impressive color change, especially at the hands of a skilled gem cutter.

rid the body of toxins. Iolite has been used in the treatment of malaria and other fever-producing disorders because of its ability to draw negative energy from the body. Purported to be especially good for athletes in training, iolite helps to increase endurance and overall stamina. Associated with the sixth chakra, or third eye, it can be used to ease migraines and lower blood pressure.

Wear iolite especially during winter or periods of bad weather to boost the immune system. By the same token, it sustains already good physical health and has been said to render those who work with it virtually impervious to infection. Considered in various indigenous cultures to be a powerful medicine stone, iolite has been used by shamanic healers to ensure the accuracy of their diagnoses.

■ BUYER BEWARE! ■

IT IS VERY important to look at an iolite from several directions before making your purchase, because the stone presents very different colors from different angles. If cut properly, the stone shows its best blue color through the top of the stone. Good-quality stones can be purchased for about the same price as fine-quality amethyst.

There is a wisdom in this beyond the rules of physic: a man's own observation, what he finds good of and what he finds hurt of, is the best physic to preserve health.
—FRANCIS BACON

■

CHARACTERIZED BY BANDS of light and dark green, malachite may be one of the most easily recognized minerals. Belonging to the monoclinic crystal system, it is usually, and almost exclusively, found as stones or in massive form, but in recent years crystal specimens are becoming increasingly available. Measuring from 3.5 to 4.0 on the Mohs scale, malachite is found in a number of locations, including Africa, Russia, Mexico, Australia, England, and several parts of the United States.

Malachite is named for the Greek word for "mallow," a green herb. It was used from antiquity for a paint pigment and has been found in Egyptian tombs. Use of malachite for pigment fell off considerably in the sixteenth century, however, probably because prolonged exposure to malachite in powdered form can be toxic. It was also considered to be a powerful talisman against witchcraft and was hung at the foot of infants' cradles to ward off evil spirits. In Germany in the Middle Ages, the stone was especially popular and was believed to protect its wearer against dizziness and losing one's balance.

For purposes of physical healing, malachite offers a soothing energy that moves through the entire system. Said to alert you to hidden physical problems, it soothes deep-seated areas of distress over time. If illness or disease can be thought of as certain systems of the body failing to communicate with one another, then malachite restores the flow of communication so that, indeed, your right hand will know what your left hand is doing.

Without this very necessary physical awareness, the body's healing forces cannot be called upon to fix the problem. Malachite's special energetic qualities improve the transmission of information at the cellular level. If, for example, you have a bone spur brewing on your right ankle that causes you no pain as yet, you may not even know it's there. But when one part of the body is made aware of the trouble spot, it's easier to stop the problem before it becomes an even worse problem.

Thus, there's no real way of anticipating malachite's effects in physical healing, save for its preventive powers, because everyone who uses it experiences completely individualized benefits. In some people it will serve to break up congestions, and in some it will increase circulation and oxygenate the blood, while still others extol its virtues as a pain reliever. In addition, it's thought to be especially good for stomach problems and useful in the prevention of kidney stones.

In any event, malachite will improve your understanding of yourself as a physical form and will deepen your appreciation of the integral beauty of that form when all systems are in communication, working for optimum wellness.

Be careful about reading health books. You may die of a misprint.
—MARK TWAIN

ALONGSIDE EMERALD AND aquamarine, morganite is probably the best-known gemstone from the beryl group. Morganite measures 7.5 to 8.0 on the Mohs scale and belongs to the hexagonal crystal group. It gets its color from a variety of other minerals, principally manganese. Today this gemstone comes mainly from deposits in Brazil, Madagascar, Afghanistan, and California, though deposits have also been found in the eastern United States, including Maine, Connecticut, and North Carolina.

Although this gemstone is millions of years old, it has only been called "morganite" for less than a hundred years. In 1911 it was named in honor of the banker and mineral collector John Pierpont Morgan. Historically, beryls were used to ward off demons and evil spirits. Ancient literature notes that Pliny the Elder used powdered beryl to cure eye injuries and infections. It is said to protect travelers from danger and to treat disorders of the heart and spine.

Morganite has been associated with the heart chakra and is said to open and balance such problems as irregular heartbeat. Offering its users a wonderful gift of what the French call *la vie en rose*, its soothing color reduces stress and is a great mood elevator. Radiating a sense of relaxation and joy in life, perhaps its principal power in healing and matters of health is that it works to prevent one from doing things that are simply unnecessary and reminds us that the body very often will heal itself. Especially useful as a natural appetite suppressant, it contributes that same energy to the area of weight control.

Also said to oxygenate the systems of the body, modern therapists have used morganite in the treatment of conditions such as emphysema, tuberculosis, asthma, and throat infections, perhaps because its powerful tranquilizing energy serves to relax the muscles and reduce the anxiety associated with breathing problems. Associated with the heart chakra, it encourages emotional release and contributes to an improved body image.

Especially good for those who are experiencing the physical manifestations of a sense of fragmentation or being otherwise overwhelmed by daily events—that is, memory loss, nervousness, sleeplessness, and so forth—morganite tends to stabilize symptoms and contributes to an improved sense of strength and renewal. Also recommended for people experiencing similar problems associated with aging, morganite improves focus, physical stamina, and circulation.

PYRITE

Spiritual energy flows in and produces effects in the phenomenal world.
—WILLIAM JAMES

PYRITE IS ALSO known as *fool's gold.* A longtime favorite among rock collectors, it is an iron sulfide that is sometimes difficult to distinguish from the mineral marcasite. Pyrite is found all over the world in every possible mineral environment. Measuring 6.0 to 6.5 on the Mohs scale, pyrite belongs to the isometric group of crystals and is found in many locations throughout the world.

The name *pyrite* is from the Greek word *pyr*, meaning "fire," probably because pyrite will spark when struck with a flint or other implement. Historically, it's been used for a wide variety of ornaments, most especially among Mexican and Central American peoples. The ancient Mexicans made wonderful pyrite mirrors, which were an antecedent of today's cosmetic or magnifying mirrors. One side was usually polished flat, while the other side was strongly convex. Frequently the convex side was carved with a variety of symbols.

Pyrite emits a powerful energy and is used in treating a wide range of physical ailments. Believed to bring the energy of the sun into the physical body, it is thought to be especially good for athletes and others whose work involves strenuous physical labor, as it protects against overall physical burnout and sore muscles.

Also said to help regulate and detoxify the digestive system, pyrite is often used in treating disorders of the blood and the liver. Others report success in treating bronchitis and upper respiratory ailments. On a more mundane level, pyrite is reported to be extremely useful for those who are suffering from overindulgence and hangovers.

■ BETTER THAN CAFFEINE? ■

OFFERING AN OVERALL energy boost, pyrite can be used without some of the side effects that can happen with other crystals, such as unwelcome or unsettling energy shifts, and it is more helpful than a cola or coffee for those after-lunch, midafternoon slumps. Particularly useful for overcoming exhaustion, it's recommended that you simply lie down and place a piece of pyrite on your solar plexus in order to draw the energy of the sun into your body. Great to have around when you wish to begin a new exercise program, it will impart the energy to continue, even at those times when the spirit is willing but the flesh is weak.

RED JASPER

(Also see chapter 4, The Stones of Protection)

I find more and more that life is better than I thought it would be.
—ANNA FREUD

■

As ALREADY MENTIONED, jasper is found in many different varieties in locations all over the world. Usually marked by interesting inclusions and patterns, these varieties are often known by their "picture names"; that is, *picture jasper, Picasso jasper, rainbow jasper,* and so forth. Red jasper is also known as *imperial red jasper* and *silex.* Belonging to the trigonal crystal system, it measures 6.5 on the Mohs scale. Major deposits can be found in Russia, the United States, Germany, France, and Egypt.

The tradition of using red jasper as a powerful protection stone dates from ancient times. The Egyptians enhanced its power by cutting glyphs into it for protection against sorcery, while the Greeks and Romans carried it as amulets or used it in seals. It was believed by many different cultures, including Native Americans, to be a bringer of rain and a protector against attacks by wild animals.

For purposes of physical healing, red jasper energy can be very useful for treating obesity. Associated with the root chakra, its nurturing energy grounds a person in such a way that nervous eating or overeating behaviors that compensate for a sense of inner emptiness begin to abate. Also associated with the organs of elimination, red jasper is good for those who are afflicted with irritable bowel syndrome, hemorrhoids, or problems with constipation. Sometimes used as an aid for infertility or for women who have had repeated miscarriages, red jasper is also said to help relieve the pain of childbirth, and in some Native American cultures, holding a piece of jasper in the hand during childbirth is said to relieve pain and guard the health of mother and child.

Red jasper is also thought to ease pain in the feet and legs and to improve circulation in the lower parts of the body. Finally, some say that these stones help to strengthen the skeletal structure and can be used to help regulate growth in children who are small for their age or otherwise experiencing slow physical development.

SMITHSONITE

The wish for healing has always been half of health.
—SENECA

■

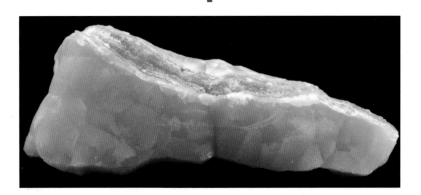

TYPICALLY FOUND IN dry climates, smithsonite ranges in colors from white to apple green, blue green, lavender, purple, yellow, tan, brown, blue, orange, peach, gray, pink, and red, and is sometimes even colorless. Distinguished by its luster, which rather resembles that of melted wax, smithsonite belongs to the trigonal group of crystals. Today it is found in many locations throughout the world, including Africa, Poland, Belgium, and many parts of the western United States.

Smithsonite is named after James Smithson, the founder of the Smithsonian Institution. The distinct grapelike clusters of smithsonite have made it highly popular with mineral collectors as well as with crystal therapists and healers. Though very little is known about the stone historically, smithsonite has gained great popularity as a so-called substitute crystal among chakra healers because of its range of available colors. Healers working with the chakra system coordinate their healing efforts according to the spectrum of colors associated with the seven energy centers of the body, and they sometimes use smithsonite to strengthen the vibrations of other stones.

Most of the information regarding the use of smithsonite in physical healing is of recent origin and experiential rather than recorded. Nevertheless, very good results can be obtained when using these crystals to strengthen the immune system.

■ THE RECOVERY STONE ■

ADDITIONALLY, THIS STONE has been used to treat various problems with addiction to alcohol and drugs. As such addictions arise from a wide variety of physical and psychological factors, smithsonite can be of great aid in helping people in recovery to come to terms with some of the unconscious factors leading to their condition. Many find it useful as well for chronic sinus problems and digestive ailments.

The most recent work indicates that smithsonite is especially useful in counteracting the side effects of drugs used in treating AIDS and HIV-related problems, as it has powerful detoxifying effects. Some have also said its steadying energies can also boost the immune system in cases where patients are enduring the ardors of chemotherapy.

TURQUOISE

Love is infectious and the greatest healing energy.
—SAI BABA

■

ONE OF THE master healing stones, turquoise is a porous hydrated phosphate of aluminum and copper that belongs to the triclinic group of crystals. Ranging in color from robin's-egg blue to a deep azure, turquoise may contain inclusions of sandstone, chrysocolla, malachite, and others. It has a hardness of 5.5 to 6.5 on Mohs scale and is commonly found in arid or semiarid climates, such as Iran or the Desert Southwest of the United States.

TURQUOISE HAS BECOME controversial in that most of the stones sold today have received so many treatments that the final product bears little resemblance to its original form. Such enhancements include plastic, wax, and oils that change the stone's color, durability, and appearance. In fact, fine specimens of turquoise are relatively rare, so imitators abound. The most common fakes include dyed howlite, magnesite, turquenite, and dyed chalcedony. In addition, a confusing number of minerals are often mistaken for the genuine article: namely, amazonite, prosopite, lazulite, hemamorphite, chrysocolla, odontolite, serpentine, smithsonite, faustite, and variscite.

The process of *reconstituting* turquoise consists of pulverizing pieces of turquoise that are then stabilized and hardened with resins to achieve a natural turquoise appearance, rather like chopping up turkey and pressing it into lunchmeat.

But assuming you find the genuine article, you should be aware that turquoise reacts to such things as hot water and household chemicals. Because it is a hydrous stone, water or light can change its color. The stone will easily absorb body or other oils, causing the stone to yellow. Never use an ultrasonic cleaner on turquoise, and avoid chlorine at all costs.

The history of turquoise begins almost with the history of civilization itself. In Egypt turquoise mines have been found in the Sinai Peninsula that date from 5500 BC. Around 3200 BC Egyptian pharaohs began annual mining expeditions to the Sinai. In Persia amulets from 600 AD contained carvings of Islamic proverbs. Turquoise is said to be one of the twelve stones of Aaron's breastplate in the Bible and rules of one of the twelve tribes of Israel.

In the Americas the Anasazi were trading turquoise with what is now Mexico by 1000 AD, and by the sixteenth century the indigenous cultures of the Southwest used it as currency. Turquoise also has a long history in Europe and Asia. As early as 500 BC it was used in Siberia, but it did not gain favor with Western Europeans until the late Middle Ages, when trade with Asia increased. The origin of the word *turquoise* is French and comes from the Venetian traders who bought the stones from the great bazaars in Turkey. Its propensity to change colors from exposure to body oils was thought to be a warning of impending danger.

As an all-around healing stone, turquoise energy benefits the whole body. A powerful immune system booster, it is said to improve communication among all systems of the body and is of particular use as a treatment for depression.

Also associated by some sources with an ability to remove toxins, turquoise is a good tonic stone. Crystal healers recommend it especially for detoxification of alcohol, poison, pollution, or radiation in the body. Its calming and grounding influence is also used in treatment of high blood pressure, asthma, infections, and dental problems.

Because it shares many healing properties with other copper-based crystals, it's a good idea to use turquoise as preventive medicine or in those instances when, indeed, the proverbial ounce of prevention is worth a pound of cure.

A FAMOUS ANECDOTE shows us that for all of the miracle properties associated with turquoise (and many other forms of crystal use!), there have always been skeptics, too.

The story goes that the Emperor Charles V once inquired of his court jester: "What is the property of the turquoise?"

"Why," replied the jester, "if you should happen to fall from a high tower whilst you were wearing a turquoise on your finger, the turquoise would remain unbroken."

8

STONES FOR EMOTIONAL WELLNESS AND HEALING

Be still my heart; thou hast known worse than this.
—HOMER

DESPITE THE FACT that it's human nature to follow our bliss, pursue our happiness, and find inner peace, a lot of things happen in the course of a lifetime that can make the journey much more difficult than it sounds. As a result, an entire industry has arisen around the various therapies, methods, seminars, and self-help approaches to healing emotional wounds.

Sometimes we know the causes of our problems: a lost love can make us hesitant to seek love again; a death can leave us unable to get on with our lives; a history of abuse or trauma can effect the way we function (or dysfunction) in other relationships. Outside events can turn our emotional lives upside down; the events of 9/11 and Hurricane Katrina are two examples that affected thousands and thousands of people. But just as often, lives can be forever changed by events

that don't make the news; a tragic accident, a fire or flood, an attack or robbery can leave victims foundering in an unfamiliar emotional landscape, resulting in depression, post-traumatic stress disorder, or a host of other problems.

Sometimes we can't identify the source of our emotional troubles. We can go for years without realizing we are repeating old patterns, making the same mistakes, or unconsciously re-creating situations that will work to our ultimate detriment. We know that we hurt, we know that we feel confused, depressed, or helpless, but we don't always get to the cause of the problem, and, indeed, sometimes even the most earnest delving into our inner lives produces no ready answers to the many emotional dilemmas we face every day.

And although we live in an age that preaches everything from religion to self-awareness to brain chemistry as an answer to why we have some of the problems we have, it's important to realize that using crystals and gemstones won't necessarily work any greater miracles on the emotional life than, say, Prozac. But, like Prozac, using such stones can go a long way to illuminating the causes of your unwelcome emotions and help you feel more stable and less at the mercy of behaviors or circumstances you may have considered beyond your power to change. Working in the same subtle yet very effective ways it works in other areas of life, crystal energy allows you to balance, regroup, and gain the objectivity necessary for real healing and recovery to be accomplished.

In a sense, all negative emotions serve to block self-esteem and creativity. Even though we never stop yearning for the things that are essentially good for us—happiness, love, needing to be fairly dealt with, getting our needs met, and so forth—we do lose the sense that we are actually perfectly able to get what we want out of life.

Like begets like, and emotions are no exception. Depression, for example, disconnects us from a sense of well-being and tends to create nothing but more depression. On the other hand, even a small shift in energy can open the way to more positive feelings. When you think about it, it really takes a great deal of energy to be depressed. That's why victims of depression often feel a lack of physical energy or enthusiasm; their available energy resources are being drained. By changing the way a person's energy flows, crystals can be of great assistance in releasing emotional blockages, overcoming resistance to change, and letting go of negative or undesirable thought patterns.

The majority of stones in this chapter fall into either the monoclinic or triclinic groups of crystals, with some exceptions. Depending upon your individual needs, you may want to experiment with these energies or use these stones in various combinations. Since the monoclinic group emits a constant pulse of energy, it can be helpful to think of these stones as aligning with your own constant heartbeat as they work to remove emotional blockages and heal emotional pain. The triclinic group offers a more constant, sustaining energy that serves to alleviate depression and inspire growth. When used in combination, they can be powerful emotional healers indeed.

But, like the old joke about how many psychiatrists it takes to change a lightbulb, a genuine desire to change is a necessary prerequisite for just how successful your work with crystals in this area will be. With time, willingness, and a conscious approach, however, they can do the work of healing, restore a sense of hope and confidence, stabilize your feelings, and prepare you for growth—even as you travel the sometimes-arduous ups and downs on the road of life.

AMAZONITE

(Also see chapter 3, Stones for Money and Prosperity, and chapter 10, The Stones of Creativity)

Those who hope for no other life are dead even for this.
—JOHANN WOLFGANG VON GOETHE

■

AMAZONITE IS A form of pale green feldspar found in Brazil, Russia, and parts of the United States. Its intense color is caused by the presence of lead, and some of the best specimens in the world are found at Pike's Peak in Colorado. A relatively soft stone, amazonite belongs to the triclinic group of crystals and ranges from 5.0 to 6.0 on the Mohs scale.

Some sources say the stone is named for the legendary Amazon women warriors, while others say it is for the Amazon River, though no deposits have been found there. Historically, amazonite has been used in jewelry in India, Mesopotamia, and the Sudan. In Egypt amazonite was fashioned into tablets in parts of the Book of the Dead and was even found in King Tut's tomb. For many years people assumed amazonite derived its color from copper, but more recent studies suggest that the blue-green color comes from small quantities of lead and water in the feldspar.

As we learned in chapter 3, on money and prosperity, amazonite puts you in touch with a sense of inner resourcefulness. Called the "hope stone" by many, wearing or carrying amazonite is an essential choice for those times when you discover a kind of misanthropic attitude coming to the surface of your consciousness. Too often we project our bad moods and ill humor onto the nearest object, thinking it a spouse, child, the smelly guy on the subway, or even the neighbor's dog, but in fact such feelings arise from a sense of frustration that we have somehow lost our ability to adequately control our environment. Amazonite is great for the times that try men's souls, because its energy will help to restore a rocky sense of self-worth and improve resourcefulness and coping abilities. Like many of the stones in this chapter, amazonite helps to filter information and keep you focused on what is essential for your own well-being. Not necessarily recommended for those who have a long-term history of emotional problems or melancholy, it is neverthe-less most useful when you're first feeling those negative feelings rise.

In much the same way people today use ribbons or jeweled pins and brooches to raise awareness of a particular social cause or concern, amazonite was once proposed as the stone for the Woman Suffrage Party as women fought for the right to vote.

APACHE TEAR

Human misery must somewhere have a stop; there is no wind that always blows a storm.
—EURIPIDES

■

APACHE TEAR IS a form of obsidian, an igneous volcanic glass. Sharing many of the protective powers of other forms of obsidian, this stone measures 6.7 on the Mohs scale of hardness. As a type of glass, it has no crystalline structure. Apache tear is found all over the world, and is especially plentiful in the western United States.

The name derives from a legend in which the United States cavalry squared off in battle with Apache warriors on a mountain overlooking what is now Superior, Arizona, in the 1870s. Rather than face defeat, the outnumbered Apache warriors rode their horses off the mountain to their deaths. The tears shed by their surviving tribe members are said to have turned to stone upon hitting the ground.

It is said that whoever owns an Apache tear

will never have to cry again, for it helps us to grieve our losses and move on. With an energy that promotes the qualities of forgiveness and protection, Apache tear is a first choice for people who are dealing with issues of loss and mourning. It is said to be of great aid in restoring a sense of balance to the emotional nature and in obtaining the sometimes-elusive sense of what psychologists call closure.

If emotional issues are causing you to obsess over past events, nurse old grudges, or beat the proverbial dead horse, Apache tear will enable you to better release the past and more fully experience the process of mourning a loss, whatever its nature.

Being a type of stone that will, in any event, help bring to consciousness what has been suppressed, Apache tear purifies the emotions through recognition and the experience of grief. Obsidian, and thus Apache tear, encourages no weak compromises, but it will help you to better comprehend your own part in any misfortunes or difficulties. In some instances it can serve to create radical changes in attitude and behavior as you learn to finally set that emotional baggage down for good.

CAVANSITE

To live is so startling it leaves little time for anything else.
—EMILY DICKINSON

■

A BEAUTIFUL AND relatively rare mineral, cavansite was only discovered in the last thirty years. It is found in only a few locations, and the majority of cavansite speci-

CAVANSITE—
CURIOUS CRYSTAL HABITS

ONE OF THE most unusual things about cavansite is its crystal habit, or the way it grows on its host rock. With cavansite, "balls" of crystals will grow opposite each other, thus creating an impression of eyes. Long ignored by mineralogists, it gained very little notice until discoveries at Poona, India, began to hit the market. Cavansite specimens proved an instant hit at the Tucson Gem and Mineral Show in early 1989. The color was vibrant blue, and the Indian specimens had needle-like crystals up to ten millimeters long, forming spherules, tufts, and "eyes" on white stilbite. This was a quantum leap in quality for an obscure species, and new finds have earned rave reviews ever since.

mens come from India. Cavansite belongs to the orthorhombic crystal group and measures a hardness of 3.5 to 4.0 on the Mohs scale. Its stunning ocean-blue crystals are usually found on zeolites, making for exciting visual contrast and beautiful mineral specimens.

Cavansite's relatively recent discovery makes historical information regarding the stone scarce, but its increasing popularity with mineral collectors has not escaped the attention of contemporary healers and crystal practitioners.

The blue to blue-green crystals are associated with the opening of the throat chakra, and it is said to encourage greater emotional expression. Its energy eases the ability to communicate difficult and complicated feelings to others, and helps you to better identify the causes of problems or pain without projecting those feelings onto others.

A crystal that bestows a greater sense of

self-possession on many levels, cavansite helps you to recognize your own shortcomings without guilt or negativity. Said to promote healing at the cellular level, it removes negative perception and patterns, even as it deepens intuitive powers, enabling those who use it to better follow their hearts with confidence and the sense of security that goes with knowing there is a larger plan.

He that cannot forgive others breaks the bridge over which he must pass himself;
for every man has need to be forgiven.
—THOMAS FULLER

■

CHALCOCITE IS AN important copper mineral ore. It has been mined for centuries and is one of the most profitable copper ores. Fine mineral specimens of chalcocite are becoming quite rare and much prized by collectors. Some new localities with well-formed crystals are promising, but so far the specimens from the now depleted mines in England and Connecticut are the only specimens available on the market. Chalcocite belongs to the orthorhombic group of crystals and measures 2.5 to 3.0 on the Mohs scale. Notable deposits of the ore occur in the states of Connecticut, Montana, Arizona, Utah, and Tennessee, and can also be found in England, Namibia, Italy, and Spain.

As an ore of copper, chalcocite shares many of the important healing properties of copper. It stimulates the flow of energy and, for emotional problems, helps those who keep it near them to overcome lethargy and feelings of powerlessness.

In general, chalcocite specimens are especially important to keep in your immediate environment as a stimulant to higher thoughts and as a deterrent to "lower" emotions, such as anger, bickering, or other long-running conflicts at home or in the office.

Strengthening and energizing, chalcocite doesn't necessarily spread good cheer, but it does cleanse and purify those nagging doubts, knee-jerk reactions, and that sense of "what's the use?" that tends to creep in when one is faced with a set of problematic people or circumstances. It is excellent for use in an environment where someone is chronically ill, for example, or where a household member is bearing the brunt of caretaking responsibilities. Equally, managers or supervisors will find it helpful in resolving problems with other personnel.

Able to revitalize and reorganize even the most stuck patterns of energy, chalcocite can help boost a sense of self-respect and serve to free you from troublesome emotional burdens, whatever the circumstances.

DID YOU KNOW that the color in fireworks comes from mineral elements? Barium produces bright greens; strontium yields deep reds; copper produces blues; and sodium yields yellow. Other colors can be made by mixing elements: strontium and sodium produce brilliant orange; titanium, zirconium, and magnesium alloys make silvery white; copper and strontium make lavender. Other features of fireworks come from minerals as well. Gold sparks are produced by iron filings and small pieces of charcoal, and bright flashes and loud bangs come from aluminum powder.

CHRYSOLITE

(Also see chapter 2, The Love Stones, Peridot)

The keenest sorrow is to recognize ourselves as the sole cause of all our adversities.
—SOPHOCLES

■

THE CHRYSOLITE FAMILY of minerals includes peridot and olivine and is used here to refer to the lightest golden-green form of the mineral. Measuring 6.5 to 7.0 on the Mohs scale, chrysolites belong to the orthorhombic group of crystals. Chemically, these stones are iron-magnesium-silicates, and the intensity of their color depends on the amount of iron contained in them. Chrysolite is found today in many parts of North America, Russia, and Italy.

A stone that has long been used to drive away evil spirits, chrysolite was once believed to protect against madness. Exerting a cheerful and calming energy, it is particularly use-

ful for those with a volatile temper or who are prone to bouts of jealousy, as it works to calm anger and soothe rage. Useful for dispelling negative emotions of all kinds, chrysolite has a cleansing energy that frees the self from sorrow and a sense of despair.

If negative emotions arise because we are disconnected from our own creativity, chrysolite will help to remind you that true creativity arises from within. It frees the imagination, restores good spirits, and will help to calm you in those moments of turmoil as you navigate through emotionally stormy periods, especially in relationships with lovers or family.

Additionally, chrysolite helps to get rid of the lethargy, apathy, and exhaustion that so often accompany bouts of the blues. It is especially useful in balancing bipolar disorder and can also alleviate symptoms of hypochondria. Chrysolite will prove of great assistance in helping you take responsibility for your own life.

DOLOMITE

Do not consider painful what is good for you.
—EURIPIDES

■

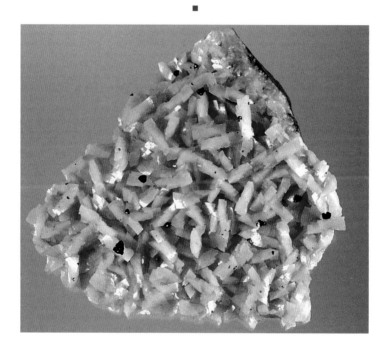

DOLOMITE IS ACTUALLY a mineral group that includes dolomite, ankerite, and others. Belonging to the trigonal group of crystals, dolomite can be difficult to distinguish from calcite. Measuring from 3.5 to 4.0 on the Mohs scale, dolomite is found in many locations throughout the world, including the midwestern United States, Canada, Spain, and Mexico.

Dolomite, named for the French mineralogist Deodat de Dolomieu, is sometimes known as *pearl spar.* Many sources say dolomite is excellent for overcoming insomnia, nightmares, and the irregular sleep patterns associated with periods of emotional turmoil, so if you're having trouble sleeping, this is the stone to place on your bedside table. It is further said to soothe loneliness and anxiety. Having the energy of the trigonal group, it will allow you to release old hurts and at the same time open you to new possibilities.

Particularly useful for those times when you're feeling at the end of your rope or that you've sunk to the bottom of the proverbial barrel, dolomite will help to restore a sense of resourcefulness. It works to alleviate the fear of failure and instead encourages a sense of generosity of spirit. By keeping dolomite close at hand, you will be able to get out of your own head to the extent that you can attend to the needs of others.

Especially good for people who lack stamina in bringing their dreams to manifestation, dolomite's gentle energy will offer you a renewed sense of inspiration, originality, and creative action. Don't be surprised if in working with this stone you suddenly discover hidden reserves of energy or give into surprising impulses and inspirations. On the physical level, dolomite also aids in oxygenating the blood and strengthening the adrenals, so the odd adrenaline rush is to be expected as well. Nevertheless, dolomite keeps you from becoming emotionally scattered and helps to center your thoughts on those issues most essential to your happiness.

HIDDENITE

Guilt is anger directed at ourselves.
—PETER McWILLIAMS

■

HIDDENITE IS A pale green to medium bluish-green mineral from the spodumene family of crystals, which includes kunzite and spinel, among others. Belonging to the monoclinic crystal system, it measures 6.5 to 7.0 on the Mohs scale. Though relatively rare, hiddenite is found in a number of locations, including Brazil, Madagascar, Afghanistan, and especially North Carolina.

Named for the town in North Carolina where it was first discovered, hiddenite is not as well known as many other minerals, but is nevertheless popular with collectors, as it is more readily available as mineral specimens than as jewelry. Hiddenite is strongly pleochroic, meaning there is a color intensity variation when a crystal of it is viewed from different directions, and because of its structure, it can be a real gem cutter's challenge.

Hiddenite is reported to have a high vibration that releases feelings of guilt, regret, and self-hatred. It's a marvelous choice when you are in search of greater clarity, or when you are having difficulty connecting the dots of your emotional patterns with your experience. Like its close cousin, kunzite, it helps to create a necessary bridge between the intellect and the spirit. It will be of great assistance, therefore, in putting you in touch with your witnessing self, allowing you to focus on specific issues as part of a bigger picture. If you carry a hiddenite and a kunzite together, it is believed the hiddenite will clarify the inner world, while the kunzite will illuminate the outer world.

Some say hiddenite acts as a protective shield and removes obstacles from the path of spiritual and emotional development. For that reason, it's recommended for adolescents or those who find themselves stuck in adolescent patterns of behavior. It will further serve to strengthen your support system and open you to the wisdom of others.

HOWLITE

He that can have patience can have what he will.
—BENJAMIN FRANKLIN

■

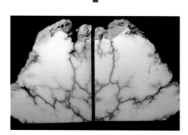

SOMEWHAT DIFFICULT TO classify mineralogically, howlite is usually thought of as a silicate, but sometimes as a carbonate. Belonging to the monoclinic group of crystals, howlite is white to grayish white and marked by prominent gray or black veins. It is frequently dyed and sold as turquoise or lapis and measures 3.5 on the Mohs scale. Today howlite is found in Canada, New Foundland, and California.

Howlite is named for Henry How, the Nova Scotia geologist who first identified it. Some Native American tribes revere the stone, calling it the "white buffalo stone," after an animal that was a symbol of peace and harmony for all the people of the world.

Especially recommended for those who are afflicted with passive-aggressive tendencies, howlite is useful for people who may unconsciously have difficulty in expressing anger, or in finding anger directed at them, without quite knowing why.

Because of its very calming energy, howlite is also good for people who struggle with an inner as well as an outer critic. It teaches patience and greater acceptance of self and others. It is especially useful as a kind of character-building stone, so if you've been struggling with issues of conscience or the sense that you're always having to backpedal, fib, or otherwise cover your you-know-what because of a sense of weakness or a failure to rise to your true potential, howlite will aid you in strengthening your will and reinforce your right to be here.

The stone's black-and-white coloration symbolizes the reconciliation of opposites— good and bad, self and other, light and shadow. With the help of howlite's energy, we can find aid for reconciling our own inner conflicts and the patience necessary to attain wholeness and healing.

■ WHITE BUFFALO TRADITIONS ■

CERTAIN NATIVE AMERICAN tribes revere White Buffalo Woman as the creator of the world—a goddess figure who came to earth to show the people how to live. By association, the white buffalo was seen as a totem animal representative of White Buffalo Woman's presence on earth. White buffalo stone is also a sacred representation of the goddess.

Today the birth of a white buffalo calf is seen by the Native Americans as the most significant of prophetic signs, equivalent to the weeping statues, bleeding icons, and crosses of light that are seen as signs, miracles, and prophecies within Christian religions. Just as the faithful who attend these signs see them as a renewal of God's ongoing relationship with humanity, so do the Native Americans see the white buffalo calf as a sign to begin to mend life's sacred hoop.

A talisman of white buffalo stone, or howlite, can serve as a powerful reminder of your own connectedness to all life, and as a sacred symbol of your personal relationship with nature.

LABRADORITE

(Also see chapter 6, The Stones of Transformation)

When you are through changing, you are through.
—BRUCE BARTON

■

THIS MINERAL IS a plagioclase feldspar that belongs to the triclinic group of crystals. Fine specimens are characterized by high degrees of iridescence containing blue, yellow, gold, and green. A great deal of labradorite is subject to twinning, where the crystals appear to be growing into or out of each other, a phenomenon caused by an error in the crystal structure. Measuring 6.0 to 6.5 on the Mohs scale, labradorite is named for the coast of Labrador, where it was first discovered. Today it comes from Canada, Madagascar, India, Finland, and Russia.

An especially good stone for those who fear or struggle with change, the energy of labradorite offers a great boost in self-esteem for anyone. Some sources recommend its use specifically for those who experience problems with, or have a pattern of, codependency, as it allows us to gain a better understanding of ourselves at a deeper level.

This mineral eases the way for change and thus is also useful in times of personal transformation. It purges negative patterns of thought, making necessary space for new insights and energies. A great healer of the kind of mental confusion that results from emotional pain or trauma, it works to set things right and restore a sense of direction and confidence. As such, it's especially useful in cases of post-traumatic stress disorder, or for those who are reeling in the aftershock of traumatic events. With a soothing and enlightening energy, it offers a rare combination of clarity, self-compassion, and insight.

(Also see chapter 5, The Power Stones)

Great tranquility of heart is his who cares for neither praise nor blame.
—THOMAS À KEMPIS

■

LEPIDOLITE IS A form of mica and has only in the past decade become available on the mineral market in any quantity. An ore of lithium, it forms in masses that contain a substantial amount of lithium. Typically ranging from pink to lilac, color is the best field test for its authenticity. A member of the monoclinic group of crystals, it measures 2.5 on the Mohs scale of hardness, and it is found in California, Brazil, Russia, and several locations in Africa.

In the work of emotional healing, lepidolite offers the gift of relaxation and a sense of greater peace. Especially good for people who tend to be tossed about by powerful and intense feelings, it alleviates stress and mood swings and is highly recommended for those with manic or bipolar disorders.

A great balancer of emotions, some sources say lepidolite eases anxiety and self-criticism. More a mitigator of symptoms of emotional disorders than a healer of their root causes, it nevertheless is very useful in helping us to recognize that all problems are not necessarily solved overnight, and that sometimes healing involves the need to take a necessary distance from the issues at hand in order to gain better understanding. Use lepidolite in meditation, especially if you have difficulty shutting out distractions. It will be of great aid in putting you in touch with the wisdom of your unconscious and guiding you toward more affirmative and constructive patterns of thought and feeling. Other sources recommend its use when differences of opinion threaten to disrupt families and relationships, for it tends to restore a sense of calm and clarity.

Many contemporary practitioners recommend lepidolite be used in conjunction with more powerful crystals, such as amethyst or rock crystals, for people who seek more profound changes in long-held emotional patterns or for those who may find themselves unduly resistant to changing circumstances.

MOQUI MARBLES

A moment's insight is sometimes worth a life's experience.
—OLIVER WENDELL HOLMES JR.

■

THESE VERY INTERESTING mineral conglomerates, or rocks, consist of mostly smooth elliptical or round balls of compacted sandstone encased in a shell of iron compounds. Variously referred to as "Moqui balls," "thunderballs," or "shaman stones," they range in size from a few centimeters to much rarer specimens that are about the size of a baseball. Moqui marbles have no determined crystal structure or measured hardness on the Mohs scale. They have been discovered in various locations throughout the world, with notable occurrences in the western United States.

Used for centuries by shamans and other mystics, Moqui marbles were considered sacred among the shamanic members of ancient tribes and were used in rituals to contact extraterrestrials, for visioning, and for out-of-body journeys. In the United States they are named after the Moqui Indians who inhabited the lands where they are found. Found also in the excavation of ancient ruins around the world, there are various theories about how these stones were formed. Some geologists believe them to be ironstone concretions formed 130 to 155 million years ago; others believe they are meteoric or even extraterrestrial in origin.

According to one legend, in the Hopi language the word *moqui* means "dearly departed one." The Hopi people believe the stones are evidence of an afterlife. Legend says that the departed ancestors of the Hopi Indians of the Southwest play games with these marblelike stones in the evening, when spirits are allowed to visit the earth. When the sun rises, they must return to the heavens, so they leave the marbles behind to let relatives know they are at peace.

Contemporary practitioners use Moqui marbles to realign the energy centers and release emotional blocks. Because some of the stones carry a magnetic charge, they can be used to move and stimulate Chi energy throughout the body. Not only will these stones act as both energizers and centering stones, but they also strengthen one's connection to the earth.

In an interesting linguistic similarity, the people of Thailand and Myanmar refer to similar rocks, or "thunderballs," as they are sometimes called, as *Moji* stones. In these countries, natives believe them to be of extraterrestrial origin and to possess a wide range of magical powers.

It is believed by many holistic and metaphysical practitioners that Moqui marbles possess great protective qualities and are essential stones to have in times of emotional stress and upheaval. Imparting the qualities of strength, calm, energy, and balance, these mysterious marbles can be truly said to be a stone for all seasons when it comes to overall emotional health.

PIETERSITE

Insanity: doing the same thing over and over again and expecting different results.
—ALBERT EINSTEIN

PIETERSITE IS A combination mineral formed when tiger's eye or hawk's eye and jasper combine with quartz. The best specimens have a beautiful chatoyancy, displaying a range of colors from blue-black to gold. Named for Sid Pieters, who first discovered the stone in Nambia in 1962, a significant deposit was discovered in China in 1993, where it is known as *eagle's eye*. Belonging to the trigonal groups of crystals, it measures from 5.5 to 6.0 on the Mohs scale. Pietersite comes from South Africa, China, and parts of Russia.

Though there's obviously a lack of historical information on the use of pietersite, contemporary sources are almost uniformly enthusiastic, claiming it brings the user closer to the source of all life and encourages the dignified use of power, in addition to imparting spiritual and intuitive guidance at

a very deep level. Known as the "tempest stone," pietersite facilitates emotional healing by helping to dispel illusion and putting you in closer touch with the soul's desires.

With modern crystal practitioners, the use of pietersite is associated with how the stone itself is formed, representing the profound movement and chaos that serves to break up emotional patterns that are resistant to change. As such, its energy works like an earthquake—jolting us into creating new patterns and forcing us to form new alliances and to transcend personal boundaries. From pietersite we can learn the art of assimilation and integration, from which all actualization arises. But when using this stone, it's likely you'll be forced out of your comfort zone first.

SAPPHIRE (BLUE)

Just to be is a blessing. Just to live is holy.
—ABRAHAM JOSHUA HESCHEL

■

SAPPHIRE IS THE nonred variety of corundum. At 9.0 on the Mohs scale, sapphire is the second hardest natural mineral and belongs to the triclinic group of crystals. While blue is by far the most popular color for sapphires, they can be almost any color, including yellow, green, white, pink, orange, brown, purple, and even colorless. Sapphire was first created synthetically in 1902 and is hard to distinguish from natural sapphires except by gemologists. Lab-grown sapphires range in price, and smaller stones are frequently used in less expensive jewelry. Today natural sapphire comes from the states of North Carolina and Montana, Myanmar, Sri Lanka, parts of Africa and India, and parts of the Middle East and Asia.

Historically, there are countless references to sapphires. The many biblical references to the stone include the Ten Commandments, which were given to Moses on tablets made of sapphire. Medieval Christians expanded on the biblical allegories with their uses of sapphires, and the

■ COLORS OF SAPPHIRE ■

BESIDES BLUE, SAPPHIRES come in a wide array of colors, and many specify sapphires of different colors for different therapeutic purposes.

Orange-pink sapphires are known as *padparadscha* and are a hot collector's item. Use this stone for increased creativity and optimism.

Pink sapphires are said to promote generosity and love.

Yellow and *golden* sapphires are used for emotional and physical balance and a sense of greater independence.

Purple sapphires improve memory and a more spiritual outlook.

Green or *white* sapphires strengthen the intellect and clarify thought processes.

Up until recently, the overwhelming favorite stone for engagement rings was not diamond, but sapphire. The shift in popular preference is largely a result of the vast improvement in gem-cutting techniques. In former times, diamond cutting was not so advanced an art as it is today, and many older stones could appear rather dull and lackluster.

stone came to be known as the "guiding stone" of kings and emperors. The British Crown Jewels include a number of magnificent examples of the gem, and the mystic Hildegard von Bingen believed it a powerful talisman against madness and demonic possession. It was also believed by some to cure the "madness of love."

Given the range of colors available in sapphires, in modern times it is a stone associated with a wide variety of healing uses. For purposes of emotional healing, however, the blue sapphire is especially thought to bring to those who wear or carry it a sense of spiritual enlightenment and inner peace. Considered a very powerful antidepressant, blue sapphire is also used to treat certain types of mental illness

■ JOAN BLUE ■

ACTRESS JOAN CRAWFORD loved sapphires so much that the press called them "Joan Blue." One of her favorite pieces was a bracelet set with three star sapphires of 73.15 carats, 63.61 carats, and 57.65 carats. She also received a 70-carat star sapphire engagement ring from her second husband and owned a 72-carat emerald-cut sapphire that she often wore on the same finger! Given her reputation as a temperamental sort, we can only guess at how things might have gone had she not had the stones to calm her down!

and has been found of particular help in overcoming obsessions.

Its particular therapeutic power seems to lie in the fact that the stone is able to focus healing power on anyone who needs it—with or without their consent. Therefore it makes a wonderful gift for anyone struggling with emotional problems who may not be getting the help they need through more conventional channels. If issues of jealousy, rivalry, or control are stirring up the waters in rela-tionships, for example, give blue sapphire as a peace offering (either to yourself or another) to dissipate the causes of conflict.

For personal use, blue sapphire helps you to remain faithful to yourself and is of special help for people who may find themselves susceptible to emotional blackmail. It bestows clarity, peace, and the kind of attitude adjustment necessary to fully enjoy the present moment, unencumbered by the issues of the past.

SODALITE

(Also see chapter 2, The Love Stones)

I have always found that mercy bears richer fruits than strict justice.
—ABRAHAM LINCOLN

■

SODALITE IS A key component in lapis lazuli, and the two are often confused. A stone that rarely forms crystals, it belongs to the isometric crystal system and measures 5.5 to 6.0 on the Mohs scale. It is most commonly found in Canada, Italy, Brazil, British Columbia, and the state of Maine.

As a mineral frequently mistaken for lapis lazuli, sodalite shares much of its appeal and history and carries much of the same kind of energy. It was not discovered in its solitary form until 1806, when it was found in Greenland. It would take another hundred years before this appealing dark blue stone would come into fashion or use on its own. When it was found in Canada's Princess mine, it became instantly fashionable, and many pieces of jewelry dating from this period include the deep blue stones.

In emotional healing sodalite is extremely useful in resolving abuse issues. Because of its gentle yet powerful energy, it is of considerable assistance in restoring a sense of trust in the aftermath of trauma. Better perhaps than any other stone for helping its owner let go of deep-seated feelings of guilt, sodalite reminds us that we are meant to be happy. Also recommended for victims of post-traumatic stress disorder, it is of special value for veterans and victims of assault or accident. For all of us, however, it is a wonderful stone for daily use in times of emotional stress, as it serves to promote all-around emotional wellness and to restore a sense of wholeness, happiness, and health.

SMOKY QUARTZ

Strengthen me by sympathizing with my strength, not my weakness.
—AMOS BRONSON ALCOTT

∎

SOMETIMES CALLED THE "Champagne crystal," this is a variety of quartz that is frequently marketed as "smoky topaz." In fact, there is no such thing as a true smoky topaz, so beware the merchant who insists there is.

Ranging in color from gray to warm brown or even black, coloration in natural specimens of this stone depends on natural radiation occurring in the environment. Most specimens today are found in Brazil,

Switzerland, the Himalayas, and Mexico, as well as in many parts of the western United States. Popular as an ornamental stone and measuring 7.0 on the Mohs scale, it belongs to the trigonal group of crystals.

Smoky quartz has a wide variety of popular uses and has been fashioned into spheres, pyramids, obelisks, eggs, figurines, and other talismans and gemstones. Smoky quartz has some varieties of its own, including *cairngorm,* which comes from Scotland; *morion,* a dark black opaque variety; and *coon tail quartz,* which is marked by black and gray bands.

A strong, steady, and powerful stone, smoky quartz increases the powers of perception, confidence, and stamina. Offering greater insight into your own stores of unconscious wisdom, it is able to dispel negativity in even the most extreme circumstances. Because this crystal promotes stability and practicality, it can be of great aid in helping you stay on a particular path and avoid the pitfalls of making decisions based on purely emotional concerns.

It offers strongly grounding energies for those who are experiencing a sense of weak-

ness, confusion, or bewilderment, and has a way of playing up your strengths while playing down your shortcomings.

I like to think of smoky quartz as an anchor stone for its ability to moderate mood swings, worry, and exhaustion. It alleviates unwarranted fears and can be of great aid for people who are suffering from insomnia. As a strong balancer of emotions and supporter of physical wellness, it works to help you better care for yourself, especially when others seem unavailable for help or comfort. For that reason alone, it is especially useful for people who are grieving a loss or otherwise coping with life's big events, such as births, deaths, moving, and marriage. Encouraging a higher sense of compassion, it enhances the spiritual aspect of any emotional upheaval without the need for martyrdom or needless self-sacrifice. Even in times of considerable stress, smoky quartz is wonderfully comforting and calming, enabling you to get through the toughest times and offering great clarity when "the smoke clears."

■ BUYER BEWARE! ■

QUARTZ CRYSTALS ARE also irradiated in the lab to create their smoky color, but since such crystals aren't recommended for therapeutic use, they are best avoided. Irradiated specimens can usually be identified by colorations that are too uniform, even, and much darker than natural specimens.

I have a simple philosophy: Fill what's empty. Empty what's full. Scratch where it itches.
—ALICE ROOSEVELT LONGWORTH

∎

COMPOSED OF AN iron aluminum silicate, staurolite is found in low- to medium-grade metamorphic rocks. Easily identified by its twinned, cross-shaped crystal formation and glassy luster, its name comes from the Greek word for "cross." Sometimes called the "fairy stone," or "fairy cross," rare examples of the stone may show a six-rayed effect. Belonging to the monoclinic crystal group, staurolite is found in the states of Georgia and New Mexico, as well as parts of Russia, and in Brazil, Scotland, Italy, and France. It is reddish-brown to dark brown and even black, and measures 7.0 to 7.5 on the Mohs hardness scale.

Long used as good luck charms, legend says the crosses were created by the tears shed by fairies when they heard of Christ's crucifix-ion. Others say the fairies wept for themselves as the rise of Christianity signaled the decline of the fairy kingdoms. We do know that stau-rolite was popular with the Crusaders, who wore it to protect them in their travels.

The healing qualities of staurolite come from the stone's association with the four elements of nature and the cross formation that unites the physical and spiritual planes of existence. Contemporary healers use staurolite with people who may feel disconnected from their emotions or who disassociate in times of external stress. A stone with extraordinary grounding properties, staurolite has been useful for those who are recovering from addictions as well as those who may have difficulty getting in touch with their feelings.

More specifically, staurolite reminds us that feelings are only feelings and are transitory. So-called emotional scars or wounds exist only insofar as we grant them power over our lives. In that sense, staurolite offers those who use it a renewed sense of control over their emotional responses, and enables them to better release the past and remain open to new experience.

9

THE PSYCHIC STONES

Intuition is the clear conception of the whole at once.
—JOHANN KASPAR LAVATER

THUS FAR, THIS book has placed a great deal of emphasis on conscious living and the importance of being as aware as possible of your own motivations, impulses, and needs when you turn to the use of stones for clarity, help, and healing. This chapter is about stones that can assist when you're not at all sure of what you desire or what you want to know. For these are the stones that will enhance what we call extrasensory perception, intuitive awareness, and even the ability to see into the future.

People have been exploring the possibilities of extrasensory perception since ancient times. In many cultures the power to see into the future; to communicate with animals, spirits, or ancestors; to see auras; or to read others in order to gain information not available through the five senses was seen as a special gift. Sometimes people who had such gifts have held positions of great honor; at other times they have been reviled or outcast because of suspicion, fear, or the belief that they had somehow made an unhealthy bargain with the powers of darkness.

Mainstream science has sought to prove the existence of human extrasensory faculties at various times with varying results. Generally, the most convincing arguments for the existence of such faculties arise outside the testing laboratory: we "know," without knowing how we know, when a loved one is in danger, when the phone is going to ring, or when we receive information about our own health or well-being that has no seeming basis in fact or our powers of reason.

Yet the very fact that human beings have developed a variety of disciplines, including yoga, tantra, meditation, and even magic rituals, as means to increase psychic awareness indicates that there is indeed a potential to be developed. If science has determined that we use less than 10 percent of our brain capacity, the millions of examples of extrasensory phenomena can be seen to indicate that the potential for further expansion and evolution is there.

In contemporary terms, we have come to think of psychic or extrasensory impressions as intuition. Psychologist Carl Jung defined intuition as one of the four functions of personality, along with thinking, feeling, and sensing. Simply put, intuition is a form of instinctive knowing without the use of reasoning processes. Though once revered (or reviled) as a rare gift, intuition is now increasingly recognized as a natural ability that all people can develop and enhance.

Many people have reported that practicing with tools such as crystals and meditation significantly helps to improve and develop our intuitive faculties. Some experience this as information coming from the "higher self"; some are better able to discern the "still small, quiet voice" within. Whatever your personal experience in working with these stones, be aware that intuition has many aspects, which can include inner guidance, greater discernment, increased awareness of self and others, inspiration, and creativity.

More than any other stones and crystals, the stones used to develop intuition are not easy to classify according to a particular crystal group or type of energy. You will find a preponderance of quartz crystals here, which belong to the triclinic or hexagonal groups, but there are many other types of stone as well, simply because different stones (and energies) work more effectively for different people in opening intuitive channels—just as there are a wide variety of shapes in meditative practice to awaken inner knowing. Some people will gravitate to a sphere, some to an egg, some to a wand, some to a carved animal totem, each fashioned of a particular material. Some will prefer to meditate with crystals that are light-colored or clear; others will prefer to gaze upon stones with a pattern that offers visual cues or pictures for interpretation. Use what works best for you.

The true power of your intuition, like any innate talent or characteristic, will better manifest with practice, conscious cultivation, and learning to use intuition to guide your decisions, actions, and movements through day-to-day reality. Far more than just playing a hunch or following your heart, intuition offers a knowledge that comes from a deep, unquestioning inner knowing that can significantly enhance your life and the lives of others.

Some of the benefits of cultivating your intuitive capacity include an overall reduction in stress, increased effectiveness, creativity, and empathy for others. In addition, you will find decisions easier to make and relationships significantly improved. With your intuitive guidance system in place, you will find it much easier to go with the flow with far less interference from external forces, or even your own critical mind. And although none of these stones or crystals can be said to endow you with the capacity to see around corners, they can help you to better anticipate events, perceive patterns, and make choices that are informed by a broader perception of life.

Though psychic crystals can be used as amulets, personal talismans, or jewelry, many people prefer to use specific examples as objects for meditation that are kept separate from their other crystals and reserved specifically for intuitive work. In that case, explore the possibilities of using readily available spheres, pyramids, geodes, or crystal specimens. Store them separately from other crystals, and use them only for purposes of personal meditation and exploration of those frontiers of inner knowledge available to us all.

AMETHYST

(Also see chapter 6, The Stones of Transformation)

All life is a manifestation of the spirit, the manifestation of love.
—MORIHEI UESHIBA

∎

AMETHYST BELONGS TO the quartz family and the tetragonal group of crystals. Available in the form of clusters, points, tumbled rocks, or cut gemstones, amethyst is available throughout the world. Though availability contributes to its affordability, the quality of amethyst differs by locale. Measuring 7.0 on the Mohs scale, amethyst from the Americas can be found in large sizes, while stones from Africa and Australia are smaller but have a higher color saturation.

The purple color of amethyst comes from small amounts (approximately forty parts per million) of iron impurities at specific sites in the crystal structure of quartz. The difference between amethyst and others of the quartz family, such as citrine, is only the oxidation state of the iron impurities present in the quartz. In its natural state, it can be found in geodes or in crystal form.

In cultivating psychic powers and intuitive capacity, amethyst is excellent, as it offers its protective and healing powers to any meditation. More a stone to put you in touch with your own inner knowing than to produce visions, it nevertheless has a powerful spiritual tradition and, as previously mentioned, is excellent for people who yearn to be in touch with higher levels of spirituality and awareness. Amethyst's color is associated with the crown chakra, the highest level of enlightenment, and it is said to open the individual to greater insight, bringing a sense of spiritual mastery to a sometimes mundane world. Some meditations even recommend placing a piece of amethyst on the top of your head while visualizing the opening of that energy center as you imagine light pouring into you from above.

For all that has been written about amethyst, however, perhaps its principal gift to those who use it for psychic development is simply that it instills the ordinary with a sense of the extraordinary—increasing the individual's awareness of synchronicity, symbolism and the sacred energies that pulse through every moment as we pursue the spiritual path.

Leonardo da Vinci wrote that amethyst could dissipate evil thoughts and quicken the intelligence.

(Also see chapter 3, Stones for Money and Prosperity)

Nature always wears the colors of the spirit.
—RALPH WALDO EMERSON

A POWERFUL COMBINATION stone, ametrine is a compound of amethyst and citrine. Sometimes called "golden amethyst" or "trystine," the rare and unusual ametrine is a member of the quartz family, and is created when amethyst and citrine reside in the same crystal. Because the color-zoning effect is entirely natural, no two ametrines will ever be exactly alike. Ametrine belongs to the hexagonal group of crystals and measures 7.0 on the Mohs scale. Today Bolivia is the foremost producer of these extraordinary stones.

Believed to be of great assistance in meditative states, ametrine raises consciousness and understanding. Imparting the qualities of spiritual clarity, compassion, and insight, ametrine's special gifts for intuitive work act on a person's ability to reconcile seemingly conflicting impressions and information. Sure to remove energy blockages, its effectiveness can be startling.

Placed under the pillow or beside the bed, ametrine is also reputed to aid you in understanding the symbolism of dreams and to facilitate lucid dreaming, enabling you to reconcile inner conflicts, make progress upon the spiritual path, and receive visions of the future while in that dream state.

Because its energy is so powerful, some may prefer to use ametrine with an additional grounding stone, as its unique clarifying qualities can prove very intense. Its extraordinarily high vibration strips away old prejudices and beliefs and can prove uncomfortable for those who are not fully prepared for its power.

ANGELITE

(Also see chapter 4, The Stones of Protection)

Dream no small dreams, for they have no power to move the hearts of men.
—JOHANN WOLFGANG VON GOETHE

■

ANGELITE IS A trade name for a form of anhydrite gypsum that has been compressed for many millions of years. Anhydrite is normally grayish, colorless, or a lilac-blue variety and is named for the angels. Though really good specimens are relatively rare, recent discoveries in Mexico and Peru are characterized by fine crystals, an internal play of light, and the typical color. Angelite belongs to the orthorhombic group of crystals and has a hardness of 3.5 on the Mohs scale. Some specimens will display fluorescence under light.

Said by some to be the fountain of youth for the new age, angelite's distinctive energy offers a true renewal of the spirit in any age, by virtue of its ability to raise and enhance your sense of spiritual power and to better align it with the will of the divine. Angelite is a stone of true universal knowledge, and opening yourself to what this stone has to teach you can be a truly extraordinary experience.

Many sources say angelite can be an aid in astral travel and in cultivating telepathic abilities. Still others say it will put you in touch with your personal spiritual guides, totem animals, and even the angels themselves.

Angelite, like all the gypsum family, is a great facilitator and has strong protective powers. Its energies are at once peaceful and expansive, allowing those who use it for psychic purposes access to a world of new knowledge and insight without fear or trepidation, knowing that the creator desires only the best for each of us.

CACOXENITE

You create your own reality.
—JANE ROBERTS

■

CACOXENITE IS A mineral that is commonly found as an inclusion in quartz, especially in amethyst. A phosphate belonging to the hexagonal group of crystals, these inclusions may appear fibrous or as tufts on the host crystals. Ranging from yellow to brownish or reddish in color, such inclusions may serve to ruin the chances for a quartz to become a gemstone, but for purposes of mineral specimens, they make for fascinating and surreal special effects. Notable occurrences of cacoxenite have been found in England, Sweden, France, Germany, and the Netherlands, as well as New York, Arizona, Alabama, and Arkansas in the United States.

As an aid to meditation and in intuitive work, the otherworldly landscapes formed by cacoxenite inclusions are very popular for awakening a sense of inner vision and intuitive knowing. Intuitives say that cacoxenite can activate the third eye and crown chakras, the energy centers at the forehead and top of the head. It is said to bring one's personal will into harmony with the higher self.

Sometimes called the "stone of ascension," cacoxenite can help in the developments of new insights and new ideas for humanity as a whole. Definitely a mineral that can help you to see the big picture, it restores a sense of how all events have a way of combining in positive, beneficial, and constructive ways.

Cacoxenite as a focus for meditation stimulates awareness, and can awaken memories, of past lives.

The shamanic tradition extols cacoxenite as a power stone. Its particular energies, especially when augmented and amplified with quartz crystals, are used to enhance many different types of types of psychic abilities, including channeling, clairaudience, (the ability to hear spirit voices) clairvoyance, telepathy, and scrying future events.

■ SCRYING ■

SCRYING IS A type of divination. Related to the modern word *spy*, *scry* is an Old English word meaning "to make out dimly" or to "discover by the eye" objects at a distance. In crystal practice the term is used to describe the act of gazing at a shiny stone or into a crystal ball to see things past and future.

Some people say scrying is a form of divination, or fortune telling, where one attempts to discern future events, while others say scrying facilitates our innate ability to bring up images from the unconscious while in an altered or meditative state. We do know that the practice has been in place for thousands of years. The Druids were among the first to practice scrying in a ritualized context, probably using beryl, which they deemed power stones.

You don't need an official crystal ball to try scrying, however; just a quiet place, a crystal or other light-reflecting object, and the willingness to open to your own intuitive capacity are all that's really required.

Who looks outside, dreams; who looks inside, awakes.
—CARL JUNG

ANOTHER MEMBER OF the gypsum family, celestite—or celestine, as it is sometimes called—exhibits sky-blue-colored crystal clusters and is orthorhombic in structure. With a hardness of 3.0 to 3.5 on the Mohs scale, celestite is becoming increasingly available, with excellent specimens found in New York, Ohio, and California in the United States, as well as in Mexico, Peru, and Madagascar.

A crystal with a variety of metaphysical properties, celestite is especially associated with what we call "the higher mind." Said by various sources to be useful for dream recall, it is also claimed to give you access to past life memories.

In intuitive work, celestite is a stone to remind us that cosmic law dictates a higher rationale behind the eternal human problem of suffering. It replaces pain with loving light, helps in recalling and interpreting dreams, and expands understanding. Some say this stone imparts the detachment necessary to attain the state of true witnessing that in turn serves to guide us each to right action.

Sharing many qualities with angelite, celestite can restore hope and faith and reminds us that everything has its purpose and that, indeed, nothing happens by accident. Finally, celestite aids the emergence of truth, as opposed to facts, and imparts the necessary discernment to tell the difference.

CHAROITE

(Also see chapter 6, The Stones of Transformation)

I did my best, and God did the rest.
—HATTIE McDANIEL

■

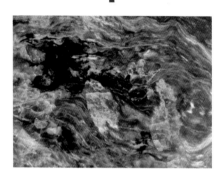

CHAROITE IS AN unusual and rare mineral that to date has been found in only one location: along the Chara River at Aldan in Russia. A colorful mix of white, lavender, lilac, violet, or purple, it has a pearly luster. Belonging to the monoclinic crystal group, chaorite has a hardness of 5.0 on the Mohs scale.

A stone endowed with powerful transformational energy, charoite's ability to release negative influences and transform them into positive impulses and actions imparts the necessary clarity for remaining open to accurate psychic impressions. When used in intuitive work, it is therefore said to be very helpful in developing clairvoyant, clairaudient, and precognitive abilities.

Associated with both the heart and crown chakras, because of its pink to violet color range, charoite is soothing yet energizing. It is of particular assistance in communicating with spirits and in channeling, because it prevents any unnecessary drain on the physical body of the medium.

■ PENDULUM, SPHERE, EGG, OR PYRAMID? ■

WHEN USING CRYSTALS and minerals for intuitive practice or as objects of your meditative attention, many people prefer to work with a specific shape, as is reflected in the many shapes and ornaments available. Usually we can find stones and minerals cut into basic geometric forms, such as a sphere, an egg, a pyramid, or a wand, but two things are important to keep in mind when choosing your meditation stone. The first is to research as much as you can about the symbolism of a particular shape. Egg shapes, for example, imply unexplored potential and rebirth. Spheres are the shape of the earth, the circle of life, and of wholeness—the circle of the self. Pyramids tend to focus energy and reinforce a sense of connection from heaven to earth. Wands tend to be symbols of power and directed energy. Only you can say which symbol is appropriate for your purposes.

Next, bear in mind that as advanced as our lapidary technology may be, some stones, because of their natural structure, will be more effective when shaped in a way that is compatible to the energy they hold. Gentle, soothing energy, such as angelite, for example, tends to be more effective in a sphere than in a wand. Stronger energies, such as those of rock crystal or amethyst, can be very responsive to the wand shape. Of course, everyone has a personal preference, but it does help to do a little extra homework to get the shape that best fits you.

Let us not be too particular; it is better to have old secondhand diamonds than none at all.
—MARK TWAIN

■

DIAMOND IS A polymorph of carbon and belongs to the isometric crystal group. It is the hardest natural substance known. It is usually clear but often comes in shades of yellow, brown, blue, red, black, or green. The youngest diamonds yet discovered on earth are more than nine million years old, making them very close to the age of the planet itself.

Measuring a perfect 10 on the Mohs scale, diamonds are found all over the world, but the best-known mines are in Africa. Contrary to popular belief, diamonds are not all that rare, and one source says that in fact there are currently enough diamonds in the pipeline to supply every man, woman, and child in the United States with more than a cupful of the crystals. Their distribution, however, is very closely regulated by the De Beers family in London. Too, diamonds have been known to finance bloody civil wars in Africa, leading to the modern policy of certifying rough stones as "conflict free."

Diamond history is rich in myth and folklore, and the ancients valued the stones more for their medicinal powers than for their brilliance. Greeks and Romans believed diamonds were tears of the Gods and splinters from falling stars. The Greek word *adamas*, meaning "unconquerable" and "indestructible," is the root word of diamond. In India the Hindus attributed so much power to the stones that they placed diamonds in the eyes of the statues of the gods.

Not only was it believed that diamonds could bring luck and success, but it was also thought that they could counter the effects of astrological events. Many people wore diamonds to heighten sexual prowess and to attract others. Plato wrote about diamonds as living beings, embodying celestial spirits. Said to be powerful talismans against evil spirits, in the Middle Ages diamonds were used to ward off contagion. It wasn't until

1477, when Archduke Maximilian of Austria gave a diamond ring to Mary of Burgundy, that the diamond engagement ring was introduced. Placing the ring on the third finger of the left hand dates back to the early Egyptian belief that the *vena amoris*, or "vein of love," runs directly from the heart to the tip of the third finger.

■ THE CULLINAN DIAMOND ■

THE CULLINAN DIAMOND, found by Frederick Wells in South Africa on January 26, 1905, is the largest rough gem-quality diamond ever found, at 3,106.75 carats. Named for the owner of the mine in which it was discovered, Sir Thomas Cullinan, the stone was eventually cut into a variety of show-stopping gems, including the magnificent Great Star of Africa, currently owned by Queen Elizabeth II, and which she refers to affectionately, along with some others, as "Granny's chips."

Today gemstone and crystal practitioners associate the diamond very strongly with the spiritual planes, and consider the stones a channel between the physical and celestial world. Considered a master stone, it is sometimes used to amplify the energy properties of other stones and minerals. Known by some as a stone of innocence and purity, it opens the energy channels in the body to make one receptive to intuitive information and impressions.

The diamond's powerful energy is also said to amplify the effects of both positive

■ PROTECTION OR POISON? ■

DIAMONDS WERE WORN by aristocratic families during the Middle Ages to ward off the plague. Noting that the disease seemed to strike the poorest first, because of their proximity to rats transmitting the infection, it became a popular notion among the rich that displaying their diamonds and other jewels would serve as protection against the disease. Paradoxically, diamonds were also regularly used as a poison throughout history. The stones were ground into powder and placed in the enemy's food and drink. Many historic figures' deaths have been attributed to diamond poisoning, which, because of the insolubility of the stones, eventually destroys the systems of the body, most notably the lining of the stomach and intestines.

■ THEY REALLY ARE FOREVER ■

ONE OF THE ideas gemstone aficionados rarely bring to public attention is that not just diamonds, but *all* gemstones are forever. They stay in circulation, are cut and recut, acquire new settings, and change hands many times through the centuries. It's quite likely that a modern American today wears a gem that once graced the gown of a lady in Charlemagne's court, and we know that many examples of engraved gems from ancient times are still in circulation. Even the gems buried with the dead have a way of rising to the surface, and not all the treasures of the pyramids, for example, are known to reside in permanent museum collections. Consider that the heart-shaped yellow diamond given by Richard Burton to his then-wife, Elizabeth Taylor, was originally a gift from Shah Jahan in 1621 to his favorite wife, Mumtaz Mahal, who was the inspiration for the Taj Mahal.

and negative forces, so one should make every effort to avoid using diamonds for intuitive development when other factors have you feeling susceptible to negativity or otherwise under par. Nevertheless, there is no better stone to use when seeking expansion of your perceptions, especially in the areas of creativity, inspiration, and brilliant insight.

It's very hard to know what wisdom is.
—JAMES HILLMAN

■

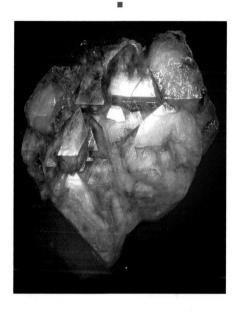

ELESTIAL CRYSTALS ARE part of the quartz family, but as this is a relatively recent designation, there are no hard and fast geological classifications as yet, since elestials may contain inclusions of all sorts of other minerals. Sometimes called "skeleton quartz," they are layered with markings and show multiple points of termination. Though elestials are found all over the world, they grow separately from other quartzes. Mined in or close to water, some elestials show inclusions of water bubbles. Elestial crystals are found in many locations throughout the world. Though scant data is available, as quartzes they would belong to the trigonal or hexagonal group of crystals and measure in the 7.0 range on the Mohs scale.

Metaphysical practitioners agree that elestials represent a synthesis of earthly qualities with high ideals. They symbolize knowledge, purification, truth, and balance.

Because an elestial crystal has numerous natural terminations occurring along the main point of the crystal formation, it is more complex, both energetically and geometrically, than a "single" crystal. Variously referred to as "bridge crystals," "library crystals," and "record keeper" crystals, elestials are said to contain stores of ancient knowledge and wisdom that can be accessed through meditation and prayer.

Reported by many to be a literal crystallization of ancient knowledge, elestial energy is said to unlock the secrets hidden within our own cellular structures and open those who are willing to the wisdom that is said to be encoded in each of us at birth.

Elestials are considered by other sources to be essential to the process of cleansing, healing, and reawakening that is occurring in our times. Offering particular strengths, they can assist in bringing body and spirit into synch, while aligning us with the wisdom of the universe. Specifically said to bring elusive intuitive realizations into focus, they help to increase the understanding that time itself is not necessarily linear in nature, so any of us may access any part of the past, present, or future at any moment. If you are seeking a sense of renewal, or a reminder that indeed all life is one, use an elestial crystal to sharpen perceptions, awaken higher consciousness, and better integrate your higher self into daily life.

FLUORITE

The art of being wise is the art of knowing what to overlook.
—WILLIAM JAMES

■

THE NAME *fluorite* is derived from the Latin word for "flow" and applies to a set of minerals in the halide group. Fluorite belongs to the isometric crystal group and may produce some spectacular specimens. It can be found all over the world, including Brazil, Canada, China, England, France, Germany, Mexico, Mongolia, Morocco, Norway, Russia, South Africa, Switzerland, and parts of the United States. It measures a 5.0 on the Mohs scale.

There is little historical reference to fluorite, but among contemporary practitioners it is believed to have extremely beneficial effects on mental and thought processes. Said to amplify and expand thinking and to improve memory, it enables you to perceive higher levels of reality.

Though its energy may at first seem tranquilizing in its effects, as it calms stress and chaos in the user's immediate environment the overall effect increases concentration, especially in meditative practice. Fluorite is regularly recommended to enhance psychic abilities and objectivity, and allows you to tap reserves of higher guidance.

Displaying fluorescence, which is a word derived from its name, fluorite does occasionally have some toxic ingredients, so overexposure or too much direct contact with the skin is better avoided. If you wear it in jewelry, make sure the stone is in a protective setting.

Said by many to be of great aid in cases of chronic insomnia, some believe fluorite will also bring prophetic and precognitive dreams through its unique ability to connect the mind with the realms of profound spiritual insight. A mineral that imparts clarity, overview, and a more refined sense of the subtler aspects of reality, fluorite offers deep intuitive insight of the kind that truly clears a space for new developments.

IOLITE

(Also see chapter 7, Stones for Physical Healing)

The only real valuable thing is intuition.
—ALBERT EINSTEIN

∎

IOLITE IS A blue silicate mineral that forms as crystals or grains in igneous rocks as a result of contamination by aluminum sediment. Ranging in color from blue to violet, the gemstone changes colors depending on the angle from which it is viewed. The name *iolite* is derived from the Greek *los*, meaning "violet," and the stone has a hardness of 7.5 on the Mohs scale. Today most iolite comes from Sri Lanka, Myanmar, India, Madagascar, and Brazil as well as large deposits in the state of Wyoming.

Blue iolite helps to open the pathway to the spiritual and connect you with the realm of spirit. When using this stone, expect to experience bursts of intuition and sudden, sometimes startling insights about yourself and others. Some people find this stone difficult to work with and best used in conjunction with a more grounding energy.

In the shamanic traditions, iolite was used to ensure the accuracy of one's visions as well as to exert influence over the spirits. Offering a marvelous energy to those not easily unsettled, iolite can impart great insight into particular problems or circumstances. Especially useful for meditation when you are curious about what's *really* going on or what someone *really* thinks of you, it should nevertheless be approached in intuitive work with a degree of caution, as it tends to remind us that it is sometimes best not to ask those questions when we are not prepared for the answer. As we saw in chapter 7, on physical well-being, iolite is a fine antioxidant. When it comes to furthering and developing your intuitive capacity, its function is somewhat similar, as it encourages development at the pace that is right for you and reminds us that taking good care of ourselves is an act of self respect.

CLEAR QUARTZ

God is a spirit. A spirit is as much matter as oxygen or hydrogen.
—ORSON PRATT

■

WHAT MOST PEOPLE tend to think of when they think of crystals, clear quartz, or "holy ice," as the ancients called it, doesn't necessarily need to be clear in order to work effectively for intuitive purposes. Some of the best examples of clear quartz contain bubbles, interesting inclusions, or "veils" which are shadows or foggy areas within the crystals themselves.

Clear quartz, or rock crystal, is found in abundance all over the world. Belonging to the trigonal group of crystals, it measures 7.0 on the Mohs scale. Today clear quartz from Arkansas offers some of the finest samples of these crystals in the world.

These clear crystals have been used from our earliest beginnings. The pre-Columbians fashioned them into jewelry and incorporated clear crystal into religious rituals in the form of crystal skulls. In ancient Rome, the emperor Nero had a huge collection of containers and goblets, all fashioned from pure, clear *Krystallos,* which is the Greek word for "ice."

Any number of spiritual traditions incorporated the use of quartz crystals. Native Americans used them in healing and in rain-making. In the East, Orientals believed that quartz was created from the breath of the White Dragon, embodying absolute perfection. Chinese Emperor Wu, a builder of shrines and temples, had the doors of these sacred places installed with large pieces of rock crystal to allow in light.

In the Middle Ages clear quartz was a popular cure, used to relieve fevers by placing the crystal under the tongue. Even today clear quartz is highly valued as a tool that teaches the body to heal itself.

Rock crystal is readily available in all sorts of appealing shapes—pyramids, wands, and spheres—and thus can be a powerful aid in meditation, intuitive development, and even divination practice. The importance of working with clear quartz in this instance is for its ability to store information, as information can be thought of as just another form of energy. Thus, it can be used to amplify and focus your meditations in specific ways.

First, quartz energy can be put to wonderful use in the manifestation of particular goals. Concentrating on a particular vision, dream, or intuitive impression can be considerably clarified in the presence of quartz energy, and even—with practice—in manifesting in the physical realm, should you so desire. Some practitioners recommend placing a piece of rock crystal on the third eye during meditation as a means of clarifying the choices available to shape the future.

Next, clear quartz can serve to charge your other crystals with your specific intention. It can also be used to cleanse your other stones of bad vibes or otherwise negative energy.

The original rhinestones were quartz pebbles taken from the Rhine River in Germany. What we now know as rhinestones evolved from cheap imitations created for tourists once the natural stones had all been taken.

In development and expansion of your psychic abilities, quartz is used in a variety of ways, though it is considered more as a stone for aiding free will than for perceived future events. Blessed with proven electrical properties, this so-called mother stone will undoubtedly respond favorably in whatever circumstance you choose to use it, as long as you take the time to properly attune yourself with a particular crystal's specific qualities. In addition, clear quartz can be used to enhance your ability to sense and commune with spirits. Essential for protection of your physical form if you're experimenting with astral travel or out-of-the-body experience, use quartz power for scrying, channeling, dream recall, and dream work, as its powerful energies will work to keep you in the light as you travel the spiritual path.

PHANTOM QUARTZ

Wisdom begins in wonder.
—SOCRATES

■

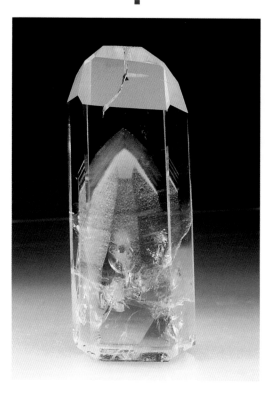

PHANTOM CRYSTALS OCCUR when the growth process of a crystal is interrupted at some point, cooling the crystal matrix before growth is resumed. They are so designated because they contain crystals within crystals and offer visual evidence of a crystal's development through the ages, leaving a partial or complete "phantom" within the crystal itself.

Usually appearing as a fine white veil, phantoms can also appear in colors and, in rarer cases, outlines and silhouettes. Most commonly found in quartz formations, they do occur in other minerals as well, giving them varying structural properties and levels of hardness on the Mohs scale.

More valuable perhaps than any other crystal type for intuitive work and expansion of psychic faculties, phantoms constitute beautiful evidence of all nature in a constant state of transformation. Associated with the crown chakra, they are said to open those who use them to universal knowledge and eternal truth.

For the psychic and spiritual seeker, phantoms offer a powerful visual reminder of how the inner being serves as the foundation for the outer life, and how the spiritual serves as the foundation of the material. A stone of great awareness, a phantom crystal is an excellent tool for meditation, for in observing nature, meditation will come very easily.

Phantoms have been reported by various sources to provide access to past life memories, to help develop clairaudient abilities, and assist in channeling the information received from other, higher realms. Others, fascinated by the idea that phantoms contain symbols of the "shadow" sides of our personal development, encourage their use as beautiful symbols of inner growth that encourage us to extend ourselves beyond our limitations and reach out for new and enticing avenues of dreams, thoughts, and expression.

ONYX

(Also see chapter 4, The Stones of Protection)

No law or ordinance is mightier than understanding.
—PLATO

■

ONYX IS A member of the chalcedony quartz family. Usually black, gray, or brown with straight white bands, it differs from banded agates, which generally display curved lines. Sardonyx is a type of onyx with bands of sard, or carnelian, alternating with the stone's white or black layers. Found worldwide, important locations for onyx include Mexico, Brazil, Madagascar, India, Algeria, and Pakistan. Onyx measures 6.5 to 7.0 on the Mohs scale.

Long renowned for its powerful protective qualities, onyx brings its unique energies to intuitive work in the form of heightened awareness. Onyx is reported to be especially useful for sharpening extrasensory gifts, bringing the user to a sometimes-uncomfortable

state of watchfulness. It won't necessarily contribute to paranoia, but its powers to ferret out the inner truth of any situation or circumstance may wind up giving you more information than you really wanted to know. As you open yourself up psychically, onyx can also prove extremely useful in keeping out undesirable elements and spirits that might threaten your well-being. One occult source indicates, for example, that onyx can be used to drive out demons in cases of possession.

As previously mentioned, onyx is very difficult to program with any specific intention, so proceed with caution when using it for intuitive pursuits. Said to be very effective, however, in banishing nightmares and troublesome dreams, this is nevertheless an uncompromising energy that doesn't work well for everyone. It strips away illusions of all kinds, even those that we might hold to be comforting, and instead will put you in touch with both the lighter and the darker aspects of inner truth.

TANZANITE

The great gift of human beings is that we have the power of empathy.
—MERYL STREEP

■

TANZANITE IS THE trade name first coined by Tiffany and Company to describe a variety of the mineral zoisite. Belonging to the orthorhombic crystal group, tanzanite has a hardness of 6.5 to 7.0 on the Mohs scale. Mined in only one location, in northern Tanzania in Africa, world supplies of tanzanite are tightly controlled, though recently a simulant called "tanzanique" has become available. Approximately one thousand times rarer than diamonds, though just as tightly controlled, tanzanite varies from a deep sapphire blue to an amethyst purple.

Since its discovery in 1967, tanzanite has become one of the world's most prized gemstones. Currently, one company controls virtually all newly mined tanzanite by purchasing a large portion of the stones coming from independent miners in the area. This is the first time a colored gemstone has been controlled in this way, and prices have increased steadily for the last several years. In August 2005 the largest tanzanite crystal ever was found, weighing in at a whopping 16,839 carats.

Associated with the spiritual and intuitive centers of the body, this stone will awaken both the mind and the heart. It has been said that it is the ultimate in balancing the mind's genius and the heart's wisdom. Above all, tanzanite is a stone of deep empathetic response, facilitating clear communication of the highest truths. Some who have worked with this stone have experienced a virtual avalanche of insights, but at the same time it possesses a grounded energy that will keep you from slipping off into "la-la land" or becoming too preoccupied with other dimensions and otherworldly concerns.

The evocative beauty of tanzanite helps you to awaken to the reflection of these same qualities in yourself. Firmly anchored in compassion, it encourages forgiveness as well as visions, messages, and insights from higher realms while keeping you firmly rooted in this one. Tanzanite energy aids you in sharing spiritual information and knowledge from a heart-centered perspective. Excellent for counselors, therapists, writers, and others who are in a position of intellectually processing and interpreting emotional and intuitive experiences, it is also very useful for highly sensitive types in expressing the kind of knowledge that is not easily put into words.

IN 1978 A massive cholera epidemic struck northern Tanzania and interrupted production of rubies, garnets, sapphires, chrome tourmaline, chrysoprase, and tanzanite. In addition, many of the known gem deposits were depleted. The resulting decrease in production caused a scarcity of quality gemstones and a rapid rise in their value.

WULFENITE

■

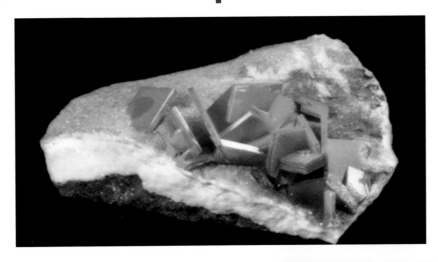

WULFENITE BELONGS TO the sulfate class of minerals and the tetragonal crystal system. With a hardness of only 3.0 on the Mohs scale, it is primarily of interest to mineral collectors yet is highly prized by others for its vivid colors, which range from yellow to deep, gemmy orange-red. Today wulfenite is found in Morocco; Tsumeb, Namibia; Mexico; Arizona; and New Mexico.

Since it is a very energetic stone, it is said that wulfenite is able to facilitate the flow of Kundalini energy, activating the chakra centers. As the chakras open, practitioners say it expands awareness and knowledge, enabling the user to access information from both the ancient past and the far future.

Wulfenite energy makes it easy to move from a grounded physical state into a psychic or trance state. Thus it is said to be very useful for psychic readers, channelers, healers, and those who work in the clairvoyant fields, but it should be approached with a degree of caution by the uninitiated.

Wulfenite is also said to facilitate contact and communication with the spirit world, opening a channel through which spirits can communicate. In individual use, it helps you to recognize karmic patterns and soul links with others in this lifetime. Supporting the use of ritual practice as meditation, it is particularly helpful in group ceremonies, traditional seances, and on spiritual journeys or quests.

10

THE STONES OF CREATIVITY

*We become creative when we realize the infinite possibilities within us and when we
understand that our function is not merely to exist but to contribute to life, to improve it,
and to make it more meaningful to others.*
—FREDERICK MAYER

How can we define the quality of creativity? Is it inspiration? Intuition?
Genius? A sort of divine intervention that
enables us to make something from nothing?

Psychology offers us more than sixty different definitions for creativity, with explana-
tions ranging from cognitive and social
processes to a sort of mental illness, genius, and
even humor. What we do know is that truly
creative people tend to have a marked ability
to combine a wide range of abilities such as
intuition, inspiration, and imagination in such
a way that they are able to fashion existing
information into something new or original.

For that reason, the stones in this chapter are
selected from a range of crystal systems. Just as
the quality of creativity must be seen as unique
to every individual, each of the stones here will
help you crystallize your creativity in a unique
way. What they do have in common, however,

is their ability to synthesize the qualities of
intuition, imagination, and experience and
help you manifest your creative impulses into
reality. Whatever your particular creative goals,
the stones here have been chosen because they
can truly be said to help you think outside the
box when it comes to a more creative and ful-
filling use of your time, energy, and talents.

Although we typically think of creativity
in terms of works of art, music, or writing, in
fact the same quality can be brought to bear
in almost any endeavor. Business requires creativity, parenting requires it, and so does scientific inquiry. As a result, whole industries
have arisen around the idea of creativity,
along with hundreds of self-help books and
methods for accessing your own.

Since so many of us spend so much of our
time in cubicles at the office or tapping away
on our laptops, it's easy to forget that we each

have a unique capacity to create (rather than merely produce) meaningful work. It's difficult at times to keep a sense of being part of a larger plan. But though technology can seem isolating, at the same time we have available to us a wider range of ideas, greater access to original works, and a much better developed sense of the big picture than at any other time in history. Indeed we are in the midst of a global conversation and the exchange of great ideas every day.

Because we are each unique individuals, we are each blessed with unique and innate talents. The challenge of creativity is to put those talents to use and contribute to the whole. Some may work in paint, some in metaphor, and some in design or multimedia. But for each of us there is a world of ideas, inspirations, and innovations waiting to be explored through the creative process.

ALEXANDRITE

Creativity is allowing yourself to make mistakes.
Art is knowing which ones to keep.
—SCOTT ADAMS

■

ALEXANDRITE IS AN extremely rare member of the beryl group, which includes emerald and aquamarine among others. Beautifully cut examples of this gemstone reveal its pleochroic qualities, and while the best examples flash from green to red, other colors are sometimes present as well. Once found only in the Ural Mountains, Russian alexandrite is only for the fortunate few. In recent years Brazilian mines have yielded some specimens, though of a different quality than the Russian stones. Russian alexandrite displays more pronounced and richer greens, while Brazilian specimens exhibit warmer red and purple tones. Other sources include Sri Lanka and Tanzania. Measuring 8.5 on the Mohs scale, most available gem-quality stones today are less than one-quarter carat.

Named for the Russian czar Alexander II (1818–1881), the very first crystals of alexandrite were discovered in April 1834 on the day the future czar came of age, and it quickly became the national stone of imperial Russia. Hardly ever used in modern jewelry, some examples still exist, as Russian master jewelers loved this stone.

Tiffany's George Frederick Kunz, for whom kunzite is named, was also fascinated by alexandrite, and Tiffany and Company produced some beautiful alexandrite jewelry around the turn of the last century. Mineralogists have determined that alexandrite differs from other members of the beryl group in that it contains both iron and titanium, but it also contains chromium, which is the key element to alexandrite's optical qualities.

Alexandrite is a stone for true connoisseurs and has a very refined energy. In appearance it is a master of understatement, but if you are fortunate enough to come across a good gemstone or specimen, expect to be fully captured by its mystery.

To really get involved with alexandrite is to become acquainted with aspects of yourself that you might have never known existed. Expect an awesome level of inspiration for your creative endeavors and bursts of imagination to equal Leonardo da Vinci himself. It will set you on new courses and propel you toward new solutions. It will truly enable you to defy all logic and perform new feats of creative daring. It's not the stone for people who like to be different just for its own sake or shock value, however. This is refined, high-class, elegant energy. Its effects may astonish you, but if you follow its very special lead, the creative results may well be nothing short of genius.

*(Also see chapter 3, Stones for Money and Prosperity, and chapter 8,
Stones for Emotional Wellness and Healing)*

Life engenders life. Energy creates energy.
It is by spending oneself that one becomes rich.
—SARAH BERNHARDT

■

AMAZONITE IS A form of pale green feldspar found in Brazil, Russia, India, and parts of the United States. Often confused with jade, amazonite belongs to the triclinic group of crystals. Its intense color is caused by the presence of lead, and some of the best specimens in the world are found at Pike's Peak in Colorado. A relatively soft stone, amazonite ranges from 5.0 to 6.0 on the Mohs scale.

Some sources say the stone is named for the legendary Amazon women warriors, while others say it is for the Amazon River, though no deposits have been found there. Historically, amazonite has been used in jew-elry in India, Mesopotamia, and the Sudan. In Egypt amazonite was fashioned into tablets in parts of the Book of the Dead and was even found in King Tut's tomb.

Just as we learned with our discussion on amazonite's powers to increase prosperity (see pg. 61 in chapter 3), its energies work in much the same way in matters of creativity. A great aid in matters of self-expression, this stone is associated with the fifth chakra, which makes it particularly useful in the more artistic and verbal forms of self-expression. Singers, writers, and actors will find it especially beneficial, as will anyone who is seeking artistic success and recognition. Very useful in situations where you are representing yourself and your artistic and creative efforts, it will help you gain the necessary financial resources to keep those engines of creation turning. Use it for auditions and verbal presentations of all kinds.

For visual types who may have a chance to present a number of works, be sure to slip a small stone in your portfolio before dropping it off for review to increase your chances of making a favorable impression.

CALCITE

(Also see chapter 3, Stones for Money and Prosperity, and chapter 7, Stones for Physical Healing)

A hunch is creativity trying to tell you something.
—FRANK CAPRA

∎

CALCITE GETS ITS name from the Greek word *chalix*, which means "lime." It is found in almost any color, but for purposes of cre-

ativity, it's important to work with the color that most attracts you. Belonging to the trigonal crystal group, calcite measures a relatively soft 3.0 on the Mohs scale. Calcite is common in many locations all over the world, with notable deposits in the midwestern United States, Germany, Brazil, Mexico, and many parts of Africa.

As mentioned in chapter 3, calcite is a terrific stone for artists, entrepreneurs, and creative types who may have deeply held fears about giving up their day jobs or are insecure about putting their art into the marketplace. With the power to better attune you to the wealth of creative ideas available to us all, calcite offers the kind of energy that will enable you to better manifest your inspiration in reality. It prevents what I like to call "creative casualties"—those who are certain they could write that book, paint that painting, or finish that project, but become stuck because they feel the "system" is somehow against them. Also, if you have convinced yourself that succeeding in a particular area is impossible or not economically viable, working with this stone is sure to help you let go of any old conditioning about what the world expects of you and draw the necessary creative opportunities your way.

Calcite reminds us to seize the moment and run with our ideas, and offers the enormous satisfaction available to us when we make the effort necessary to turn our dreams into reality. The energy of this stone is also good to work with when you want to strike out on your own, make a career change, or become self-employed against the wishes of loved ones.

Creativity is not the finding of a thing, but the making something out of it after it is found.
—JAMES RUSSELL LOWELL

DANBURITE IS A mineral species belonging to the orthorhombic crystal system. Characterized by its appealing pale pink to clear white crystal forms, it was named for Danbury, Connecticut, where it was found. Danburite crystals range from relatively small and very thin to up to a foot long and several inches across, and are characterized by a steeply slanted, prism-shaped termination. Danburite has a hardness of 7.0 to 7.5 on the Mohs scale. The major sources are Mexico, Myanmar, Japan, and Madagascar, as well as parts of the northeastern United States.

Not a well-known mineral, danburite is nevertheless gaining increasing popularity among mineral collectors, crystal practitioners, and other aficionados. In creative pursuits it's especially recommended for visual artists, sculptors, and graphic or fashion designers. In addition, anyone who works with color is said to benefit enormously from this stone's energy, as it works to open up the channels between the heart center and what are called the "vision chakras," located right behind the eyes. In short, danburite encourages you, whatever the medium, to manifest the kind of creative effort that indeed comes right from the heart.

It enhances creativity because it helps give form to pure feeling, without the need to dissect or analyze it first. Considered a stone of joy and celebration, it's great for joint or group artistic efforts that require a level of cooperative effort among divergent artistic egos and temperaments. For more personal purposes, use the pink variety of this crystal to increase a sense of self-worth, especially if you're feeling creatively uninspired or doubtful of your own talents.

The orthorhombic energy of danburite helps us to connect the dots between ourselves and the rest of existence, and the clear variety of this stone has been said to add an almost visionary quality to creative efforts. A stone that heightens an overall sense of awareness, it is sure to assist you in finding creative outlets and producing the kind of art that will move the spirit of anyone who encounters it.

EPIDOTE

Opportunity is missed by most people because it's dressed in overalls and looks like work.
—THOMAS EDISON

■

EPIDOTE IS A mineral species in the epidote group, which also includes zoisite, clino-

zoisite, and allanite. Usually characterized by a green color, specimens can range from very light green to almost brown. Belonging to the monoclinic crystal system, epidote has a hardness of 7.0 on the Mohs scale. Today the main sources for epidote are Austria, Brazil, Finland, France, and Mexico.

Epidote is the stone to use for creative blocks of all kinds, offering a kind of jump start to the creative life. Many who are drawn to this little-known mineral are looking on some level to be shaken into greater awareness and creative effort. As more people are experiencing and experimenting with more conscious choices and lifestyles, epidote is becoming increasingly popular.

Specifically, epidote has a not-so-subtle way of clearing out the old and making way for the new. Expect an encounter or two with some of your best-kept repressions, and then expect to let them go once and for all. If you're the type who has a multitude of projects you can't ever seem to finish, or who keeps promising yourself that someday you will sit down and write that book, or paint that painting, epidote will be very helpful in seeing to it that your days of creative procrastination come to a merciful end.

This stone is especially good for creative types who just can't seem to put the necessary effort into realizing their higher potentials. It mitigates feelings of self-pity or the sense that you're just not good enough or talented enough to be successful. Epidote also helps you stabilize those feeling of restlessness and distraction and overcome the avoidance that is sometimes typical of creative personalities.

More important, this energy helps you to become more authentically yourself in the world. If our creative efforts are the truest statements of who we really are and what we have to offer, then epidote will make sure your statement is made loud and clear. No more excuses.

Mystery is at the heart of creativity. That, and surprise.
—JULIA CAMERON

LARIMAR IS THE name given to a distinct blue variety of the mineral pectolite. Found only in the southern portion of the Dominican Republic and in the Bahamas, the stone is volcanic in origin. Larimar belongs to the triclinic crystal system and measures 4.5 to 5.0 on the Mohs scale.

Though there is some indication that islanders were aware of the stone as early as 1916 when a local priest applied for exploration and mining rights, larimar was not formally introduced into world markets until 1974. Discovered by Norman Rilling, who at the time was a member of the Peace Corps, along with a Dominican named Miguel Méndez, the two men found samples

of this beautiful turquoise to sky-blue stone at the seashore, and with some further exploration, followed its trail upstream to the Bahoruco River to the remote mountainside where it is mined today. Named *larimar* for Mendez's daughter, Larissa, and the Spanish word for sea, *mar,* this stone has taken its place among the most popular of semi-precious contemporary gemstones.

Part of the deep fascination people hold for larimar is its association with the lost continent of Atlantis. Among the prophecies of the famous psychic Edgar Cayce was his prediction that on one of the Caribbean Islands, a blue stone of Atlantean origin would be found that possessed extraordinary healing attributes.

Some people believe that the ancient Atlanteans were able to communicate with dolphins. For this reason, larimar is also sometimes known as the "dolphin stone."

Whatever your feeling about the existence of Atlantis or this stone's ancient origins, anyone who has encountered this blue Caribbean beauty is in for a truly inspiring experience. Larimar energy works to open your sense of perspective and allows you to view ordinary events and ideas through the different lenses of intuition, imagination, and inspiration. Able to instill the ordinary with a sense of the extraordinary, larimar is finely attuned to the throat chakra and is especially recommended for writers and singers, or anyone seeking a higher level of creative self-expression. Encouraging a sense of patience, acceptance, and going with the flow, larimar works to bring forth the kind of creativity that arises from complete inner serenity.

PREHNITE

Our dreams are firsthand creations, rather than residues of waking life.
We have the capacity for infinite creativity; at least while dreaming, we partake of the power of the Spirit, the infinite Godhead that creates the cosmos.
—JACKIE GLEASON

■

PREHNITE WAS NAMED after its discoverer, Colonel Hendrik von Prehn. Characterized by a distinct pale green, it is popular with collectors. Sometimes confused with smithsonite, prehnite belongs to the orthorhombic crystal system and has a hardness of 6.0 to 6.5 on the

Mohs scale. Found all over the world, notable deposits occur in South Africa, the eastern United States, Europe, and parts of China.

Offering a powerful energy that can be quite disconcerting at times, prehnite is especially useful for those who work with dreams and symbols as sources of creative inspiration. It increases dream recall and is said to intensify and deepen meditative states as well. So if you've been struggling to get a better grasp of that elusive image or great idea that's been teetering on the tip of your consciousness, use prehnite to get it out in the open.

Some say that this stone enhances your ability to communicate with unseen entities and to bring back information regarding past and future events. Others claim that it will increase your powers of prophecy.

Not a stone to be taken lightly, prehnite can have a profound impact on your life, especially your creative life. It doesn't allow for a lot of half measures, though, so if from a creative standpoint you've been guilty of producing only what you believe the market will bear, it is sure to show you how and when it's time to pull out all the stops.

For some, prehnite has a peculiarly futuristic quality, so if you are involved in trend spotting or struggling to come up with the next right thing, this is sure to help you get you what you need by way of insight. Strongly associated with the visual arts and imagery of all kinds, it is especially good for people whose creative efforts involve abstract, symbolic, or nonrepresentational art.

Creativity often consists of merely turning up what is already there.
—ANON

■

A TRADE NAME FOR a unique compound of minerals, Quantum Quattro Silica comes from Namibia in South Africa. A rare and special mineral combination of blue shattuckite, light blue chrysacolla, green dioptase, and smoky quartz (all silicas) combined with pastel green malachite (a nonsilica), it is unique among rocks as it constitutes a combination of minerals not usually found together, all of which come from the mono-clinic, trigonal, and orthorhombic systems, and range from a hardness of 2.0 to a hardness of 7.0 on the Mohs scale.

If we consider the variety of properties that come together in this stone, we can begin to gain a sense of its creative power. The word *quantum* in its name is a good indicator of the energy properties of this most unusual stone. One dictionary defines the word as "an abrupt change, sudden increase, or dramatic advance," which is what you're likely to experience in your creative life if you work with this stone for any length of time.

In essence, Quantum Quattro Silica is a stone of synergy and offers the seemingly magical energy that causes things to suddenly fall into place, take that giant step forward, or experience a much-required moment of "aha!" It has a way of making you see diverse elements in a way that you have never seen them before. It alerts you to the infinite possibilities that are available and will doubtless give you the burst of energy you need to fire and inspire your creative processes.

There have been many hyperbolic claims as to Quantum's healing powers since its appearance in September 1996, including the assertion that it creates an "instant state of perfect physical and emotional health." That being rather a daunting reputation to live up to, suffice it to say that Quantum is definitely good for making breakthroughs of every description in almost every area of your life. If creativity can indeed be defined as the ability to synthesize diverse elements and combine them in new and unexpected ways, then Quantum Quattro Silica is definitely a stone to keep close at hand.

■ RUNNING OUT? ■

THOUGH THERE HAVE been similar rock and mineral combinations discovered at various locations in the United States, including Arizona, as yet Namibia is the only true source of Quantum Quattro Silica. It is still readily available, but rumors persist that the original mine is no longer producing the rocks. As such, Quantum Quattro Silica may well prove a profitable investment for collectors in the coming years.

Creativity is the power to connect the seemingly unconnected.
—WILLIAM PLOMER

■

RHYOLITE IS SOMETIMES called "streaming rock" because of its beautiful bands, bubbles, and crystal-rich layers that form in lava flows. An igneous volcanic rock, rhyolite is usually buff to pink colored, but will display any number of variations in specimens and samples. Rhyolites that cool too quickly to grow crystals result in a form of obsidian, and the two are related mineralogically. As a volcanic rock, rhyolite has no defined crystal structure, and has a Mohs scale rating of 7.0. Found in many locations, significant deposits occur in Nevada and New Mexico.

Interestingly enough, rhyolite serves as a matrix, or host rock, to many extraordinary crystal specimens. Used in all kinds of construction work, crushed rhyolite is much lighter than its counterparts in ordinary sandstones and is especially popular in stucco facing and finishes as well as in a variety of other uses.

Metaphysically, however, opinions tend to vary, just as the many formations of rhyolite vary. Some associate this stone with structure; others associate it with change, variety, and progress, though on closer examination, the two concepts are not mutually exclusive.

What we do know is that rhyolite sparks necessary creativity in people who are ready to move on and make things happen for themselves. If you imagine laying the basic foundation from which a perfect emerald crystal can grow, you will gain a better sense of the role rhyolite can play in your creative life.

It offers the kind of energy that allows you to reach beyond your own sense of boundaries and into a greater sense of what you are capable of achieving. It is sure to help you overcome any creative blocks and put you in touch with a profound level of inner knowing. Especially beneficial in overcoming any feelings of apathy, boredom, or lack of inspiration, rhyolite energy is what the alchemists have called the *prima materia,* the "first matter." They believed that all substance, being composed of one primitive matter, could be found by imposing different qualities upon it—a highly creative concept, to be sure.

Yet working with this energy is very much in keeping with that idea, for rhyolite is so adaptable, it can serve as the host for an emerald, or it can be carved into a pueblo.

Anasazi cliff dwellers carved their homes into the large deposits of rhyolite located in New Mexico about one thousand years ago in what is now called Bandelier National Monument. They dug into the relatively soft cliffs composed of compressed rhyolite and built adobe- or pueblo-style homes against the cliff face.

Rhyolite reminds us of the profound resources available to us, and encourages creativity by offering a constant reminder of the sheer power of adaptation and variation that exists in nature herself.

I can't understand why people are frightened of new ideas.
I'm frightened of old ones.
—JOHN CAGE

RANGING FROM YELLOW orange to deep red and brown, zincite belongs to the hexagonal crystal group. A relatively soft stone, it measures 4.5 on the Mohs scale. Thought at one time to be found in only one location, Franklin, New Jersey, where it is found in abundance, other locations where it occurs in much smaller quantities include Italy, Namibia, Poland, Spain, and Australia.

Zincite has a way of putting you in touch with your creative passions, and can be put to great use in almost any creative endeavor, whether it's writing a book or starting a family. It helps you set aside doubts and dithering thoughts that are interfering with your process and puts you down the path you were truly meant to travel.

Not thought to convey an especially healing energy, zincite is nevertheless a true energy transmuter, changing fear to courage, doubt to decisiveness, and worry to confidence. It clears a space for inspiration to enter and fires you up with the life force necessary to turn even the most tragic events and darkest hours into creative efforts.

In nature, zincite crystals are formed by a rare process known as *sublimation*, in which they grow from a very low state of being (fire or gas) to a much higher one (crystals) without passing through what we normally think of as

MINERALS FOUND IN the Franklin and Sterling Hill mining district, located in the north-western corner of New Jersey, comprise some of the most unusual mineral species on earth. Including two large deposits of zinc-manganese-iron, from which zincite is formed, the mines have been worked for more than 150 years—one on Mine Hill in the town of Franklin, and the other on Sterling Hill in the town of Ogdensburg. The two deposits are closely related and share much of the same peculiar mineralization that is quite unlike any similar mineral deposit anywhere on earth.

All told, more than 340 different species, some 80 of them fluorescent under ultraviolet light, have been discovered in the Franklin-Sterling district—a world's record.

stages or growth. As such, zincite crystals are seen as physical evidence of the kind of creative transformation that occurs all around us every day and are believed by many people to be a collective symbol of our human transformation to a higher state of being.

Many people have found that zincite works most effectively for them when used with other stones in a kind of creative collaboration. Used with amazonite, for example, it stimulates and facilitates self-expression in vocal form, but when used in conjunction with danburite, zincite will provide a transformative aspect in areas of visual creativity.

A powerfully moving example of the forces of nature, zincite offers an opportunity for the synthesis and deepening of a sense of personal power, joyful creativity, and physical energies in a more complete and passionate approach to life.

Trade Names

WHEN PURCHASING ANY stone, be aware of trade names, misleading names, and the all-too-common industry practices of marketing gemstones and minerals as something other than what they are. Below is a list of common trade names for various stones and minerals. While it is by no means complete, as merchants and marketers are inventing new names all the time, it's a good insider's guide for making your purchases.

DIAMOND

Synthetic stones are sometimes sold as:

Absolute

American diamond

Diamonite

Quartz is another stone sometimes sold as diamonds under the names:

Arkansas diamond

Alaska diamond

Arkimer diamond

Bohemian diamond

Brighton diamond

Bristol diamond

Cape May diamond

Colorado diamond

Herkimer diamond

Hot Springs diamond

Lake George diamond

Mexican diamond

Occidental diamond

Pecos diamond

Quebec diamond

Radium diamond

Tasmanian diamond

Other stones that are sometimes sold as diamonds:

Alpine diamond (pyrite)
Arabian diamond (colorless or yellow corundum)
Alaskan black diamond (hematite)
Ceylon diamond (colorless topaz)
Moguk diamond (colorless topaz)
Nevada black diamond (obsidian)

EMERALD

Synthetic stones are sometimes sold as:

Chatham emerald
Gilson emerald

Other stones that are sometimes sold as emerald:

Bastard emerald (peridot)
Bohemian emerald (green fluorite)
Cape emerald (prehnite)
Congo emerald (dioptase)
Emeraldine (dioptase)
Emeralite (green tourmaline)
Evening emerald (peridot)
Indian emerald (treated quartz)
Mother of emerald (green fluorite)
Night emerald (peridot)
Uralian emerald (green garnet)

RUBY

Synthetic stones are sometimes sold as:

Geneva ruby
Wyse ruby

Garnets are frequently sold as ruby under the names:

Adelaide ruby
Alabandine
American ruby
Arizona ruby
Australian ruby
Black Hills ruby
Bohemian ruby
California ruby
Cape ruby
Colorado ruby
Elie ruby
Fashoda ruby
Montana ruby
Mountain ruby
Rock ruby
Rocky Mountain ruby

Red tourmaline is sold as ruby under the names:

Brazilian ruby
San Diego ruby
Siberian ruby

SAPPHIRE

Lab-grown sapphire is sometimes sold as:

Burma sapphire

Other stones that are sometimes sold as sapphire:

Hope sapphire (blue tourmaline)
Lux sapphire (iolite)
Lynz sapphire (iolite or cordierite)
Meru sapphire (blue zoisite)
Sapphirine (blue spinel)

Uralian sapphire (blue tourmaline)
Water sapphire (iolite)

AGATE
◆

Obsidian is sometimes sold as agate under the trade names:

Glass agate
Iceland agate

AMETHYST
◆

Synthetic stones are sometimes sold as:

Desert amethyst
False amethyst
Japanese amethyst
Lithia amethyst

ANDALUSITE
◆

Synthetic andalusite is sometimes sold under the trade name:

Earth stone

AQUAMARINE
◆

Synthetic aquamarine is sometimes sold as:

Mass aqua

Other stones that are sometimes sold as aquamarine:

Siam aquamarine (zircon)

CITRINE
◆

Synthetic stones are sometimes sold as:

Madeira citrine
Spanish topaz

Other stones that are sometimes sold as citrine:

Smoky citrine (quartz)

CORAL
◆

Synthetic stones are sometimes sold as:

Chinese coral
Japanese Moro coral

GARNET
◆

Synthetic stones are sometimes sold as:

Vesuvian garnet
White garnet

IDOCRASE
◆

Synthetic stones are sometimes sold as:

Bohemian garnets
Malaya garnet
Rhodolite

IOLITE
◆

Synthetic stones are sometimes sold as:

Spanish lazulite
Water sapphire

JADE

◆

Synthetic stones are sometimes sold as:

Andesine jade
Fukien jade
Hunan jade
Imperial Mexican jade
Jadine
Korean jade
Manchurian jade
Mexican jade
New jade
Pectolite jade
Serpentine jade
Shanghai jade
Soochow jade
Styrian jade
Vesuvianite jade

Other stones that are sometimes sold as jade:

Feldspar is sold under the names:

Amazon jade
Colorado jade

Garnet is sold under the names:

African jade
Transvaal jade
Garnet jade

Jasper is sold under the names:

Jasper jade
Oregon jade
Swiss jade
Malachite is sold under the name silver

peak jade
Opal is sold under the name fire jade

Quartz is sold under the names:

Australian jade
Red jade
Indian jade

KUNZITE

◆

Synthetic stones are sometimes sold as:

Pink sapphire

LAPIS LAZULI

◆

Synthetic stones are sometimes sold as:

Canadian lapis
Copper lapis
Faience lapis
Italian lapis
Nevada lapis

Other stones that are sometimes sold as lapis lazuli:

Dyed jasper
False lapis
German lapis
Sodalite
Swiss lapis

MOONSTONE

◆

Synthetic stones are sometimes sold as:

Beach moonstone

Other stones that are sometimes sold as moonstone:

Blue moonstone
California moonstone
Chalcedony
Mojave moonstone
Oregon moonstone
Prismatic moonstone

PEARL

◆

Synthetic pearls are sometimes sold as:

Antilles pearl
Atlas pearl
Cave pearl
Delta pearl
Fire pearl
Ivory pearl
La beau pearl
La tausca pearl
Oil pearl
One-year pearl
Red Sea pearl
Roman pearl
Tecla pearl

PERIDOT

◆

Other stones that are sometimes sold as peridot:

Bohemian crystal (glass)
Ceylon peridot (tourmaline)
Hawaiite (yellow quartz)

SPINEL

◆

Synthetic stones are sometimes sold as:

Balas rubies
Cobalt spinel
Kandy spinel
Pleonast
Rubicelle
Sapphire spinel

Lab-created stones are sometimes sold as:

Almandine spinel
Aqua gem
Rozircon
Zircon spinel

TOPAZ

◆

Synthetic gems that are sometimes sold as topaz:

Hawaiian golden yellow topaz
Hyacinth topaz
Nevada topaz

Occidental topaz
Palmyra topaz

Other stones that are sometimes sold as topaz:

Quartz is sold under the names:

Hinjosa topaz
Madeira topaz
Orange topaz
Rio topaz
Scottish topaz
Smoky topaz
Spanish topaz
Topaz quartz
Topaz saffronite

Citrine is sold under the names:

Bohemian topaz
Colorado topaz
Jeweler's topaz
Madeira topaz
Salamanca topaz
Saxon topaz
Scotch topaz

TOURMALINE

◆

Synthetic gems are sometimes sold as:

Aqualite
Indigolith
Verdelite

TURQUOISE

◆

Synthetic gems are sometimes sold as:

Australian turquoise
Chinese turquoise
Fossil turquoise
Gilson turquoise
Ivory turquoise
Nevada turquoise
Sacred turquoise
Tooth turquoise
Turquosite
Utah turquoise
Vienna turquoise

ZIRCON

◆

Synthetic gems are sometimes sold as:

Ceylon
Cubic zirconia
Matura diamond
Siam zircon
Starlite

Crystal FAQs

What's the difference between a rock and a mineral?

Minerals are made of substances whose atoms are arranged in patterns, like crystal. One or more minerals together form a rock.

What is a gemstone? What's the difference between precious and semiprecious stones?

Gemstones are high-quality precious minerals. This special category of minerals is usually clearer, rarer, and more stunning than other minerals. There's no definite way of distinguishing which mineral is a gemstone. What decides its value is basically age-old ideas and uses as well as its newfound value. The terms *precious* and *semiprecious* are designations based on cost, rarity, and popular perception.

What does it mean when a crystal is said to "morph"?

In essence, it means that while crystals are growing, they may take on some of the physical characteristics and shapes of the host rock or nearby minerals, imitating shapes and colors while retaining their basic crystal structure.

Are there any guidelines to keep in mind before I purchase a gemstone, mineral specimen, or crystal?

The main thing you should remember is to buy something you love and that you plan to use for a purpose. Next, make sure you're really getting what you're paying for, and always deal with reputable merchants. If someone can't answer your questions about a stone's origin or authenticity, shop elsewhere.

What are the four C's?

Color: The old wisdom insists that the more unadulterated and radiant the color, the more valuable the gemstone. With the advent of heat treatments and other enhancements, that's not always the case, so ask questions to ensure you're purchasing a natural stone.

Cut: All gemstones must be cut well to attain maximum brilliance. A well-cut gemstone will radiate a firelike quality that ordinary gemstones just don't have.

Clarity: Although most gemstones hold inclusions or silk (a quality that helps determine its origin), there shouldn't be so many that the clarity of the gemstone is affected. The clearer it is, the more valuable and prettier it is, but only in the case of untreated stones.

Carat Weight: The larger gemstones are the rarer ones. However, some gemstones, such as amethyst, occur abundantly in larger sizes. The stone's relative size must be checked in order to obtain one that's rarer and holds more value.

In jewelry, does the metal setting influence a gemstone's power?

Generally speaking, the answer is yes. Gold is ruled by the sun, which is considered masculine, and therefore imparts a more assertive energy to crystals and minerals that are mounted in it. Silver is ruled by the moon, which is considered feminine, and therefore imparts a softened, less assertive emotional energy to crystals and minerals that are mounted in it.

Copper is usually not advised for jewelry setting, simply because it carries a pronounced healing property of its own. Therefore it should only be used with stones that have a high copper content in order to strengthen the energy of stones such as turquoise or malachite.

What does it mean when a crystal shatters while working with it?

It simply means that the energy exchange between the user and the stone has caused the stone to fracture. You can continue to work with such a stone if you so desire, but most people prefer to retire that particular piece.

What is the piezoelectric effect?

Crystals have both piezoelectric and **pyroelectric** properties. Piezoelectricity is electricity produced by pressure. Many early cultures used to strike rocks and crystals, resulting in a flash of light. Compression releases electrons from a crystal's atomic bonding—producing a flash of light—and then returns to the atomic nuclei.

Pyroelectricity is produced by temperature. Simply holding a crystal in your hand gives enough heat to generate the pyroelectric effect.

What's the best way to carry my crystals?

In order to derive the greatest benefits of a stone, I recommend just putting it in your pocket or wearing it as a piece of jewelry, simply because the energy is more efficiently exchanged through regular contact with the skin. Should you carry your stones in a purse or backpack, it's advisable to keep them in a pouch of some kind, but remember to touch them often.

Does it make any difference if my stones are in tumbled, rough, crystal, or faceted form?

The main difference is what it means to you and your budget. The important thing is to choose stones that are aesthetically pleasing to you, the user. And although quite a business has grown up around carved wands, spheres, and the like, such designs really aren't necessary to access a stone's energy or power.

I've heard that a crystal only works if someone gives it to you. Is that true?

Definitely not. But if you receive one as a gift, it can carry a special energy.

The jewelry cleaner I used to clean my diamond ring cleaned the metal but ruined the gemstone. What happened?

Keep in mind the kind of chemical cleaners you pick up from the market. While silver and metal react one way to these cleaners, gemstones set in the metal will react differently. Ultrasonic cleaners are to be avoided as well, simply because their vibrations can harm your stones, even shattering them. If you have any doubts, the best option would be to consult a jeweler and get your jewelry cleaned professionally.

What's the best way to meditate with crystals?

There are many ways, but the only "best way" is the one that works best for you. Simply finding quiet time while holding a crystal and allowing yourself to feel its energy makes the crystal's energy part of your meditation.

Birthstones

Like just about everything that attempts to delve into the history of crystals and gemstones, getting the hard facts about where the custom of associating certain gems with the months of the year or signs of the zodiac is a journey that reaches so far back into history, the truth is just about impossible to pin down. Most gem scholars agree that the tradition of birthstones probably arose from the Breastplate of Aaron, a ceremonial religious garment set with twelve gemstones that represented the twelve tribes of Israel and first described in the Book of Exodus.

But since human history didn't begin with the Bible, birthstones may very well be far older, deriving from the twelve signs of the zodiac and the twelve months of the year. But neither did history begin with Egyptian and Babylonian astrologers or the Julian calendar, so again, we're looking at a very deep human response to the power of stones that probably began with a long forgotten tribal elder or medicine woman first passing a colored stone over a newborn baby, asking for blessings from the deities.

Different cultures around the world have developed different birthstone lists over the centuries, altering birthstone choices according to availability and price. Thus a variety of birthstone choices exist for both those who want to honor tradition and those who want to own or give a stone with more contemporary connotations.

There's a great deal of dispute and considerable overlapping from month to month, but for people who are interested in the ever-evolving tradition of birthstones, the following list includes ancient, traditional, and modern choices organized by the month of the year.

JANUARY

◆

Ancient: garnet
Traditional: garnet or amethyst
Modern: moss agate, opal, or sugilite

FEBRUARY

◆

Ancient: amethyst
Traditional: amethyst
Modern: aquamarine, bloodstone, jade, or sapphire

MARCH

◆

Ancient: bloodstone
Traditional: diamond
Modern: aquamarine

APRIL

◆

Ancient: sapphire or diamond
Traditional: diamond
Modern: rock crystal or Herkimer diamond

MAY

◆

Ancient: agate or emerald
Traditional: emerald
Modern: rose quartz, turquoise, or azurite

JUNE

◆

Ancient: agate or pearl
Traditional: citrine or pearl
Modern: chrysoprase, moonstone, or alexandrite

JULY

◆

Ancient: ruby or onyx
Traditional: ruby
Modern: moonstone, pearl, or onyx

AUGUST

◆

Ancient: carnelian or sardonyx
Traditional: peridot
Modern: golden topaz or tourmaline

SEPTEMBER

◆

Ancient: zircon
Traditional: sapphire
Modern: jade, jasper, or moss agate

OCTOBER

◆

Ancient: aquamarine
Traditional: opal or tourmaline
Modern: lapis lazuli, opal, or peridot

NOVEMBER

◆

Ancient: topaz
Traditional: beryl
Modern: Apache tear or obsidian

DECEMBER

◆

Ancient: ruby
Traditional: topaz or garnet
Modern: turquoise or tanzanite

Zodiac Birthstones

THE SELECTION FOR birthstones is even more widely varied for the signs of the zodiac. The selections below are comprehensive, but are traditionally believed to correspond with the energies and characteristics of each sign, as described by the Western astrological tradition.

Aries (March 20–April 19):
ruby, diamond, red jasper, bloodstone

Taurus (April 20–May 19):
emerald, topaz, sapphire, carnelian, amber, lapis lazuli

Gemini (May 20–June 19):
agate, pearl, tourmaline, tiger's eye, chrysoprase

Cancer (June 20–July 19):
moonstone, pearl, ruby, emerald

Leo (July 20–August 22):
tiger's eye, tourmaline, sardonyx, onyx, citrine

Virgo (August 23–September 22): jasper, carnelian, jade, sapphire, peridot, amazonite

Libra (September 23–October 22): opal, sapphire, green aventurine, emerald

Scorpio (October 23–November 21):
topaz, malachite, aquamarine, topaz, rhodonite

Sagittarius (November 22–December 21): sapphire, turquoise, amethyst, topaz

Capricorn (December 22–January 19): onyx, jet, ruby, garnet, smoky quartz

Aquarius (January 20–February 19): aquamarine, amethyst, garnet, moss agate, opal, amethyst, malachite

Pisces (February 20–March 19): amethyst, moonstone, rock crystal, sapphire, bloodstone

Aaron's Breastplate

REFERENCES ABOUND, THROUGHOUT this book and others, to the use of gemstones in Aaron's breastplate, an easily accessible reference to how deeply gemstones are woven through our civilization, and how closely connected they are to a sense of the divine.

In the Old Testament Book of Exodus, there is a description of twelve sacred gemstones from the Mountain of God, where the Ten Commandments were presented to Moses. In Jewish rabbinical text these stones are described as being sacred to the twelve angels who guard the gates of Paradise. In turn, these twelve precious stones were fashioned into a sacred breastplate, which Moses gave to his brother, the high priest Aaron, and were symbolic of the twelve tribes of Israel.

The text of this story is quoted below:

And thou shall make the breastplate of judgment with cunning work; after the work of the ephod thou shalt make it; of gold, of blue, and of purple, and of scarlet, and of fine twined linen shalt thou make it.

And thou shalt set in it settings of stones, even four rows of stones: the first row shall be a sardius, a topaz, and a carbuncle; this shall be the first row.

And the second row shall be an emerald, a sapphire, and a diamond.

And the third row a ligure, an agate, and an amethyst.

And the fourth row a beryl, and an onyx, and a jasper; they shall be set in gold in their enclosings.

And the stones shall be with the names of the children of Israel, twelve, according to their names, like the engravings of a signet; everyone with his name shall they be according to the twelve tribes.

And thou shalt make upon the breastplate chains at the ends of wreathen work of pure gold . . .

And Aaron shall bear the names of the children of Israel in the breastplate of judgment upon his heart, when he goeth in unto the holy place, for a memorial before the Lord continually.

And thou shalt put in the breastplate of judgment the Urim and the Thummim; and they shall be upon Aaron's heart, when he goeth in before the Lord; and Aaron shall bear the judgment of the children of Israel upon his heart before the Lord continually.

EXODUS 28:15–30

(*Sardius*, as referred to in the above passage, is what we call carnelian. *Carbuncle* is an ancient name from what is probably a ruby or garnet. Finally, it is thought that *ligure* refers to a zircon, or quartz crystal, but opinions vary.)

Resources

Amethyst Galleries Mineral Gallery

"The First Internet Rock Shop" includes a mind-boggling array of solid scientific information and stunning specimens for sale. http://mineral.galleries.com

Broad Horizons

Online shop with a crystal guide, specimens for sale, and a guide to rock and mineral shows around the country. http://broadh.com

Crystal Balance

An informative site offering healing course, crystals and minerals for sale, and a wide variety of instructional materials. http://www.crystalbalance.com

Alan Guisewite's Online Rock and Mineral Collection

A huge visual resource gallery put together by Alan Guisewite of the Robotics Institute of Carnegie Mellon University. Scientifically organized and absolutely invaluable. http://www.cs.cmu.edu/~adg/adg-piimages.html

Emily Gems

A beautiful site with great information and tumbled stones and crystals for sale. http://www.crystal-cure.com Gemological Institute of America All the up-to-date informations you need from the publishers of Gems and Gemology. http://www.gia.com

Geologic Desires

Mike Walters auctions, photographs, and a wealth of invaluable information for buying minerals. Organized by country of origin, a must for any collector. http://www.geologicdesires.com

Irocks.com

Dr. Rob Lavinsky's spectacular specimen gallery features online auctions of fine minerals for the collector.
http://irocks.com

Mineral Miners

Offering direct links to rock shops, lapidary resources, and a spectacular amount of information.
http://www.mineralminers.com

Mama's Minerals

Straight from Mother Earth to you. Rocks, minerals, fossils, and a wide assortment of lapidary supplies.
http://www.mamasminerals.com

Multistone International

Wholesaler of tumbled and rough stones from around the world.
http://www.multistoneintl.com

Peacefulmind.com

Andrew Pacholyk's wonderful selection of writings, seminars and resources for healing body and soul.

YupRocks Mineral Photography

Your source for fine mineral photography, featuring a huge selection of quality photos of rocks, fossils, and minerals for interested students and others.
http://www.yuprocks.com

Glossary

Below is a list of commonly recognized terms that you will doubtless encounter in your work with crystals, minerals, and gemstones.

ABSORPTION: a term for how the spectrum of light is absorbed in a stone, which in turn imparts its color. An amethyst, for example, absorbs the various colors of the spectrum, with the exception of purple, which is dispersed rather than absorbed, causing it to appear the purple color we recognize.

ASTERISM: a dense, microscopic, fibrous inclusion that causes the mineral to reflect a starlike formation. Usually asterisms are limited to a cabochon-type cut. Star sapphires or star rubies are perhaps the best-known stones featuring asterisms.

AVENTURESCENCE: the effect caused by small inclusions of a mineral with a highly reflective surface, which causes it to exhibit a glistening effect.

CABOCHON: a gemstone fashioned with a domed or convex smooth surface.

CARAT: a unit of measurement pertaining to the weight of gemstones; one carat is equal to .2 grams. Not to be confused with *karat* (see below).

CAT'S EYE EFFECT: see *chatoyancy*.

CHATOYANCY: the property where a stone displays a narrow band of light across the surface of the stone, such as in tiger's eye.

CLEAVAGE: the tendency of a crystal to split along definite planes to produce smooth surfaces.

CRAZING: condition in opal that causes it to form small, internal cracks, and in some severe cases eventually disintegrates the opal.

CRYPTOCRYSTALLINE: composed of tiny, microscopic crystals.

CRYSTAL: any particular three-dimensional form a mineral exhibits; classified by the distance ratio and angle of its parts.

CRYSTAL SYSTEM: the primary method of classification of crystals. The crystal system classifies crystals in six groups: *isometric* (or *cubic*), *tetragonal*, *hexagonal* (which includes *trigonal*), *orthorhombic*, *monoclinic*, and *triclinic*.

CUBIC (CRYSTAL SYSTEM): synonym of *isometric system*. Crystals of this class generally form six mirror planes, just as a cube has six sides.

DENDRITIC: an aggregate, usually an agate, composed of skeletal or treelike formations. May be a single entity or a formation that forms from mineral-rich solutions that deposit the mineral in rock and form a tree or plant structure embedded in the rock.

DEPOSIT: an accumulation of certain minerals within a rock formation.

DICHROISM: the tendency to show two different colors from different angles when looking at the gemstone. Tourmaline is a common example of a dichroic stone, appearing green or pink depending on the angle from which it is viewed. See also pleoochroism.

DISPERSION: refers to the color that is allowed to disperse, or pass through, a stone. A high-quality diamond disperses virtually all colors and is therefore colorless to our eyes. See *absorption*.

DOUBLY TERMINATED: exhibiting a pinched crystal form or point on both ends of the crystal.

DRUSE: cavity in a mineral or rock filled with protruding crystals.

FACET: a desired surface displayed in a gem, which may grow naturally but may also be hand cut.

FLOATING CRYSTAL: a crystal that developed without being attached to rock, such as being grown artificially in a lab or grown in clay or water.

FLUORESCENCE: the property of certain minerals to display a multicolored effect when illuminated with ultraviolet light.

FRACTURE: the characteristic way a mineral breaks when put under stress.

GEODE: a hollow rock that contains crystals.

HARDNESS: the resistance of an object to scrapes and scratching. The harder it is, the greater its resistance.

HEXAGONAL (CRYSTAL SYSTEM): a crystal with seven planes, each running perpendicular to the axis, or center. This system is divided into two groups—the hexagonal and trigonal.

INCLUSION: material locked inside a mineral as it is forming. Such materials may be gaseous, liquid, or solid.

ISOMETRIC (CRYSTAL SYSTEM): see *cubic (crystal system)*.

KARAT: a unit of measurement describing the content of gold. The karat measurement determines the percentage of gold on a 1 to 24 scale, with 24 karats being pure gold.

LABRADORESCENCE: an effect that causes dark, metallic-like color shimmers, commonly blue and green, to be displayed on a few minerals, including labradorite and spectrolite.

LUSTER: the optical property that describes the appearance of a gem in terms of the reflected light. The stone may be described as "metallic," "resinous," "greasy," "silky," "pearly," or "dull." Luster is most importantly used in referring to the uncut gem.

MOHS HARDNESS SCALE: a measurement devised by Austrian scientist Fredrick Mohs (1773–1839) to determine the hardness of a mineral.

MONOCLINIC (CRYSTAL SYSTEM): crystals with three unequal axes, two of which incline toward each other at an oblique angle, while the third runs perpendicular to the other two.

ORTHOHOMBIC (CRYSTAL SYSTEM): crystals with three axes of unequal length that intersect at right angles to each other.

PETRIFICATION: a process in which organic substances, such as wood and shells, are replaced by silica.

PHANTOM GROWTH: an interesting phenomenon exhibited when a crystal grows, then a new growth grows over the old crystal in the same direction, leaving an inscription of the previous growth on the crystal.

PIEZOELECTRIC: a substance that generates an electrical charge when under stress.

PLEOCHROISM: the tendency in a mineral to exhibit two or more separate colors when viewed at different angles. Pleochroism and dichroism are synonymous, except dichroism refers only to two colors, but pleochroism can be more than two.

POLYMORPH: a type of solid material that may exist in more than one form or crystal structure.

PSEUDOMORPH: a mineral that chemically replaces another mineral without changing the external form of the original mineral.

PYROELECTRIC: a substance that generates an electrical charge during a temperature change.

REFRACTION: the bending of light within a stone, caused by different spectrums of light traveling at different speeds through the stone. The greater the refractive index, the greater the dispersion of color, and therefore the greater brilliance, or sparkle.

ROCK CRYSTAL: transparent, colorless quartz crystal.

SCHILLER EFFECT: color reflections or flashes present in a mineral. The individual color flashes of opal are known as *schillers*.

SPAR: any nonmetallic, lightly colored mineral with good cleavage.

SYNTHETIC: man-made.

TETRAGONAL (CRYSTAL SYSTEM): crystals with three perpendicular axes, two of which are horizontal and of equal length, while the vertical axis is of different length and may be either shorter or longer than the other two.

TRICLINIC (CRYSTAL SYSTEM): crystals with three unequal axes, all of which intersect at oblique angles. None of the axes are perpendicular to any other axis.

TRIGONAL (CRYSTAL SYSTEM): see *hexagonal (crystal system)*.

TWINNING: the tendency of some crystals to intergrow in a distinct way or form specific repeated patterns.

VUG: a cavity in rock that is lined with long, slender crystals. A vug forms when air pockets form in cooling magma and allow crystals to form in the hollow area.

Acknowledgments

M Y HEARTFELT APPRECIATION to all those who dedicated their time talents and energies to this book, especially, Jim Butterbrodt, Mike Walters, Rob Lavinsky.

Special thanks to my editor, Renée Sedliar, for her helpful comments and infinite patience; Andrew Pacholyk of peacefulmind.com for his very generous insights, and most especially to my husband, Andrew Earley, for his design skills in the daunting task of pulling it all together—but and most especially, for getting well!

Photo credits

The photos on the following pages are courtesy of Jim Butterbrodt:
xv, 29, 36, 43, 58, 62, 71, 78, 79, 80, 81, 84, 87, 90, 103, 105, 128, 132, 149, 186, 201, 202, 205, 227, 238

The photos on the following pages are courtesy of Alan Guisewite:
45, 47, 63, 199, 217, 218, 246

The photos on the following pages are courtesy of Rob Lavinsky, irocks.com:
32, 82, 119, 139, 148, 160, 210

The photos on the following pages are courtesy of Mike Walters:
4, 30, 44, 50, 59, 69, 116, 130, 134, 135, 150, 163, 167, 168, 172, 174, 175, 176, 179, 236, 237, 241, 252, 255, 256,

The photos on the following pages are courtesy of Rob Weller, Cochise College:
164, 165, 223

The photos on the following pages are courtesy of yuprocks.com:
119, 175

All other photos courtesy of Kennedy and Company.

Index

cyanite, 138
cyclops, 132

D

danburite, 254–255, 265
dark powers, 113
debt, 61, 65, 69
decisions, 37, 131, 150, 264
dedritic agate, 89
defensive energy, 107
Delong star ruby, 131
dementia, 178
demons, inner, 169
dentistry, 104, 177, 182, 195
depression
    emotional wellness stones, 197, 205, 215
    love stones, 49
    physical healing stones, 195
    power stones, 126, 136, 150
    prosperity stones, 73
    protection stones, 93, 99, 107, 109, 120
desert roses, 70, 116
desire, 44, 49, 213
despair, 204
destiny, 113
devotion, 27
diabetes, 176
diamond, 1, 134–135, 232–234, 267–268, 281
digestion, 51, 173, 176, 190, 193
diopside, 130–131
dioptase, 171, 260
direction, personal, 49, 73, 109
disappointment, 120
discipline, personal, 113
discretion, 157
disthene, 138
divination, 240
divinatory power, 152
divine will, 142
divine within, 133
divorce, 52–53, 155
dolomite, 7, 134, 205–206
dolostone, 134
dolphin stone, 258
doubt, 264
dreams, 102, 138, 225, 229, 237, 241, 243, 259
Drusy chrysocolla, 156

dumortierite, 76–77
dyeing, of stones, 13

E

eagle's eye, 213
egg shaped stones, 231
elbaite, 87
electromagnetic qualities, 95
elestial crystals, 235–236
emerald, 11, 13, 26–28, 172, 268, 281
emeraldine, 11
emeraldite, 11
emotional health, 261
    emotional wellness stones, 201, 202, 207, 209,
        210, 212, 220
    love stones, 26, 31, 40, 46, 52
    physical healing stones, 189
    power stones, 123–124, 136, 144
    prosperity stones, 59, 69, 70
    protection stones, 95, 97, 99, 106, 120
    transformation stones, 150, 157, 163, 167
empathy, 97
emphysema, 189
employment, 59, 61, 71, 86
endocrine system, 176
endurance, 31, 178, 185
energy, of stones, 3–4, 6, 70, 264
energy, personal, 7. *see also* chakras; Kundalini energy
    creativity stones, 264
    emotional wellness stones, 202, 203, 212
    love stones, 36, 49
    physical healing stones, 174, 176, 179
    power stones, 126, 129, 139
    prosperity stones, 79, 88
    protection stones, 104, 119, 120
    psychic stones, 224
    transformation stones, 159, 165
enhancements for gemstones, 12–13
environment, natural, 97, 107, 142, 164
envy, 106
epidote, 255–256
evil, 25, 100, 109, 188, 204
evil eye, 98, 132
exhaustion, 190, 205
extrasensory perception, 221, 243
extraterrestrials, contacting, 211
eye agate, 132–133

high quartz, 7
historical uses of stones, 15–21
Holy Grail, 141
holy ice, 239
honesty, 79, 139, 140
hope, 25, 61, 95, 100, 198
hormone fluctuations, 156, 181
hostility, 120
howlite, 35, 194, 207–208
hypochondria, 205

I

Idar-Oberstein, Germany, 68, 73
identification, minerals, 2–3
idocrase, 160–161, 269
illness, 117, 128, 187, 203. *see also* organ systems; specific conditions
illusion, dispelling, 213
imagination, 50, 91, 159, 204, 258
immortality, 39, 144
immune system, 185, 192, 193, 195
immunity, 150, 178
imperial jade, 32
imperial red jasper, 107, 191
Imperial topaz, 85
Inca Rose, 43
indecisiveness, 31
independence, 215
Indian topaz, 10–11
infections, 95, 102, 119, 177, 188, 195, 233
infertility, 191
infidelity, 31, 33
inflammation, 180
influence, over others, 135
influences, negative. *see* negative energy
injustice, 108
inner demons, 169
inner evolution, 142
inner peace, 215
inner voice, 135
innocence, 30, 40, 234
insight, 108, 165, 224, 225, 234, 238–239, 245
insomnia, 183, 189, 205, 218, 237
inspiration, 163, 206, 234, 250, 255, 258, 263
integration, 120
integrity, 40, 84
intellect, 131, 144, 215

intuition, 8–9, 221–222
    creativity stones, 258
    emotional wellness stones, 201, 213
    love stones, 37
    power stones, 128, 144
    prosperity stones, 61, 75
    psychic stones, 225, 228, 234, 236, 237, 238, 240, 245
    transformation stones, 150, 151, 156, 163
investments, financial, 64
investments, stones as, 155, 261
iolite, 184–185, 238–239, 269
ionic crystals, 5
iridescence, 209
iron, 2, 6, 203
    creativity stones, 250
    emotional healing stones, 148, 211
    love stones, 25, 42, 45
    prosperity stones, 72, 79
    protection stones, 100
    psychic stones, 223
iron aluminum silicate, 219
iron oxide, 81, 98, 103, 152, 182
iron sulfide, 189
iron-magnesium silicates, 204
irradiated stones, 12–13
irritability, 174
irritable bowel syndrome, 191
isolation, 49

J

jade, 17, 32–33, 60, 68, 101, 119, 171, 251, 270
jadeite, 32
Japanese amethyst, 11
jasper, 17, 213, 270, 282
jealousy, 106, 204, 216
jet, 108–109
jewelry, metal settings and, 274
Joan Blue, 215
joint health, 174, 177, 180
joy, stone of, 255
justice, 99, 108

K

Kalpa tree, 169
karmic patterns, 247
kidney ore, 183

kidneys, health of, 181, 183, 187
kindness, 144
knowledge, 163, 235, 246
Korean jade, 119
Krystallos, 240
Kundalini energy, 51, 129, 144, 181, 246
Kunz, George Frederick, 137, 250
kunzite, 136–137, 206, 270
kyanite, 64, 138–139

L

La Peregrina, 40
lab-grown gems, 13–14, 27, 214
labradorite, 161, 162–163, 209
lapis, 208
lapis lazuli, 17, 34–36, 52, 76, 171, 216, 270
larimar, 257–258
lasering, of stones, 13
lazulite, 79–80, 194
lazurite, 34, 80
lead, 60, 251
leadership, 126
legal matters, 104, 108
lepidolite, 139–140, 210–211
lethargy, 179, 202, 205
library crystals, 235
light blue chrysacolla, 260
lignite, 109
ligure, 281
lilalite, 140
limestone, 34, 134, 175
lithium, 139, 210
liver, 183, 184, 190
lodestone, 81
logic, 52, 130
loneliness, 49, 206
longevity, 124, 133
love
        crystal energy and, 23–24
        emotional wellness stones, 215
        love stones, 27–28, 30, 33, 40, 42, 46
        physical healing stones, 173
        power stones, 124, 126
        protection stones, 100
        transformation stones, 149
lover's stone, 50
low quartz, 7

loyalty, 27, 124, 160
luck, 39, 54, 68, 78, 84, 100
lungs, health of, 178, 189, 190
luster, 2
lymphatic system, 170

M

Madagascar Star, 43
magic, 39, 113, 153, 178, 212
magnesite, 194
magnesium, 79, 203
magnesium aluminum oxide, 143
magnetic properties, 81, 118
magnetite, 81–82
malachite, 8, 17, 68, 171, 179, 186–187, 193, 260
malaria, 185
manganese, 118, 188
manic disorders, 210
marble, 176
marcasite, 189
marriage, 37, 218
martyr's stone, 98, 152
masculine energy, 129
master crystal, 14, 148
master stones, 234
meaning, seeing true, 91
Mecca stone, 25–26, 100
mediation, 150
medicinal uses, 22, 158, 170, 178
medicine wheel rituals, 55
meditation, 275
        creativity stones, 259
        emotional wellness stones, 210
        prosperity stones for, 65
        psychic stones, 228, 230–231, 237, 239, 240, 242, 247
memory, 65, 139, 178, 189, 215, 237
menstrual problems, 181, 183
mental abilities, 63, 75, 79, 237
merchant's stone, 73
Mesmer, Anton, 81
metabolism, 150, 180
metal settings, jewelry, 274
metallic crystals, 5
metastability, 122
meteorites, 42, 141, 142, 212
Mexican, 132

pessimism, 97
petrified wood, 114–115
petroglyphs, 115
phantom quartz, 241–242
phobias, 93, 102
phosphate group, 174, 227
Picasso Jasper, 107, 191
Picture Jasper, 107, 191
pietersite, 213–214
piezoelectric effect, 274
pineal gland, 170
plagioclase feldspar, 8, 162, 209
playas, 90
pleochroic, 185, 207, 249
Pliny the Elder, 39, 49, 113, 125, 188
Poppy Jasper, 107
positive thinking. *see* optimism
postpartum depression, 107
post-traumatic stress, 97, 209, 217
power, 67, 84, 97, 121–122, 136, 202, 228, 265
precious gemstones, 273
precognitive abilities, 230
pregnancy, 191
prehnite, 258–259
prenatal development, 181
prima materia, 263
problem resolution, 203
problem solver's stone, 163
procrastination, 108, 256
progress, 262
prophecy, 259
prosopite, 194
prosperity, 54, 56–57, 78–79, 84, 88, 90, 126, 140
protection
        emotional wellness stones, 200
        physical healing stones, 172, 183
        prosperity stones, 82, 86
        protection stones, 95
        psychic stones, 224, 227
        transformation stones, 153, 167, 169
Prussian amber, 95
pseudochrysolite, 142
psychic abilities, 240, 247
psychic attack, 109
psychological pain, 97
pure vessels, 20
purity, 30, 40, 169, 177, 179, 234, 235

purpose, sense of, 71, 82, 97
pyramid shaped stones, 231, 240
pyrite, 6, 34, 109, 189–190
pyroelectric properties, 274
pyrope, 29

Q

quantum quattro silica, 260–261
quartz, 7, 89, 134, 156, 222, 267, 270, 272, 282.
        see also individual stone names
quartzite, 68

R

Rainbow Jasper, 107, 191
rainbow sheen, 110
rationality, 52
reawakening, 236
receptive energy, 72, 78
record keeper crystals, 235
recovery stone, 193
red jasper, 99, 106–108, 171, 183, 191–192
red onyx, 113
red spinel, 143–145
red tourmaline, 268
regeneration, 49, 73
regret, 207
Reiki, 176
rejuvenation, 151, 189
relationships, 7, 31, 33, 37, 52, 155, 161, 204, 216
relaxation, 210
reproduction, 31, 40, 47
resolve, 49, 70
resourcefulness, 151, 199, 206
respiratory system, 95, 173, 176, 178, 189, 190, 195
rheumatic disease, 180
rhinestones, 240
rhodochrosite, 43–45
rhyolite, 262–263
ring agates, 132
rock art, 115
rock crystal, pure, 14, 211
rocks vs crystals, 1
rocks vs minerals, 273
romance, 55
rose quartz, 45–47, 171
rough stones, 275
rubies, 1, 11, 50–51, 143, 268, 282

ruby corundum, 143
ruby slippers, 51
rutilated quartz, 48–49

S

sacred energy, 224
sacred objects, stones as, 15–21
safety, 97, 173
sagenite, 48
San Diego ruby, 11
sandstone, 193, 211
sapphires, 1, 50, 131, 171, 214–216, 268–269, 281
sard, 25, 100, 112, 243
sardius, 25, 100, 281
sardonyx, 243
satin spar, 116
scapolite, 163–164
scheelite, 164–165
schiller effect, 37, 67
scrying, 166, 228, 241
security, 65, 92, 97, 137, 173
seduction, 129
seeing stone, 65, 158
selenite, 78, 116–117, 171
self, sense of, 52, 133, 151, 163, 175, 208, 263
self-actualization, 99, 126, 144, 214
self-control, 61, 76, 113, 129, 136
self-damaging behaviors, 61, 111, 163
self-employment, 61
self-esteem
 creativity stones, 255, 256
 emotional wellness stones, 199, 203, 207, 209, 210
 love stones, 25, 31, 43, 47, 52, 55
 power stones, 144
 prosperity stones, 61, 63
 protection stones, 100
 transformation stones, 163
self-expression, 55, 59, 97, 126, 251, 265
self-pity, 49, 256
self-possession, 128
self-revealing energy, 67
semi-precious gemstones, 273
senses, physical, 26, 168
serenity, 63, 258
serpentine, 118–119, 194
sexual abuse, 53

sexual anxiety, 37
sexual attraction, 51, 100, 181
sexual dysfunction, 47, 176
sexual energy, 24, 31, 37, 55, 128, 129, 144, 233
sexual enjoyment, 55
sexual healing, 26, 53
sexual relationships, 26
shaman stones, 211
sheen obsidian, 110
Siam zircon, 168
Siberian ruby, 11
silex, 107, 191
silicates, 118, 132, 207, 238
silk, in rubies, 51
sillimanite, 64
silver, jewelry settings, 274
silver-gray hematite, 183
simulated stones, 12
sinus problems, 193
skeleton quartz, 235
skin disorders, 117, 149, 182
skulls, crystal, 16–18
smaragdos, 27
smithsonite, 192–193, 194, 258
smoking, 111, 178
smoky quartz, 109, 171, 217–218, 260
smoky topaz, 217
snowflake obsidian, 110, 166–167
sodalite, 52–53, 76, 171, 216–217
sodium, 203
sorcery, protection against, 191
sorrow, 204
soul links, 247
spectrolite, 161
specularite, 183
spessartine, 30
sphere shaped stones, 231, 240
spine, health, 188
spinels, 11, 206, 271
spirit guides/voices, 129, 168, 213, 221, 227, 228, 241, 245, 247, 259
spirit quartz, 148
spiritual clarity, 165, 215, 225, 245
spiritual growth
 emotional wellness stones, 207, 215
 love stones, 43, 49
 power stones, 120, 144

transformation, 8, 63, 136, 140, 146–147, 265
transition, 149, 169
trauma, 120, 209
travel, 101, 102, 169, 188
treatments for gemstones, 12–13
tree agate, 89–90
tribes of Israel, 98, 152, 194, 276
trust, 53, 217
truth, 35, 52, 153, 174, 235, 242, 244, 245
trystine, 62, 225
tuberculosis, 189
tumbled stones, 275
tungsten, 164
turmoil, 153, 168
turquenite, 194
turquoise, 1, 13, 156, 171, 193–195, 208, 272
TV stone, 90–91, 116
twinning, 162, 209, 219

U

ulexite (TV stone), 90–91, 116
ultrasonic cleaners, 194, 275
unconscious thoughts, 102, 117, 138, 167
understanding, 46, 49, 67, 131, 167, 225, 229
unification, 149
universal knowledge, stone of, 227, 242
uvarovites, 30

V

variety, 262
variscite, 194
veils, 239
Venus of Willendorf, 141
Venus-hair stone, 48
verbal skills, 131
verdite, 87
vesuvianite, 160
Vietnamese ruby, 10–11

violan, 130
virility, 51, 55
vision, of eyes, 172, 188
visions, 135, 144, 166, 211, 225, 228, 245
vitality, physical, 43, 178, 179
vitamin absorption, 181
Vogel, Marcel Joseph, 7, 8

W

wands, 116, 231, 240
waxing, of stones, 13
weather, 178, 191
weight loss, 106, 189
white buffalo stone, 208
White Buffalo Woman, 208
will, personal, 228
willpower, 84, 107, 208
wisdom, 99, 135, 163, 166, 236
wise stone, 156
wishes, granting of, 37
witchcraft, 109
worry, 80, 104, 105, 129, 218, 264
wulfenite, 21, 246–247

Y

yang energy, 126, 165
yellow topaz, 73
yu, 32

Z

zeolites, 105, 167, 201
zinc, 58
zincite, 264–265
zircon, 7, 168–169, 272, 282
zirconium, 203
zodiac signs/birthstones, 17, 276, 279–280
zoisite, 11, 244, 255